DIONYSIOS C. TSICHRITZIS
University of Toronto

Dr. Tsichritzis graduated in Electrical Engineering from the Technical University of Athens. He subsequently attended Princeton University where he obtained his M.A. (1967) and Ph.D. (1968). He joined the University of Toronto in 1968 and is currently an Associate Professor, Department of Computer Science, and a member of the Computer Systems Research Group.

Dr. Tsichritzis worked for EAI, IBM, and Arthur D. Little. He has served as a consultant for various business organizations and is a member of ACM and CIPS, an associate editor of *INFOR Journal,* and a president of the Computer Science Association of Canada.

He has a wide range of research interests including computational complexity, operating systems and information systems design. He has published over 25 papers in journals and conference proceedings. Dr. Tsichritzis was one of the initiators and participants in Project SUE, and is now involved in research in different aspects of operating systems design and data base management systems.

PHILIP A. BERNSTEIN

Philip A. Bernstein received a B.S. in Computer Science from Cornell University (1971). He received a M.Sc. in Computer Science from the University of Toronto (1972), and is enrolled in the doctoral program at the University of Toronto. His current research interests include models for parallel computation and data base management systems.

OPERATING SYSTEMS

This is a volume in
COMPUTER SCIENCE AND APPLIED MATHEMATICS
A Series of Monographs and Textbooks

Editor: WERNER RHEINBOLDT

A complete list of titles in this series appears at the end of the volume.

OPERATING SYSTEMS

Dionysios C. Tsichritzis and Philip A. Bernstein
University of Toronto

ACADEMIC PRESS   New York and London

A Subsidiary of Harcourt Brace Jovanovich, Publishers

ACADEMIC PRESS, INC.
111 Fifth Avenue, New York, New York 10003

United Kingdom Edition published by
ACADEMIC PRESS, INC. (LONDON) LTD.
24/28 Oval Road, London NW1

Library of Congress Cataloging in Publication Data

Tsichritzis, Dionysios C
    Operating systems.

    (Computer science and applied mathematics)
    Bibliography: p.
    1.   Electronic digital computers.   I.   Bernstein,
Philip A., joint author.   II.   Title.
QA76.5.T738   001.6′44′04   73-18959
ISBN 0–12–701750–X

CONTENTS

PART I.   PRINCIPLES

Chapter 1.   Operating System Functions and Concepts

Chapter 2.   Processes

Chapter 3.   Processor Allocation

Chapter 4.   Memory Management

Chapter 5.   Virtual Memory

PART II.   TECHNIQUES

Chapter 6.   I/O and Files

Chapter 7.   Protection

Chapter 8.   Design

Chapter 9.   Implementation

Chapter 10.   Examples of Systems

Appendix I.   Data Structures

Appendix II.   Computational Structures

Appendix III. A Toy Operating System

Annotated References

PREFACE

The concept of an operating system is difficult to define precisely. The word "system" is used with a multitude of meanings in both computer science and engineering, and the word "operating" does not add much context. Traditionally, users have wanted facilities which are different from those which the hardware provides. To solve this problem, a set of programs is usually written which translates the hardware capabilities into facilities which satisfy user requirements. This set of programs is referred to as an *operating system*. At this point, we will not attempt to further clarify or confuse the term. In Chapter 1 we present our view of what constitutes an operating system. We hope that by the end of the book the reader will be able to recognize an operating system when he sees one.

Most users do not need a thorough understanding of the operating system within which their programs run. They only have to abide by the constraints which the system imposes, such as memory partition size or job control language. Analogously, the Fortran programmer does not have to understand all the details of the Fortran compiler which he uses. There is general agreement, however, that an exposure to operating system principles is a necessary background for a "computer scientist." The purpose of this book is to provide that necessary background to the reader. We do not attempt to define a general methodology for designing operating systems. Rather, we try to present in a concise and lucid manner the fundamental concepts and principles which govern the behavior of operating systems.

We have tried to keep our notation as consistent as possible with the literature. In the case of hardware this has been difficult to do, since manufacturers frequently use conflicting definitions. When in doubt, we have yielded to the force of large numbers and have adopted IBM's notation. We have not used any particular programming language to describe our algorithms, taking a good deal of liberty with control structures and basic operators where appropriate. Commonly used programming languages, such as PL/I, are cumbersome to use for descriptive purposes while more appropriate programming languages, such as PASCAL, are not widely known. Nuances in notation are clearly defined in the sections which introduce them.

This book is primarily intended as a text for a one-semester course directed toward fourth-year undergraduates and first-year graduate students, similar to the course I4 outlined by ACM Curriculum '68. Such a course has been taught at the University of Toronto with about a hundred students per year since 1969. The course (and the book) has been developed according to the recommendations of the COSINE task force on operating systems [Denning *et al.*, 1971]. We strongly recommend the report of the task force as a guideline to the lecturer who plans to institute a course on operating systems.

The students taking the course in our university have had a course on data structures and a course on language and compiler design. This background is not absolutely necessary, but it does give the students some maturity in the area of systems programming. We did not make any strong assumptions about the background of the students for whom the book is intended. We only presume some experience in computer science. Specifically, it is helpful if the students have written some long programs and have some idea of the problems encountered in interfacing with computer systems, such as fighting with job control language restrictions. It is also important that the reader have some knowledge of lists and queues. This material, which is outlined in Appendix I, can be presented in an early tutorial section for those students whose background is weak.

Many issues regarding the structure of operating systems are well understood. The problems of managing processes, processors, and memory, which are covered in Part I, have found extensive treatment in the literature for some time. Although there are still many open questions, these areas can be discussed in a reasonably neat way. Unfortunately, not all the issues are quite so elegant. Part II deals with subject matter whose formal development is still in its incipient stages. Input–output, files, security, protection, design methods, reliability, performance evaluation, and implementation methods are all important aspects of operating systems. Despite the rather *ad hoc* flavor of many of the techniques associated with these topics, we feel they are nevertheless relevant and should be part of any introductory presentation of operating system principles.

Some of the basic concepts of operating systems come rather late in the book, such as virtual machines in Chapter 8. Our experience is that students find these concepts hard to appreciate before they have enough knowledge to relate them to examples in operating systems. Although some of the early material can be made more elegant using these concepts, we feel it may be too confusing in an introductory book.

There are many papers in the literature treating analytical problems of operating systems. Such work has generated important results which often give much insight into operating system behavior. We have tried to avoid most of these analytical results for two reasons. First, the results are more related to branches of applied mathematics than to the world of operating systems. Second, this material is more appropriate for a separate graduate course on modeling and analysis of operating systems than for an introductory course which emphasizes basic concepts. Theoretical work is well documented throughout the book; the annotated bibliography can serve as a guide to interested readers. We did, however, choose to make one exception. In Appendix II there is a short survey of computational structures, material relating directly to Chapter 2. Since most of the references for this subject are not widely available, we thought that it would be worthwhile to add a short discussion for the interested reader.

ACKNOWLEDGMENTS

Many of the ideas discussed in this book are the result of work done by the Project SUE group: J. W. Atwood, B. L. Clark, M. S. Grushcow, R. C. Holt, J. J. Horning, K. C. Sevcik, and D. C. Tsichritzis. Project members have influenced not only the material but also the spirit of the book. We very gratefully acknowledge their vast contributions and their continuous encouragement.

Many local students and faculty members have given us considerable help in editing early versions of the chapters. Their comments are responsible for many merits of the final manuscript. In particular, we would like to thank A. J. Ballard (Chapters 8 and 9 and Appendix III), C. C. Gotlieb (Chapter 7), R. C. Holt (Chapter 8), J. J. Horning (Chapters 1 and 2), R. N. S. Horspool (Chapter 4 and Problem Sets), E. Lazowska (Chapters 4 and 5), J. Metzger (Chapter 9), K. C. Sevcik (Chapters 3, 7, and 10), and F. Tompa (Chapters 4–6). The Annotated References are based on an earlier version by R. Bunt. We would also like to thank B. Liskov for her assistance in clearing up many foggy points in our description of the Venus Operating System in Chapter 10. Overall comments on a late version of the manuscript by B. W. Kernighan were quite helpful in locating and correcting a number of weak sections.

Special thanks go to our friend and associate J. R. Swenson whose careful reading of the final draft led to many changes on both a technical and pedagogical level. In particular, many of his ideas on memory management had a considerable influence on the organization and content of Chapters 4–6.

We are also indebted to many other colleagues, too numerous to mention by name, for exciting and informative discussions on various aspects of operating systems principles.

Finally, we would also like to thank M. Oldham, V. Shum, and P. Steele for clerical assistance rendered during various stages of the writing.

NOTES TO THE INSTRUCTOR

In parallel with the lectures, we have found that tutorial sections which cover a particular system in some detail are quite helpful in showing students how the ideas of the course fit together. In Chapter 10 we present two examples of operating systems. Further examples can be found in the books by Hoare and Perrot [1972] and Sayers [1971]. We recommend these discussions be held early in the term in order to motivate the material. Most students, especially undergraduates, have very little exposure to real operating systems. They can hardly be expected to be enthusiastic about solutions to problems which they do not appreciate.

The material in the book is complemented by problems at the end of the chapters, which serve many useful purposes. First, they elaborate on points which receive only cursory treatment in the text. Second, they help relate some abstract concepts to the real world of operating systems. Third, they point to papers in the literature for further reading. Many of the problems are necessarily open ended; that is, they have no single correct answer. Such problems are meant to provoke students to consider different alternatives. These problems can be used as topics for discussion sessions as well as for homework assignments.

The requirements of the course as given at the University of Toronto are as follows:

1. an examination in class to verify whether the students follow the course lectures;

2. a long take-home assignment with more substantial, thought-provoking problems which the students can develop in depth;

3. a project which brings the students closer to the real world of operating systems.

If the class is small, several short assignments may be substituted for the exam. Problems for both the test and assignment(s) can be taken from the chapter problems.

We will elaborate on the project requirement, because it presents a serious challenge to both the instructor and the students. It is not easy to design, supervise, and evaluate one hundred projects per year. We have tried several approaches.

1. An essay surveying some aspect of operating systems. In the problem sets we incorporate suggestions for essay topics. Essays from past years at the University of Toronto have been retained and put on reserve in the library for the benefit of future students. We have found essays to be particularly useful the first few years the course is given. They require a minimum of supervision, and they generate a nice local library on subjects which are too obscure to be included in the course lectures. In particular, developing a collection of descriptions of popular operating systems can be quite valuable. After the course is given several times, it is difficult to avoid duplicating topics. At this point, emphasis can be placed on other types of projects. However, essays should always remain as an alternative for some types of students, such as part-time students who are good programmers but do not have much exposure to the literature.

2. A joint effort in evaluating some aspects of the design or implementation of operating systems. The Rosetta Stone project, originally proposed by W. Wulf, for evaluation of system programming languages is an example of this type of activity [Wulf *et al.*, 1972]. A set of standard problems, such as process synchronization and memory management algorithms, are programmed by many students in two or three languages. In addition to the programs, students are asked for comments comparing the different languages. We have tried this type of project with limited success. The main problem is that it takes a good deal of maturity to evaluate languages. Since most students do not do much evaluating, the main value of the project for them is in learning a few new languages and in solving several small problems. We feel that this project, although

worthwhile, is probably better suited to a course in software engineering or systems programming than one in operating systems.

3. A "toy" operating system using a pedagogical, simulated hardware environment. In Appendix III we outline the basic issues in designing and supervising such a project. The students, working in teams of two or three, simulate a simple machine and then write a small operating system for it. We have tried this project repeatedly with great success. It can be somewhat expensive in computer time, but the students get some real experience in how complex systems are constructed. As a side benefit, the students get a taste of real programming problems by having to build a relatively large program in a team. They have to deal with project management, which has been the nemesis of more than one operating system design. At the University of Toronto we are currently using a toy operating system assignment which was designed by R. C. Holt for use with the TOPPS programming language [Holt and Kinread, 1972]. The TOPPS system [Czarnik *et al.*, 1973] can be run under any system which supports the XPL compiler writing system [McKeeman *et al.*, 1970]. Hopefully, a distribution tape and documentation will be available in the near future for universities which would like to try the project.

4. A programming project for a minicomputer in an environment of a software laboratory. This type of project can be very exciting, but it presumes the presence of a highly accessible minicomputer system. If the proper facilities are available, a number of interesting software packages would make good term projects, such as a simple executive, a spooling system, or a simple file system. There are several reports describing such an environment, for example Corbin *et al.* [1971] and Marshland and Tartar [1973]. In our university this approach will be adopted for an advanced course on operating systems. However, the supervision of a large number of projects of this type can be a problem.

5. A real contribution to the university computer center or to industry. We have a cooperative agreement with our computer center by which ten to fifteen students work on assignments proposed, supervised, evaluated, and ultimately used by computer center personnel. Both the center and the students are very enthusiastic, but we doubt that the number of participating students can be increased without serious organizational difficulties. To be successful, each student requires close supervision, and the number of available supervisors is limited. This project is particularly well suited to students who have little practical experience. Students with industrial experience generally do not choose to write one more systems program. For the same reason that a real programming

assignment is a thrill for an inexperienced student, a survey type of essay is very beneficial for an experienced systems programmer.

Availability of facilities will be the primary influence on which projects are most suitable for a given school. If there are any questions about the specifics of a given project, we will be happy to assist in any way we can.

PART I

PRINCIPLES

The first five chapters of this book discuss the allocation of the basic resources of a computer system, namely, processors and memory. Chapter 1 provides a general overview of what operating systems do and how they are usually structured. Chapter 2 introduces the primary concept of *process* as a means for understanding the interactions among active computations in a computer system. Chapter 3 uses processes to show how a single processor can be allocated to several independent computations. Chapters 4 and 5 cover the allocation of main memory and ways of extending main memory using peripheral storage devices.

Methods of managing processes, processors, and memory have found extensive treatment in the literature. The fundamental issues are well understood. Therefore, the main problem is to present the material in a technically sound and pedagogically lucid manner.

1

OPERATING SYSTEM FUNCTIONS AND CONCEPTS

1.1 Introduction

Most modern computer systems are "unwieldy beasts." A typical medium-sized installation is a complicated interconnection of many hardware devices, such as central processors, core memory, drum storage, disk and tape drives, typewriter terminals, card readers, and line printers. To overcome the complexity of managing all these devices, the system provides programs, or *software,* which make the hardware system more convenient to use. Those people, namely, users, who have programs which they want to execute on the computer system's hardware are relieved by the software of having to deal with the peculiarities of each device. They request operations, such as "execute this program" or "store that file"; the system software takes care of the details of allocating storage and a processor to the program, or of assigning disk space for the file. In addition to making the machine easier to use, software is needed to facilitate sharing. Modern computer systems are very expensive. The average user simply cannot afford to buy his own system or to pay for solitary occupancy of a large system. Hence, out of economic necessity he must settle for sharing the system with others.

Again, he relies on the software to manage the resources of the system so that sharing is possible.

The purpose of this chapter is to give the reader a feeling for the functions and performance requirements of that part of the computer system's software which is called the operating system. However, before narrowing down the discussion to the subject of operating systems, it is important to understand the basic characteristics of the components of computer systems, that is, hardware and software.

1.1.1   Hardware

Computer system hardware is composed of one or more *central processing units* (also called *CPUs* or *processors*), which can execute machine-language instructions; processor addressable *memory* (also called *main memory* or *core*); and *peripheral devices* (also called *peripherals* or *I/O devices*), which provide a means of input and output (I/O) for the system and provide *secondary storage* space. The processor usually consists of several fixed-length *registers* for storage and an *arithmetic unit,* which executes instructions. *Main memory* is divided into fixed-length blocks of bits called *words,* generally the same length as the registers. Each word in memory is given a unique name, called its *address* or *location.* Words can contain either instructions or data. One of the processor's registers, the *instruction address register,* contains the location of the next instruction that the arithmetic unit will interpret. Instructions are usually executed sequentially in order of increasing address until an instruction chooses to *branch* to a new location by altering the contents of the instruction address register. It should be pointed out that other quite different structures for computer system architecture are possible [Organick, 1973].

Although the foregoing description of processors and memory is a gross simplification of hardware in the real world, it does present a common vocabulary for talking about the devices. Although the properties of processors and main memory are well known, the characteristics of peripheral devices are probably unfamiliar to many readers, and consequently will be covered in more detail.

Peripheral devices move information between core and some type of storage or display medium, such as punched cards, magnetic disk or tape, or printed paper. Devices differ with respect to the medium on which information is stored and the method and speed by which the information is accessed. Some devices, such as magnetic tape drives and card readers, are strictly sequential. Data can only be processed as a single stream in first-in–first-out (FIFO) order; to read the tenth data item, the first nine items must also be read. Other storage devices allow a more *random accessing* of data. Magnetic drums and disks are organized as a set of *tracks*. Instead of accessing a piece of data as the Nth item on a tape, it is accessed on a drum as the Nth item on the Mth track. Since the drum or disk heads can switch relatively quickly from track to track, the average time required to access a data item (that is, *access time*) is considerably less than in the strictly sequential case. On virtually all magnetic devices, the rate at which a piece of data can be moved once it is located (called the *transfer rate*) is substantially faster than the access time to find it. This property of devices makes it advantageous to move information in large blocks. For example, if ten words are stored sequentially on a disk, it is much faster to retrieve them as a block on one access than to access them one at a time. For small blocks of data, the transfer time is negligible compared to the access time; moving the words one at a time is nearly 100 times slower than moving all ten at once.

Despite the wide range of speeds among device types, their connection to the computer system is relatively uniform. Peripheral devices are usually attached to the CPU through special-purpose computers called *channels*. The connection from the peripheral to the channel is effected through a *device control unit*. The device control unit is an electronic device which accepts commands from the channel and causes the device either to operate in some way (for example, backspace or switch tracks) or to move data either to or from the channel (that is, read or write). When a program initiates an I/O operation, the system receives the request, generates the necessary program, and sends it to the channel. Using the information contained in the I/O program, the channel selects the device and causes it to perform the appropriate action, for example, to read into or write from its storage medium. After the I/O operation is complete, the channel must notify the system of the completion. This notification is usually done through a hardware interrupt.

An *interrupt* is a transfer of control forced on the running program due to some external condition. An interrupt is said to be *enabled* if a *request* for its invocation will be honored; the requesting and enabling of interrupts is generally done by setting special interrupt bits in the processor. When the interrupt is both requested and enabled, the central processor stops what it is doing and branches to an agreed upon location in main memory. Beginning at this location, the interrupt registers are examined to ascertain the reason for the interrupt. For example, the interrupt may have occurred because a device terminated or because an illegal instruction was executed. The appropriate action can then be taken, such as sending another command to the channel or aborting the program.

Channels and the central processor can execute concurrently. In most machines, since a CPU program is responsible for telling the channel what to do, interrupts must be used to synchronize the operation of these independent devices. As will be seen in Chapter 2, interrupts are not necessarily the best method by which to synchronize concurrent operations. However, their ubiquitous presence in hardware systems makes them important in understanding system design.

1.1.2   Software

If the hardware provided exactly those facilities which were needed by users of computer systems, there would be no need for system software. However, the hardware facilities are not in the most convenient form for most users. Also, it is difficult for users to share the system safely and efficiently without software assistance. Therefore, users require system software to support the operation of their programs.

1.1.2.1   SHARING

A *resource* is any object which can be allocated within the system. Hardware resources are rarely shared in the sense that two programs are simultaneously accessing a single resource. Rather, a resource is said to be *shared* if several programs are each given exclusive control of the resource for some subinterval of a time period. For example, five programs can share a processor equally if each program is allowed to execute for one second out of every five. Virtually all hardware devices are shared in this way, although the time scale over which programs are given control of different devices may vary considerably. For example, a program may be allowed to use part of main memory for several minutes, but may never be given control of the processor for more than a second at a time.

There are basically two ways to implement sharing. In the decentralized method, if several programs want to share a resource, and if the programs "know of each other's existence," then the programs can cooperate by passing the resource among themselves. In most systems, though, users do not care to be bothered communicating with each other. In the centralized method a separate program is put in charge of allocating the resources of the system equitably and efficiently, so that programs no longer need to cooperate in order to fill their resource requests. When a program needs a resource, it merely requests the re-

source from the "resource allocator." The notions of resource allocation
and resource sharing are central to the concept of an operating system.
The main functions of resource allocation and techniques for implementing them are investigated further in later sections.

1.1.2.2 OTHER SOFTWARE FACILITIES

Peripheral devices move data at speeds which are substantially slower
than the speed at which the CPU can process the data. To avoid having
the CPU waiting for its data, the device should move data into core
before the CPU explicitly needs it. When the CPU does start processing
data from core, the device will already have a head start and will be
able to keep the processor busy for a while before the CPU must stop
and wait. This activity is called *buffering,* and the area in which the
device stores advanced information is called a *buffer.* One common
buffering technique in computer systems is called *spooling.* The processor typically obtains much of its input data from a card reader, but
the card reader is many orders of magnitude slower than the processor.
To compensate, the cards are moved (or *spooled*) from a small memory
buffer onto a disk. The disk now acts as a buffer between the CPU
and the card reader. Instead of physically reading cards, the CPU reads
card images from the disk. A similar technique can be used to buffer
output to the printer. The program that implements the spooling of
data is an integral part of most complex computer systems.

One of the most heavily used facilities offered by a computer system
is language translation: compilers, assemblers, and interpreters. This
is also the class of system programs about which the most is known.
As with many other software facilities, language translators must interact
with the computer system on which they run. The places where the
system and the translator ·interact, called the *interface,* require careful
design. For example, the translator must be able to obtain certain resources from the system, such as file storage or typewriter terminals.
This implies that the translator must communicate with that part of
the system which governs resource allocation. Similarly, if the translator
generates machine code, that code should adhere to system conventions,
such as the system's rules for linking programs. From the system side
the interface should be both simple and flexible to permit the connection
of a wide variety of translators.

The area of translation has been given a great deal of special attention.
The field has progressed to the point where translators can be bought
commercially in much the same way as hardware devices. There are
a number of good books on both the theoretical and practical aspects
of translation (for instance, McKeeman *et al.* [1970] and Gries [1971]).

In this book it is assumed that translators either are available or can be built to meet stated requirements. In fact, they are treated in the same way as hardware devices, which can be built to specifications. Although this is a gross simplification in some cases, it is a reasonable assumption for the purpose of understanding operating systems.

A second important facility provided by computer systems is the ability to manipulate large amounts of data. Data is organized into logical units, called *files,* and then stored in a way which is related to its use. Elements within the file, usually called *records,* can be accessed by a variety of techniques, depending on how the file is structured. For example, in a sequentially structured file, records are accessed in the same order in which they were originally stored (for example, a tape file). The ability to store large blocks of structured data within the system for long periods is a powerful and convenient tool. Files are often placed in secondary storage rather than main memory. File systems make it easier for several users to share the data; if well structured, they can provide rapid average access time to an arbitrary data element. Since the file system requires the use of the computer system's resources, it must interact with the computer system in order to obtain peripheral devices, core storage, and processing time. Thus, the interface between the file system and the computer system requires the same careful design as that discussed under translators.

There are a number of other software facilities which are frequently offered by computer systems. Mathematical subroutine packages, statistical subroutine libraries, and utility sort and merge libraries add to the convenience of the system for some users. The inclusion of application programs, though, is generally considered to be of less importance than that of language translation and file manipulation. The construction of such routines is the subject of numerical analysis, statistics, and data structures, and consequently is beyond the scope of this book.

1.2   Operating Systems

The *operating system* is that part of the software which supports the sharing of resources. Not every operating system restricts its operation to include only facilities which aid in sharing. In the early days language translators and utility programs were usually considered to be part of the operating system. Although these facilities can be clearly distinguished from the operating system in most recent implementations, there are still vestiges of the broader view. Most systems include a file system that is significantly more complex than what is minimally required to share I/O devices. File systems are mostly a convenience factor, rather than a requirement for sharing of I/O devices; their presence in an operating system enables the user to have a simple access to I/O devices. However, the *nucleus* of the system—the software that is directly responsible for the sharing of hardware—has functions which are reasonably invariant across a wide variety of machines. The nucleus provides a means by which processors, main memory, and peripheral devices can be shared. The parts of the operating system which interact with users, such as a batch system or a text-editing system, use the nucleus functions as a software base in much the same way that the nucleus uses physical devices as a hardware base. The nucleus provides facilities mainly to other operating system components, which provide further facilities to users. Techniques for structuring and implementing the nucleus of an operating system constitute the main body of material covered in this book.

The notion of "user of an operating system" is rather vague. Quite simply, a *user* is a person who has a program to run on the system. That program, though, can have widely varying characteristics. Its requirements for processing time, memory space, and peripheral devices can be anywhere in the range from an insignificant fraction of the resources to the entire machine. In subsequent discussions it will be assumed that a user is a person with a computation to do, and that the computation is within the capabilities of the system.

Independently of what functions it provides, an operating system should satisfy certain performance constraints [Hoare and Perrot, 1972]. Specifically, the system should be

1. *reliable*   The system should be at least as reliable as the hardware on which it runs. If a software or hardware error does occur, the system should detect the error and either try to correct the problem, or at worst try to minimize the damage to the users of the system from the error.

2. *protected*   A user does not want other users to interfere with him. Therefore, the system should protect users from being affected both by each other's errors and by malicious attempts at tampering.

3. *efficient*   The operating system is usually a complex program which uses a large part of the hardware resources for its own functions. Resources consumed by the operating system are not available for users. Consequently, the system itself should be as efficient as possible. In addition, the system should manage user resources to minimize their idle time or, equivalently, to maximize *utilization* (that is, percent of time not idle).

4. predictable   User demands on the system are generally unpredictable. At the same time, users prefer to get service which does not vary widely over extended periods of time. That is, after reading his program into the system, the user should have a rough idea when to expect his output, based on previous runs of the same program.

5. convenient   Users share a system because of economic necessity, not necessarily by choice. Since the operating system is forced upon them, it should be flexible and convenient to use. After all, the users are in closest contact with the system; therefore, the system should be designed with them in mind.

To allow the sharing of resources and at the same time meet the performance goals just listed, the operating system must be in complete control of the allocation of the computer system's resources. Only by being the sole allocator of resources can the operating system achieve a balance between user requirements and performance constraints.

1.3   Resource Allocation

Resources are allocated by an operating system according to user needs and system capabilities under the usual constraints of efficient and reliable operation. In simple systems the key resource to be allocated is time on the main processor. Without it, a computation can make no progress. In more complex and powerful systems both hardware devices and software services can be thought of as scarce resources which can be allocated separately. Ideally, users should be able to obtain these resources whenever they need them. Unfortunately, this is not always possible. For instance, there are times when user requirements exceed the amount of available system resources. In such circumstances the system must compromise and fill those requests it believes to be most important. The importance of a request depends not only on the urgency of the user's need, but also on the effect on the system of granting the request. Allocating a resource slows down service for other waiting requests but increases utilization of that resource. One goal of the system is to utilize resources efficiently while maintaining good service.

It is the nature of a system that no single figure of merit exists by which to judge its quality. A system is by its nature a multidimensional object. Even worse, however, is that a system generally provides facilities which are more complex than those provided by any single component. This probably complicates the task of system analysis hopelessly. Perhaps the only fruitful point of view is to design the system with specific measurable goals in mind and then hope for the best as regards the intangibles. In this section some thoughts are presented about the allocation of main resources provided by an operating system.

1.3.1 Processor Time

In an unsophisticated system the entire system is allocated as a single resource unit. A user either controls the machine, or he is waiting to control it. Although this strategy is easy to implement, it does not necessarily utilize the equipment efficiently. The running program may not use any peripheral devices. Clearly, those resources which are not used by the running program remain idle, thus reducing their utilization. This problem can be alleviated somewhat by exercising the inherent concurrency of the hardware.

Since peripherals can operate concurrently with the main processor, it is possible for one program to be executing an I/O operation while another program is executing on the main processor. Although the details of such an implementation are complex, this scheme does have the advantage of making more use of each device. However, since a program must be running on the processor to initiate an I/O device, the allocation of main processor time becomes difficult. For example, assigning the processor to a program which does not need peripheral devices can significantly increase the idle time of these devices. Trying to optimize the usage of all resources, though, can lead to intolerably slow service for some programs, in particular those programs which do not need peripherals. Such dilemmas are frequently encountered and not easily resolved. Methods of allocating the processor in a system which exploits device parallelism are discussed in Chapter 3.

1.3.2 Memory Management

Memory management and processor allocation are closely related. Programs can execute only while they are situated in main memory, but they should not stay there unless they have a good chance of obtaining the processor. Otherwise, the memory they are using is wasted. Main memory is an expensive resource and promises to stay relatively expensive in the foreseeable future. Consequently, the system spends a considerable amount of time packing it effectively, in the attempt to keep useful programs in core and to eliminate gaps between programs.

To eliminate memory "holes" between programs, the system may choose to *relocate* programs. That is, programs are moved around within core to reduce wasted space. Special methods of memory organization can make relocation much easier. These strategies give the operating system considerable flexibility in moving information in and out of core. However, such strategies usually require special hardware and sometimes generate quite a bit of overhead. To justify added complications in the memory allocator, a significant improvement in memory utilization must be realized over more conventional schemes. Unfortunately, the net effect of a complex memory allocation strategy on the entire system is very difficult to quantify. Despite the large amount of research into memory allocation strategies, optimal methods are still difficult to analyze and implement.

Techniques for allocating memory are introduced and analyzed in Chapters 4 and 5, respectively.

1.3.3 I/O Devices

Methods of allocating I/O devices and their associated controllers and channels vary, depending on the speed of the device. Some devices, such as card readers, line printers, and tape drives, are allocated to one job at a time. The job uses the peripheral device for as long as it needs it and then relinquishes control. Fast random access devices, such as drums and disks, can be shared on an operation by operation basis. That is, instead of assigning the unit to one job for an extended period, several jobs are permitted to use the device concurrently. A delay results if two jobs try to do an I/O operation on a device simultaneously; but since the devices are fast, the delay is tolerable. The latter mode of operating is not feasible on a card reader or a tape unit, because the physical nature of the device requires unloading when it is switched from one job to another.

The method of allocating devices has an important effect on both correctness and efficiency. For example, in a system with one reader and one printer, improper allocation policy can bring execution to an unexpected halt. If user A possesses the reader but needs the printer to finish, and user B possesses the printer but needs the reader to finish, both A and B will sit and wait forever (or until one of them has the foresight to release his resource to allow the other one to finish). The resource allocator must prevent such situations from occurring.

Allocation policy also affects device utilization. For example, consider a system with three tape drives where jobs A and B have requests for two and three tape drives, respectively. When two drives are free and one is still in use, it may be better to wait for the third drive in order to grant B's request, rather than give the two drives to A right away. If B already possesses an expensive resource (like another peripheral device or a large amount of core), it may be more efficient to push him through the system quickly, even though the two drives will remain idle temporarily. Such scheduling decisions, which may be counterintuitive in a local situation, actually increase global efficiency.

Efficient allocation of peripherals is difficult to implement for two reasons. First, the analysis required in finding optimal methods of allocating several different types of devices is beyond current mathematical techniques. Many good *ad hoc* methods are known, but the balancing of multiple resource systems is still as much art as science. Second, it is difficult to measure the performance of the resource allocation policy in a given system. Knowing that performance is "poor" does not aid in isolating specific problems. Unfortunately, most presently available monitoring techniques cannot locate specific system inefficiencies; only general manifestations of improper allocation can be measured. Analytic and empirical techniques are even less promising when interactions due to main memory and the central processor are included. Although effective methods are known for allocating processors or memory in isolation from other resources, it is difficult to predict performance when these allocation methods are conjoined in a complex system.

Methods for sharing I/O devices, controllers, and channels are highly device dependent. The organization of one possible scheme is discussed in Chapter 6.

1.3.4 Software Resources

A successful general-purpose operating system often contains extensive system and user libraries of application programs. As resources to be allocated, these libraries have much in common with hardware. Compilers, interpreters, and special utilities, such as text editing and utility sort–merge, can be shared if they are reentrant. A program is *reentrant* if it has completely separate data and procedure sections; "store" operations are applied only to the data section. Reentrant code can be shared among several users by giving each user a private copy of the data section and allowing all users to share a single copy of the procedure section. If a program is not reentrant, then each copy must be allocated to one user at a time, in the same way as any hardware device. Sharing software is somewhat more flexible than sharing hardware in that extra copies of the former can be produced at an acceptable cost when needed. With hardware, one generally must make do with whatever exists. In software sharing the same questions of efficiency and correctness must be considered as in the hardware case.

1.4   The Supervisor

In operating system design the traditional approach is to group a number of processes providing the key facilities under a "master" program called the *supervisor*. As the centralized authority, the supervisor ties the rest of the system together. It organizes cooperating programs by granting privileges and occasionally inflicting punishment; it provides the means for communication and synchronization among processes and physical devices. Traditionally, messages passed between processes, initiation and termination of devices, and hardware signals are all handled by the supervisor. (Some systems spend as much as half of their time in the supervisor.) However, there is no intrinsic reason for the supervisor to be very large. A decentralized organization can have advantages for more streamlined operation of the system.

The supervisor generally controls the allocation of all the resources and facilities of the system to the user population. When a system function, such as language translation or file system maintenance, becomes too big, it is separated from the supervisor. Although the facility is "outside" of the supervisor, it is still responsible for doing that which the supervisor requests. In most systems a program must notify the supervisor of the use of any of the system's resources, even if the program is not a direct part of the supervisor. Therefore, even if the supervisor is small, it retains most of the control of the system.

1.4.1   Supervisory Functions

The main purpose of an operating system is to permit sharing. To do this effectively, the supervisor is put in control of the facilities which the operating system provides. The supervisor's functions can be roughly divided into four areas: controlling and monitoring, communication, protection and enforcement, and utilities [Mealy, 1967].

1.4.1.1   CONTROLLING AND MONITORING

The supervisor is responsible for sequencing and controlling the jobs in the system. Scheduling job execution, accounting for the resources which jobs consume, and interpreting a job control language all facilitate job manipulation. These functions can be implemented independently of the supervisor, or they can be subsumed under it. The user specifies his requirements in a job control language. The supervisor interprets the requirements and notifies various resource allocators what resources and tasks the job is requesting. The resource allocators service the requests, perhaps in priority order. The accounting procedure records the quantity of resources consumed by the user and charges them to the appropriate user code for later billing.

1.4.1.2 COMMUNICATIONS

The supervisor provides links to connect different programs. When two independent programs, such as the file system and the memory manager, want to communicate, they must ask the supervisor to establish contact. After the supervisor establishes initial contact, the programs are allowed to communicate by a system-defined mechanism, such as passing "letters" through a common "mailbox." The communication has to be initialized via the supervisor, since only the supervisor has the privileged knowledge of where the independent programs are located and how they can be contacted. The supervisor's privileged information also allows it to perform other communication activity, such as linking system programs with user programs. Indeed, much of the supervisor's power comes from simply knowing more than any of its users.

1.4.1.3 PROTECTION AND ENFORCEMENT

To ensure smooth operation, the supervisor must enforce constraints on both the system and users. A set of routines monitors hardware signals, especially abnormal conditions. When an error condition occurs, usually via an interrupt, the supervisor must decide to restrain or even abort a job. Limits for execution time and quantity of output must be enforced. The supervisor may also provide a protection scheme by issuing special "tickets." Protected resources are then only accessible by presenting the correct ticket, which hopefully is unforgeable.

In view of its large concentration of information, the supervisor constitutes a very sensitive part of the system. Consequently, the supervisor must be suspicious both of the rest of the system and of users in order to avoid accidental or malicious tampering with its private storage area. To permit protection of the supervisor, some systems have two types of execution modes: supervisor and user. Privileged instructions, such as starting I/O operations or accessing special core locations, can only be executed in supervisor mode. This provision gives the supervisor special power over unprivileged system and user programs. The supervisor can protect itself by keeping its sensitive information in protected storage which is only accessible in supervisor mode. This hardware scheme protects the supervisor from being tampered with.

1.4.1.4 UTILITIES

In addition to allocating resources, the supervisor provides some facilities itself. It contains a set of utility routines for emergency dumps, access to program libraries, on-line message handling, etc. A storage area for communication purposes and tables for the protection system are often located inside the supervisor. It also may be responsible for job control language processing, the system–console interface, and accounting. When more elaborate functions are required, the supervisor generally invokes special software processors.

1.4.2   Evaluation of Centralized Control

There are advantages and disadvantages to the philosophy of centralizing the key system functions in the supervisor. One advantage of centralization is the straightforward implementation of protection. Supervisor mode provides a method of isolating certain parts of the system from users. A second advantage relates to simplicity of organization. It is conceptually easier to group the crucial system functions under the supervisor instead of spreading them throughout the system. This philosophy works best if the supervisor is made very small, since control of the system is then concentrated within an easily locatable boundary. Unfortunately, it is very tempting to incorporate many functions, in which case the distinction between supervisor and operating system loses its advantages.

However, there are significant disadvantages to the centralized supervisor. Programs are not permitted to communicate on their own. Hence, every time something important happens, the supervisor must be invoked. When a large number of programs are trying to communicate simultaneously, only a few will get through to the supervisor. This is an example of a *bottleneck:* A large amount of information must be forced through a channel which has only a limited capacity. Invocations of the supervisor and the services it provides generate overhead. Since it is frequently invoked, the supervisor can become a major (or even *the* major) bottleneck in the system.

In addition to efficiency considerations, the merging of many functions into the supervisor makes modification difficult. Functions may be interdependent, making specific functions hard to isolate. A change to one part of the supervisor affects all other related parts. In this way a small modification can cascade into a major overhaul.

Despite these problems, recent research has given strong evidence supporting the use of a supervisor or a structured group of cooperating supervisors [Brinch Hansen, 1970]. For example, a program can be associated with each major hardware resource, such as main memory, disks, readers, printers, and terminals. By cooperating with each other, these programs together perform the same functions as a supervisor. The modularization of functions within single programs reduces the complexity of each component; however, it also increases the amount of communication needed among components. Successful systems have been built using both the centralized supervisor and the cooperating supervisors methods. A variety of approaches to structuring systems are treated in Chapters 2, 8, and 9.

1.5 Conclusion

The function of an operating system within a computer system is comparable to the function of management in a corporation. It provides an important function in exchange for incurred overhead. Management personnel are responsible for organizing the useful work done by the corporation and distributing the corporation's resources to the working groups. Even with the advent of automation in an industry, the need for management remains. The same is true in computer systems. Even as hardware becomes able to accomplish more complex tasks, the need for the operating system does not diminish. However, the details of the work that an operating system performs may change considerably.

It is anticipated that many of the low-level techniques for managing some resources, particularly memory and peripheral devices, will be subsumed by the hardware in the not too distant future. This is not to say, though, that the subject being presented is guaranteed to grow obsolete. Rather, the problem of sharing resources will always be with us. Although the detailed specifications of the resources may change, the basic techniques for sharing them are likely to find broad application in many areas of computer system design for a long time to come.

Problems

1.1 Prepare a list of storage devices and their characteristics in terms of speed and cost per bit stored. Complete the table with entries corresponding to the years 1950, 1955, 1960, 1965, and 1970. Discuss the trends indicated in the table.

1.2 Many peripheral I/O devices can be attached to a computer. Prepare a list of different I/O devices together with their characteristics, including speed and cost per character. Compare special devices, such as Computer Output Microfilm, character readers, and mark readers, with traditional devices like card readers and line printers.

1.3   Consider a minicomputer serving as a special-purpose device, such as a front-end data concentrator or a network interface. What functions are needed in the operating system of such a computer system? What functions available in general-purpose systems lose their importance?

1.4   What is the difference between a channel and a modern minicomputer? Could a minicomputer serve as a channel? How might it be interfaced to a central computer?

1.5   Prepare a list of equipment used at a particular installation, associating with each device its purchase price. Compare the cost of the processor, memory, and peripheral devices. How do the equipment costs compare with the overall computer center budget?

1.6   Spend some time observing an operator performing his duties at your local computer installation. Prepare a job description for an operator. As a system designer, how much would you trust an operator? Give examples of decisions which the system should make. What activities are operators best equipped to handle?

1.7   Suppose you were asked to design operating systems for a series of machines of increasing size and speed with upward compatibility. Would you design one operating system or would you design one operating system for each machine? Think about the advantages and disadvantages in marketing, maintenance, design, and implementation.

1.8   Suppose a computer system were dedicated completely to numerical analysis applications with small I/O requirements. How would this environment affect the computer system architecture and the operating system's facilities?

1.9   Assume you were asked to design an operating system for a new minicomputer. Make a list of those facilities you would build into the system. Order the list according to decreasing importance of the facilities.

1.10   Grosch's law states that the effectiveness of a computer system is proportional to the square of the capital cost [Sharpe, 1969]. This argument has been a major justification for large, centralized computer installations. Attempt to verify Grosch's law with respect to CPUs, computer systems, minicomputers, communications equipment, etc.

1.11   Supply and demand of goods in the economy is controlled by pricing schemes. Discuss the relative merits of various pricing schemes for computer facilities. Outline a pricing scheme which is fair, equitable, and efficient to implement.

2

PROCESSES

2.1 Introduction

The subject of this chapter is the definition and properties of the basic unit of computation within an operating system, the *process*. Consider first the familiar type of computation, the sequential program. A large sequential program written in a language such as ALGOL or PL/I can be subdivided into smaller sequential programs called *procedures*. If recursion is excluded, then a procedure never has more than one activation at a time. Hence, any computation being performed can be uniquely identified by the procedure which is active. However, in operating systems this simple relation between computations and procedures is lost. One procedure may be executing simultaneously in several parts of the system. For example, several disk channels may share a single input procedure. Conversely, a function which is conceptually a single operation, such as "input," may use one or more different procedures each time it executes. When a job says "read a card," the system takes different actions, depending on where the next card is located. It may already be in core; it may be residing on a disk; or perhaps it has to be physically read in from the card reader. In some cases the command "read a card" may be a multistep operation involving steps which are executed concurrently. Thus, for a given computational task, there may be more than one associated procedure; or a single procedure may be active in more than one computational task. The one-to-one correspondence between procedures and computations that is present in sequential programming languages does not exist in operating systems. Therefore, the concepts of computation and procedure cannot be equated.

Computations within an operating system are not inherently sequential. The central processor, channels, and devices all operate concurrently. It is natural that the software reflect this concurrency. Typically, an operating system consists of a number of computations which progress almost independently, such as input, output, and CPU activity. The *process* is a formalization of this notion of an "independent computation." Processes are a convenient model for understanding what happens within an operating system. The motivation for concurrent processes can be best explained by examining the concurrency which is built into the computer system itself.

2.1.1 Concurrency in Hardware Systems

From the hardware viewpoint, parallel operation has almost always been present at the bit level. Traditionally, the way to build faster arithmetic units, such as adders and multipliers, is to increase the amount of work which can be accomplished in parallel. There is good reason for taking this approach. The current technology in digital electronics is approaching physical limits in terms of speed of individual components. Devices operate with speeds on the order of tens of nanoseconds, and light travels about 1 foot in 1 nanosecond. Further miniaturization will increase device speed somewhat. However, major improvements in the computational capacity of machines will probably be due to increased parallelism.

Peripheral devices and their channels work concurrently with the central processing unit. The central processor can also exploit hardware parallelism. A number of machines have increased their computing power by increasing the number of processors (for example, ILLIAC IV). In a hardware system with several arithmetic processors and a number of channels all working simultaneously, organizing the computations associated with these devices is a complex task. To organize them efficiently is even more difficult.

One user does not usually exercise the facilities of the system uniformly. If he is doing a lot of I/O, he is probably not using the arithmetic unit very much. Conversely, if he is doing a lot of computation, he is likely leaving the I/O peripherals idle. By allowing several users to be active at the same time, the system has a better chance to utilize the equipment fully. While one user is printing and a second user is reading, a third can be computing on the central processor. Therefore, in addition to having a number of hardware devices operating concurrently, there may be several user jobs which are executing concurrently.

2.1.2   Concurrency in Software Systems

User jobs, when executing concurrently, generally should not be aware of each other's existence. When a job issues a print command, it is not concerned that another job is currently reading in cards. Hardware devices act in a similar fashion. The printer is usually unaware of the reader's presence. To model this adequately, a unit of computation is needed which reflects this concurrency, namely, the process. Since computations proceed independently, the processes which represent the computations should be independent. In addition, since devices operate at different speeds, the relative speeds of processes should also be independent. Therefore, by examining computer systems, several properties of processes have been isolated: processes are independent computations which execute concurrently and at varying speeds.

Computations do occasionally have to exchange information. To the extent that computations must communicate with each other, they are not completely independent. Processes, which are being used to model computations, must reflect this ability to communicate. If processes were allowed to communicate in a random fashion, it would be difficult to understand their complex interactions. Therefore, communication among processes is permitted only through explicit, well-defined mechanisms. Methods for communication among processes are described in later sections.

Although concurrency has been shown to be present among hardware and software components, programs are usually sequential. This is not always the case. There are programming languages which allow the specification of concurrent computations. However, the human mind seems better adapted to mastering sequential programs. Consequently, in this book processes are assumed to be sequential. That is, operations within the process are applied in a well-defined sequence. Intuitively, one can think of a sequential process as the execution of an ALGOL program. In subsequent sections the word "process" is used as an abbreviated form of the term "sequential process" without further comment.

2.2   Process Definition

The concept of process appears in many papers; it is probably the most frequently used and least precisely defined term in operating systems. Loosely speaking, a *process* can be thought of as a group of memory cells which changes according to certain rules. In a computer these rules are usually specified by a *program,* which is interpreted by a *processor.* Although the underlying intent is clear, definitions have varied considerably. Nearly every new system or system model has redefined the term with a slightly different connotation. In OS/360 the term "task" is used and defined as "the basic multiprogramming unit under the control program" [IBM, 1965]. Saltzer [1966] states that "a process is a program in execution by a pseudo-processor." Dijkstra [1968b] defines a sequential process to be what happens during the execution of a sequential program on a computer. Horning and Randell [1973] have constructed a formal definition of the process concept. To clarify the concept, we present a formal model for processes very similar to that of Horning and Randell, [1973].

Let $X = \{x0, x1, \ldots, xN, \ldots\}$ be a possibly infinite set of state *variables,* called the *state variable set.* A *state* is an assignment of values to the elements of the state variable set. A *state space* for the state variable set consists of the set of states that the variable set can assume. An *action* assigns values to some of the variables of the variable set. A sequence of states from the state space is called a *computation.* One way of obtaining a computation is by successive applications of various actions. Each action generates a new state, and the sequence of states is a computation. An *action function* is a function which maps states into actions. An action function can also generate a computation given an initial state. It merely specifies an action to apply at each state, and the action yields a new state. The action function interprets new states, ad infinitum, thus producing a series of states. Intuitively, the variable set is memory, a state is the contents of memory, and the action function is a program.

A *process* can now be defined as a state space, an action function in that state space, and some special elements of the state space called the *initial states.* Consider the process P, which has two variables x and y. A computation of P can be described by a sequence of states: $\{(2, 1), (4, 2), (6, 3), (8, 4), \ldots, (2i, i), \ldots\}$. A computation of P can also be described by a state space $\{(i, j)$ where i and j are natural numbers$\}$, one of its initial states $(2, 1)$, and the action function which for all states yields the action $(x, y) \rightarrow (x + 2, y + 1)$.

Each state of the process represents a "snapshot" of the progress of the computation which the process performs. Suppose a program, together with its variables, is stored in main memory. The execution of the program can be visualized by observing the memory locations and registers associated with the program. At any given time each memory location will contain a certain value. The status of the program's execution is given by the values of all of its memory locations at a particular moment—hence, the notion of state. A sequence of states describes the progression of the program's computation in a given environment. A program, or action function, with an initial state is just another way of describing that sequence of states.

Some states of a process will be rather uninteresting to some observers. For instance, when a procedure is invoked, the interesting states from the viewpoint of the calling program are at the invocation and at the return, with particular emphasis on the parameters. Most of the "internal" states of the procedure do not warrant any special attention, since the calling program's main interest rests on the results of the procedure call. Similarly, only some of the variables are particularly interesting, namely, those which get returned at the conclusion of the computation. Both of these ideas are easily formalized by considering only subsets of states and state variables.

The foregoing model exhibits the properties of processes discussed in the last section. For example, it was said that processes are nearly independent. Clearly, if two processes have disjoint state variable sets, then they cannot interact. Communication among processes is modeled by shared variables. It was noted that several processes may execute the same code. This corresponds to equivalent action functions which act on different variable sets. In fact, most of the concepts relating to processes can be stated in terms of the Horning and Randell model. For our purposes, the important point is that formal definitions are available. That the nature of the remainder of this chapter is rather informal should not be interpreted as a lack of precision in the ideas. Rather, precise concepts are treated informally primarily for convenience of explanation.

Although processes have been conceptualized as abstract entities, they model real components of operating systems. Action functions and state variables represent procedures and memory locations. One implementation of processes as software components is discussed in the next section.

2.3   Process Implementation

The following hypothetical implementation of the process concept, although not an exact copy of any particular system, closely resembles processes as implemented in many systems, such as RC4000, THE, Project SUE, and Venus (see Chapter 10). In a real system a process models an execution of one or more procedures on a physical processor which is provided by the hardware. Each software process is uniquely identified by a data structure called the *process descriptor*. In a typical system the process descriptor contains

1. a state variable, which defines the status of the process (for example, ready-to-run, running, blocked);

2. a save area, which holds the current values of registers when the process is interrupted in the middle of its execution;

3. information about the resources that the process either owns or is entitled to use.

The descriptor may also have, among other things, space reserved for communication activity with other processes. The discussion of communication is deferred to later sections.

In Section 2.2 a process was defined to be an abstract unit of computation which was claimed to be convenient for describing the activity in an operating system. The machine representation of a process consists of a descriptor and a block of memory. It is important to distinguish between an abstract process and a software process. Frequently, a software process will be a process, and conversely—but not always. In the remainder of this section "abstract processes" will be clearly identified as such. Since in this book discussion will be almost exclusively centered on software processes, the term "process" will refer only to software processes.

Somehow, the descriptor and memory area which constitute the software process must be allocated from the machine's available resources. There are two approaches to the creation of software processes. A system may be built which has a fixed number of software processes which always exist. Therefore, software processes are created at the same time as the system. To perform a computation, one need only get control of one of the existing software processes. There may be more abstract processes than there are software processes. An abstract process may therefore have to wait until a software process becomes available, so that the computation can be performed. Alternatively, a mechanism can be built into the system which creates and destroys software processes when requested to do so. This mechanism, which is *not* a software process itself, provides the system with the ability to manipulate software processes. This mechanism is called the *kernel*. In the remainder of this section the view is taken that a kernel exists and that the system already consists of one or more software processes.

Processes are able to cause the creation and destruction of other processes. One process can request that the kernel create another process. The kernel initializes a new process descriptor, allocates some memory for the process, and signals the completion of the activity to the creator process. The creator process now stores a program (that is, a representation of an action function) in the new process's memory. The kernel provides the *start* command, which allocates a processor to a process. By invoking the start operation with the created process as a parameter, the creator can initiate the execution of the created process. Similarly, the command *stop* deallocates the processor, and the command *destroy* deallocates the descriptor and the resources of a process.

In a system with only one processor, there can still be multiple processes. The kernel gives each process the use of the processor when appropriate. For example, with ten processes, the kernel may give each process a tenth of every processing second. Each process behaves as though it has its own CPU (albeit a slow one). Actually, all processes share one CPU. The starting and stopping of processes is implemented by granting or revoking access to the shared processor.

Processes may exist as unrelated units, or they may be related in a structured manner. In an unstructured system one part of the system, usually the supervisor, is responsible for creating processes as they are needed. When a task arises, the supervisor creates a process to do the task. When the task is completed, the process is destroyed. Thus, all processes are "equal" within the system structure. Each is created and destroyed by the supervisor. In a more structured system not all processes are equal. For example, processes can be structured as a tree [Brinch Hansen, 1970; Sevcik *et al.*, 1972].

In a tree-structured system a process is said to be the *father* of all the processes it creates, and a process is said to be a *son* of the process that created it. *Ancestors* and *descendants* are defined in the obvious way (that is, grandfathers, grandsons, etc.). A *creation tree* for the system is defined to be a directed graph where each process is represented by a node, and an arc connects node A to node B if and only if A is the father of B (see Fig. 2–1). The creation tree describes the ordering of processes within the system at any point in time.

A tree-structured system may have very strict rules regarding the passing of resources and the location of control. For example, each process, when created, might receive only resources that are "owned" by its father. In addition, a father could have control over the actions of its sons and could take measures to remedy abnormal situations. Specifically, one might permit only a father to inspect or modify the process descriptor of its sons, thereby changing their status.

There are clear advantages to this highly structured scheme. First, the allocation of resources is strictly controlled. Each process's resources were at one time the property of each of its ancestors. If a process wishes to release some of its resources, it can give them up only to its father. There is never any ambiguity as to which process owns which

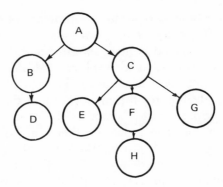

FIG. 2–1 Creation tree. (Each node is a process. A directed arc from node A to node B means that A is the father of B.)

resource. Second, the overall structure gives some processes more control than others, providing a simple mechanism for division of labor. If a process is assigned to do a task, it can create several sons, each of which will do part of the task. These sons may further divide the sub-tasks until the task is complete. Again, the structure always makes it clear which process is in control, namely, a father is in control of its sons. In an unstructured system the supervisor knows all; that is, every process has the same father. Although the centralized control allows more freedom in dividing tasks, it complicates the bookkeeping, since the supervisor must keep track of every process in the system. Most systems are structured to some extent. Local protocols among certain groups of processes give some processes more power than others. Some systems are built in "levels" where each succeeding level is somewhat less powerful than its creator. This arrangement roughly corresponds to a tree which has degenerated into a long chain. There are advantages and disadvantages to each of these structuring techniques. Examples of the tree structure and level structure are provided in Chapters 8 and 10.

So far, processes have no means of communication. Once created and started, they operate independently until stopped or destroyed. However, processes have a need to exchange information. To allow them to exchange information, mechanisms for process communication must be introduced.

2.4 Process Communication

Both hardware and software resources must be shared if they are to be utilized efficiently. Consider a user job that executes within the system as a single software process. It is rare that such a process needs exclusive control of a hardware device during its entire lifetime. Assume the process is using a channel to access a peripheral device. In general, the channel will be able to service requests much faster than the process generates them. Consequently, it makes sense to have several processes sharing a single channel. A shared channel services requests from all of the processes, and therefore is better utilized.

Software sharing is equally important for reducing inefficiency. Consider a utility program, such as a compiler. When a process needs to translate a program, it can copy the compiler into its own memory area and then execute it. If several processes are using the compiler simultaneously, much memory is wasted with duplicated code. By having only one copy of the compiler in storage and allowing processes to share this copy, memory can be saved. Thus, in both hardware and software, shared resources improve system efficiency.

Notice that hardware and software resources have common properties. Consider a file system that can service requests from only one process at a time. Even though the file system is a software resource, it is shared in the same way as many hardware resources. When several processes are trying to use it, the file system can be as serious a bottleneck as a disk drive or a CPU. Physical devices are called *physical* or *natural* resources. A piece of software that behaves as if it were a physical resource is called a *logical resource*. Logical resources exist only in their incarnation in software. For example, to allow several processes to share a disk, the system may implement a number of logical disks which share a physical drive. Each logical disk is a process which communicates with the disk channel. When a process uses a logical disk, it "thinks" it has a whole disk. In reality all it has is a logical disk which simulates a complete physical unit by sending and receiving commands from the disk channel. A process using a resource does not care whether the resource is a logical one implemented in software or a physical one implemented in hardware. The process's only concern is that the resource do what it is supposed to do. When discussing resource sharing, logical and physical resources are generally not distinguished, since their external behavior is essentially equivalent.

2.4.1 Process Synchronization

Although natural and logical resources may be shared, they can generally be used by only one process at a time. A resource that allows only one user at a time is called a *critical resource*. If several processes wish to share the use of a critical resource, they must synchronize their operation so that at most one of them is ever in control of the resource. If one process is using the resource, then all other processes that want the resource are temporarily excluded and must wait until the resource is freed. Within each process, the regions which access critical resources can be isolated. These regions, called *critical sections,* must have the property that they be *mutually exclusive.* That is, at most one process can be executing a critical section with respect to a resource at one time.

Many natural resources, such as tape drives and card readers, are critical. However, shared variables which can be modified by a number of processes are also critical resources. For example, assume two processes, named A and B, share a variable named COUNT. If both A and B attempt to increment COUNT by one simultaneously, the final value of COUNT may be incorrect. Suppose the following sequence of events occurs:

1. process A stores the value of COUNT in a local variable called TEMPA;
2. process B stores the value of COUNT in a local variable called TEMPB;
3. process A increments the value of TEMPA by one and stores it in COUNT;
4. process B increments the value of TEMPB by one and stores it in COUNT.

Even though two processes have each incremented COUNT by one, the final value of COUNT is augmented by only one, not two. To prevent this kind of undesirable behavior, the incrementing of COUNT must be treated as a critical section. In fact, whenever several processes have the capability of incrementing a shared location, to avoid erratic behavior, the variable must be manipulated as a critical resource.

Consider the two independent processes described in Fig. 2–2. Each process successively executes its critical section and then performs some other work. The critical sections represent a group of operations that access a shared critical resource. To forbid simultaneous execution of the two critical sections, a mechanism that synchronizes the two processes must be implemented. This mechanism must have two properties. First, if one or more processes want to access their critical sections, then at least one must eventually be permitted to enter. Second, at most one process is allowed to be in its critical section at a time. A number of solutions to the problem of synchronizing critical sections are discussed later in the chapter.

```
parbegin
    PROCESS 1:    do      while (true);
                          begin
                              critical section 1;
                          end ;
                          remainder of process 1;
                  end;
    PROCESS 2:    do      while (true);
                          begin
                              critical section 2;
                          end
                          remainder of process 2;
                  end
parend
```

The construct:
```
    parbegin
        statement 1;
        statement 2;
          .
          .
          .
        statement N
    parend
```
indicates that statements 1 through *N* can be executed
concurrently.

FIG. 2–2   Critical section problem.

In addition to synchronizing themselves for purposes of mutual exclusion, processes must also communicate to exchange data. For example,
user processes have to communicate with the console operator to request
tape and disk mounts. This type of communication is easily effected
by allowing processes to pass messages.

Let PRODUCER be a process which transmits blocks of data to another process called CONSUMER. These blocks of data can be thought
of as messages. For example, PRODUCER may be a user process generating lines of output, and CONSUMER may be the process which outputs the lines on a printer.

One way to implement the passing of messages is to have a pool
of empty buffers, where each buffer can hold one message. Between
PRODUCER and CONSUMER there is a queue of full buffers containing messages. When PRODUCER wishes to send a message, it adds
a buffer to the end of the queue. CONSUMER receives a message by
removing the buffer which is on the front of the queue. Although the
solution appears trivial, PRODUCER and CONSUMER must cooperate

in many ways. For instance, they must keep track of the number of full and empty buffers. PRODUCER can transmit only as long as empty buffers are available. Similarly, CONSUMER can receive only when the queue is nonempty. Clearly, shared variables are needed to count the number of full and empty buffers. However, since variables are being shared, critical sections are required. Therefore, altering the count of full and empty buffers must be done in a mutually exclusive way. A similar problem is encountered in the implementation of the message queue. Assume the queue is implemented as a linked list. If PRODUCER adds a message to the queue just as CONSUMER is removing the very last message from the queue, a misdirected link may result. This situation is not unlike the example where COUNT was incremented from two processes. Therefore, the manipulation of queue pointers also constitutes a critical section. In short, implementing a "simple" producer–consumer relationship requires much care.

Processes such as PRODUCER and CONSUMER, which communicate on an equal basis through some external mechanism, are called *coroutines* [Conway, 1963]. Coroutines are not related by a "calling" and "called" procedure, as in the subroutine. Rather, they cooperate by calling each other. Unfortunately, the word "coroutine" has been given a variety of conflicting definitions in the literature. To eliminate confusion about coroutines, we choose to use the notion of "cooperating processes" instead of coroutine in this book.

In the producer–consumer example messages travel in only one direction. If it is important for PRODUCER to know that its message was received, then CONSUMER must acknowledge the receipt of each message. This requires a response to travel in the other direction. If there are a number of producer–consumer pairs operating within the system, empty buffers can be shared through a common pool. Such additional complications are more representative of real producer–consumer problems encountered in system design.

In this section, two basic problems of process communication were discussed: the critical section problem and the producer–consumer problem. In the next two sections these problems are solved by outlining different mechanisms that enable processes to communicate effectively while avoiding undesirable interaction.

2.5   Low-Level Synchronization Primitives

The most basic process synchronization primitive operations operate close to the hardware: memory interlock, test and set, and semaphores.

Each of these mechanisms is sufficient for implementing both mutual exclusion and producer–consumer relationships among independent processes.

2.5.1 Memory Interlock

Mutual exclusion is implemented in hardware by making store operations indivisible. That is, if two processes each try to store a value in a single location, the hardware arbitrates; one access is permitted to store right away, and the other process must wait until the first completes. This arbitration, called *memory interlock,* is sufficient for the implementation of mutual exclusion among two or more processes.

Recall the critical section problem as described in Fig. 2–2. A solution must guarantee that at most one process can enter the critical section at one time, and if one or more processes desire entry to the critical section, then one will definitely be allowed to enter. Since the speeds of the two processes are independent, the foregoing conditions must hold no matter how fast each process is executing relative to the other. The following example is an attempted solution which fails because of the latter restriction.

In Fig. 2–3, each process has associated with it a switch which has the value "true" when that process is in its critical section, and "false"

```
Begin boolean switch 1, switch 2;
      switch 1 := false;
      switch 2 := false;
      parbegin
          process 1 :        do      while (true);
          loop 1 :                   do while (switch 2);
                                     end;
                                     switch 1 := true;
                                       /* critical section 1 */
                                     switch 1 := false;
                                       /* remainder of process 1 */
                             end;
          process 2 :        do      while (true);
          loop 2 :                   do while (switch 1);
                                     end;
                                     switch 2 := true;
                                       /* critical section 2 */
                                     switch 2 := false;
                                       /* remainder of process 2 */
                             end
      parend
end
```

FIG. 2–3 Incorrect critical section solution.

otherwise. Before entering the critical section, a process tests the other process's switch to make sure it is safe to enter. It then turns on its own switch and uses the critical section. However, the safety of this "solution" is illusory. Assume process 1 is in loop 1 while process 2 is in its critical section. Process 2 finishes its critical section and turns switch 2 to false. This frees process 1 from executing loop 1. Since speeds are arbitrary, suppose that process 2 is moving much faster than process 1. It moves so much faster, in fact, that after process 1 finds switch 2 to be false, but before it has the chance to set switch 1 to be true, process 2 rushes through the rest of its cycle, and skips through loop 2 (since switch 1 is still false). Both processes may "safely" proceed to set their respective switches to true and execute the critical section. The arbitrary speed assumption has led us to a sequence of events that allows both processes to execute their critical sections simultaneously. Thus, Fig. 2–3 does not solve the critical section problem.

The reader is encouraged to try to modify this program so that it satisfies the restrictions of a critical section solution. It is a nontrivial exercise. The first correct solution, due to Dekker, is shown in Fig. 2–4 (rewritten without GO TO statements by R. C. Holt). In this solution the variable $c1 = 1$ when process 1 wants to enter its critical section, $c2 = 1$ when process 2 wants to enter its critical section, and "turn" specifies whose turn it is to try to enter, given that both processes want to use their critical sections. To appreciate the subtlety of Dekker's algorithm, one should attempt to execute it by hand with different relative processor speeds. The solution, which has been proved correct [Dijkstra, 1968a], has also been generalized to the case of an arbitrary number of processes competing for the critical resource [Dijkstra, 1965; Knuth, 1966].

2.5.2   Test and Set

To implement mutual exclusion, many machines provide hardware instructions that are easier to use and more efficient than the simple indivisible store operation. One such operation is the "test and set."

The hardware instruction *test and set* significantly simplifies the solution to the critical section problem over memory interlock. Test and set is invoked with two parameters, LOCAL and COMMON. The instruction takes the value of COMMON and assigns it to LOCAL, and then sets the value of COMMON TO ONE. The main property of the operation is that it is indivisible. When a process executes a test and set operation, no other action can intervene between the initiation and termination of the operation.

```
Begin integer   c1 , c2, turn ;
                c1 := 0 ;
                c2 := 0 ;
                turn := 1 ;
        parbegin
        process 1 :   begin c1 := 1 ;
                            do while (c2 = 1) ;
                              if turn = 2
                              then   begin c1 := 0 ;
                                            do while (turn = 2) ;
                                            end ;
                                            c1 := 1
                                     end
                            end ;
                            critical section for process 1 ;
                            c1 := 0 ;
                            turn := 2 ;
                            remainder of process 1
                      end ;
        process 2 :   begin c2 := 1 ;
                            do while (c1 = 1) ;
                              if turn = 1
                              then   begin c2 := 0 ;
                                            do while (turn = 1) ;
                                            end ;
                                            c2 := 1
                                     end
                            end ;
                            critical section for process 2 ;
                            c2 := 0 ;
                            turn := 1 ;
                            remainder of process 2
                      end
        parend
end
```

FIG. 2–4   Dekker's algorithm.

The variable COMMON is shared among the processes which are being synchronized with respect to some critical resource. Each process has its own private variable LOCAL. In the IBM/360 implementation of test and set, the condition code of the machine acts as the local variable. COMMON = 1 implies there is a process in the critical section. Initially, COMMON = 0. In Fig. 2–5 the mutual exclusion problem for two processes is solved using the test and set instruction. In this solution it is assumed that the machine has memory interlock, that is, the instruction COMMON : = 0 is indivisible.

```
Begin      integer      COMMON ;
              COMMON := 0 ;
         parbegin
           process 1 :    begin  integer LOCAL 1 ;
                              do while (true) ;
                                 LOCAL 1 := 1 ;
                                 do while ( LOCAL 1 = 1) ;
                                     Test and set  (LOCAL 1, COMMON)
                                 end ;
                                 critical section 1 ;
                                 COMMON := 0 ;
                                 remainder of process 1
                              end
                       end ;
           process 2 :    begin  integer LOCAL 2 ;
                              do while (true) ;
                                 LOCAL 2 := 1 ;
                                 do while (LOCAL 2 = 1) ;
                                     Test and set  (LOCAL 2, COMMON) ;
                                 end ;
                                 critical section 2 ;
                                 COMMON := 0 ;
                                 remainder of process 2
                              end
                       end
         parend
      end
```

FIG. 2–5   Mutual exclusion problem using test and set.

Although memory interlock and test and set are each sufficient for implementing mutual exclusion, they are both very inefficient. Whenever one process is executing its critical section, any other process which tries to enter ends up in a loop, waiting for permission to proceed. This indefinite looping, called *busy waiting*, wastes processor time. Until the process which is using the critical resource decides to relinquish it, all other processes that are waiting might just as well "go to sleep" and give away the processors on which they are executing. When the critical section is free again, one of the "sleeping" processes can then be awakened, have its processor returned, and be granted access to the critical resource. One simple synchronization mechanism which allows processes to wait without busy waiting is the "semaphore."

2.5.3 Semaphores

A *semaphore*, sometimes called a *general semaphore*, is an integer variable whose value can only be altered by the operations P and V

[Dijkstra, 1968a,b]. Let S be a semaphore. When a process executes $P(S)$, then S is decremented by one and

1. if $S \geq 0$, then the process continues execution; or
2. if $S < 0$, then the process is stopped and put on a waiting queue associated with S; it remains blocked until a $V(S)$ operation by another process releases it.

When a process executes $V(S)$, S is incremented by one and

1. if $S > 0$, then the process continues execution; or
2. if $S \leq 0$, then one process is removed from the waiting queue and is permitted to continue execution; the process which invoked $V(S)$ can also continue execution.

In addition, the operations P and V are indivisible. Only one process can execute a P or V operation at a time on a given semaphore. Therefore, if $S = 1$ and two processes try to execute a $P(S)$ simultaneously, only one process will be permitted to continue. The other process will be blocked and put on the waiting queue for S.

Recall that in Section 2.3 a kernel, which implements processes, was defined. The kernel is responsible for allocating and deallocating processors to processes. P and V can be implemented within the kernel, since the kernel has the power to start and stop processes. There must be the added proviso that the kernel service only one P or V operation on a given semaphore at a time, to ensure indivisibility of the operation. With the additional power of the P and V commands, the critical section problem is now solvable without a busy wait.

A semaphore which has a maximum value of one is called a *binary semaphore*. Using a binary semaphore S, processes can implement mutual exclusion merely by bracketing their critical sections by $P(S)$ and $V(S)$ (see Fig. 2–6). If there are two processes using S to synchronize their critical sections, then by the definition of semaphore, S takes on a value of 1, 0, or -1. If $S = 1$, then neither process is executing its critical section. If $S = 0$, then one process is executing its critical section. If $S = -1$, then one process is executing its critical section and one process is on the waiting queue for S, waiting to be allowed to enter the critical section. This simple solution using binary semaphores works equally well when more processes are added. Whereas Dekker's algorithm becomes quite complex with more than two processes, the semaphore solution remains trivial. This is a main advantage of the semaphore approach.

Using general semaphores, the producer–consumer problem is easily

```
Begin      integer  free ;
           free := 1 ;
           parbegin
               process 1 :   begin
                                 do while  (true) ;
                                     start of process 1 ;
                                     P (free) ;
                                         critical section 1 ;
                                     V (free) ;
                                     remainder of process 1
                                 end
                             end ;
               process 2 :   begin
                                 do while  (true) ;
                                     start process 2 ;
                                     P (free) ;
                                         critical section 2 ;
                                     V (free) ;
                                     remainder of process 2
                                 end
                             end
           parend
           end
```

FIG. 2–6   Critical section problem using semaphores.

solved (see Fig. 2–7). AVAIL is a semaphore whose value is the number of empty buffers in the buffer pool. FULL is a semaphore whose value is the number of full buffers that have been sent to the consumer. The semaphore MUTEX (MUTual EXclusion) is binary and guarantees that only one process can operate on the buffer pointers at a time.

General semaphores provide a natural means for managing resources. In the producer–consumer solution general semaphores were used to count full and empty buffers. They can be used equally well to allocate tape drives, disk drives, or typewriter terminals. Let DISK be the number of disk drives available. A process requests a disk by invoking P(DISK). A disk is released by invoking V(DISK). There is no chance that one disk drive will be allocated to two processes, since DISK will only be decremented by one process at a time.

Semaphores can also be used for synchronization. For example, process 1 may ask process 2 to do some work for it. Until process 2 finishes, process 1 has nothing to do; so it invokes P(WAIT), where WAIT is a semaphore with initial value zero. When process 2 completes the work, it signals process 1 by executing V(WAIT). Process 1 is now "awakened" and can continue processing. This use of semaphores is not conceptually different from the critical section problem, since process

```
Begin       integer  avail, full, mutex ;
            avail := number of empty buffers ;
            full := 0 ;
            mutex := 1 ;
            parbegin
               producer :   begin
                               do while (true) ;
                               prepare message ;
                               P (avail) ;
                               P (mutex) ;
                               send message ;
                               V (full) ;
                               V (mutex)
                            end
                          end ;
               consumer :   begin
                               do while (true) ;
                               P (full) ;
                               P (mutex) ;
                               receive message ;
                               V (avail) ;
                               V (mutex) ;
                               process message
                            end
                          end
            parend
      end
```

FIG. 2–7 Producer–consumer semaphore solution.

2 can be considered to be a resource that is protected by the semaphore WAIT. However, in using semaphores for synchronization and resource management, complications arise in scheduling the semaphore waiting queue.

If a semaphore S goes negative, then one or more processes are on a waiting queue associated with S. When the next $V(S)$ operation is performed, the kernel must choose a process to remove from the waiting queue. The kernel may use a first-come-first-served (FCFS) discipline and remove the longest-waiting process from the queue. Or a more complex scheduling algorithm, such as highest-priority-first, may determine the next process to be released. The scheduling discipline must be chosen based on the purpose for which the semaphore is used.

For example, consider a semaphore solution to the critical section problem. If a critical section is too long, it quickly becomes a bottleneck for the processes which share it. Therefore, critical sections are usually kept quite short. This implies that no process ever has to wait very long to enter the critical section. Since processes do not spend much time on the semaphore waiting queue anyway, the simplest scheduling discipline might just as well be used, namely, FCFS. However, resource management and synchronization often require more complex rules, since waiting times can be significant.

Recall the semaphore DISK used to allocate disk drives. Assume all the disks are being used and that several additional processes are requesting drives, that is, DISK < 0. When the next process releases a disk with V(DISK), it may be important which of the waiting processes is released. For instance, one of the processes may already have three tape drives. It is clear that this process should receive the newly freed disk before a process that possesses no expensive resources. In this case, a priority-based scheduling rule is desirable. The priority of the process can be determined dynamically by the number of expensive resources that the process controls. This example shows that a single scheduling rule is generally not sufficient in implementing semaphore queues.

Semaphores are generally considered to be sufficient for the synchronization and communication requirements of an operating system. The THE Multiprogramming System (see Chapter 8) and the Venus Operating System (see Chapter 10) both use semaphores as the basic communication mechanism. However, semaphores are often quite inconvenient because they are too primitive. For example, the implementation via semaphores of a sophisticated message-passing scheme among a group of parallel processes is reasonably complex. One can simplify the solutions to such common synchronization problems by choosing more elegant communication tools. Several of these more elegant communication mechanisms are described in the next section.

2.6 High-Level Synchronization Primitives

The synchronization mechanisms discussed so far are logically complete and quite powerful, but their use presents many dangers. Their primitive nature often leads to complex constructions that are difficult to comprehend and rather sensitive to minor changes. Slight perturbations of critical section and producer–consumer solutions sometimes yield catastrophic results. The synchronization primitives described in this section yield solutions which are easily understood. Hence, the programmer has a high degree of confidence in his code. Although they provide an elegant communication mechanism, the higher-level primitives frequently require an elaborate and costly implementation. However, there is some evidence that the expense is justified by the decrease in the likelihood of programming error.

2.6.1 *Mailboxes*

Mailboxes derive their name from the conventional mechanism for sending mail. If process P1 wants to communicate with process P2, then P1 requests that a mailbox be created which connects the two processes so that messages can be passed between them. To communicate with P2, P1 merely puts in the mailbox a message, which P2 may pick up at any time. The mailbox ensures that P2 eventually receives the message, if and when P2 requests it.

A *mailbox* is a data structure with associated rules which describe its operation. Logically, it consists of a *header* element, which describes the mailbox, and a number of *slots* in which messages are deposited. The size of each slot and the number of slots are generally fixed when the mailbox is created. The operation rules vary, depending on the complexity of the mailbox. In the simplest case messages are passed in only one direction. Process P1 can send messages as long as there are empty slots. If all the slots are full, then P1 can either wait, or it can continue doing other things and try to send the message later. Similarly, P2 can receive messages as long as there are full slots. If there are no messages, it can either wait for a message or continue executing. This simple mailbox design can be complicated in several ways to obtain a more sophisticated communication mechanism.

2.6.1.1 TWO-WAY COMMUNICATION

It is often desirable for P1 to receive an acknowledgment from P2 that the latter received the message and took some action. This can be accomplished by allowing communication through the mailbox in both directions. Now, each slot contains either a message from P1 or an acknowledgment from P2. One problem with this scheme arises if P1 is sending messages faster than P2 can acknowledge them. P1 may fill up all the slots, leaving no room for acknowledgments from P2. This situation is resolved by requiring that acknowledgments be sent in the same slot that carried the original message. When a message is sent, the slot is reserved until the acknowledgment is received. This restriction prevents P1 from bombarding P2 with messages that it does not have time to answer.

2.6.1.2 MULTIPLE-INPUT MAILBOXES

Frequently, many processes want to communicate efficiently with one process that provides an important utility, such as the file system or accounting manager. This situation is sometimes called the *demon problem*. Mailboxes with only a single input and output handle this problem very inefficiently. Each process has to have a separate mailbox to communicate with the utility. Furthermore, the utility must poll each of these mailboxes for requests. A multiple-input mailbox allows several processes to deposit messages. The messages may be received according to any priority discipline. Needless to say, multiple-input mailboxes are more difficult to implement than the single-entry kind. However, the multiple-input mailbox can represent an improvement in efficiency over multiple mailboxes in solving the demon problem. Multiple-output mailboxes can be defined analogously.

2.6.1.3   PORTS

A process must know the name of a mailbox in order to send a message to it. This is occasionally an inconvenient restriction. For example, consider a system with several disk drives where each drive has an associated driver process which routes read and write requests to the channel. When a process wants to use a particular drive, it hooks up a two-way mailbox to the driver process and sends disk commands to that mailbox. The driver process returns messages, such as "the write command is completed" or "here is the record you asked me to read." Clearly, the driver process does not care who is asking for its services, since read and write requests are the same, no matter who sends them. To avoid requiring a process to know the name of the mailbox it is using, processes can communicate by means of ports. A *port* is a connector that links a process to a mailbox. After a mailbox is connected to the port, the process need only give the name of the port to send the message. In the foregoing example, the disk driver process sends its message and its replies through one of its ports, with complete indifference regarding whose mailbox the port is connected to. Mailbox names are only needed when the mailbox is physically connected to two ports.

The operation of mailboxes is best understood by means of an example. The following mailbox system was designed for (but not implemented in) the SUE System [Atwood *et al.*, 1972].

2.6.1.4   SUE MAILBOX SYSTEM

Assume processes are implemented as in the kernel of Section 2.3. The SUE design uses two-way mailboxes connected via ports. Processes have two types of ports: *input ports* and *output ports*. Each mailbox is connected to one input port and to one output port. A message sent through an output port is called a *query*, and a message sent through an input port is called a *reply*. Each mailbox slot is in one of the following four states: waiting-for-query, containing-query, waiting-for-reply, containing-reply. The commands provided by the system for message passing include *create mailbox, destroy mailbox, connect, send,* and *receive.* In this design an unconnected port may be considered connected to a "dummy mailbox"; an unconnected mailbox is connected to a "dummy port."

The *create mailbox* command constructs a mailbox with the specified slot size and number of slots. The owner of the mailbox, namely, the creating process, must provide space for the header and slots. When the mailbox is created, it is connected to two dummy ports.

Once created, the mailbox is connected to a port using the *connect* command. Disconnecting is accomplished by connecting to a dummy port or dummy mailbox.

A message is sent through a specified port using the *send* primitive. The mailbox connected to the specified output (or input) port is checked for the availability of a slot in the state waiting-for-query (or reply). If any are present, then the message is copied into the slot, and the slot is marked containing-query (or reply). If there are no available slots, then the message is not sent, and the calling process is warned. This does not affect the state of the calling process; that is, the process is not blocked.

A message is requested by invoking the *receive* command, specifying a number of input (or output) ports as parameters. The mailbox connected to each port is successively checked for the availability of a slot in the state containing-query (or reply). If one of the ports satisfies this condition, then the message is copied from this slot to the area supplied by the calling process. The calling process can request that it be blocked if no message is available, or alternatively that it merely be informed that there is no message and be allowed to continue.

A mailbox may be destroyed at any time by its owner using the *destroy* primitive. If the mailbox is not already connected to two dummy ports, then it is replaced by a dummy mailbox. The space occupied by the mailbox is returned to the owner process.

2.6.1.5 REMARKS

In all of the communication mechanisms previously described, it is necessary to be able to identify uniquely the process with which one wants to communicate. In a mailbox system, process identification is needed to connect a mailbox. The knowledge of a process's name is a source of power within the system. It gives a process the ability to tamper with other process's ports and mailbox connections and perhaps even to read their messages. To prevent malicious processes from creating havoc, the system must enforce rules to protect process names and mailbox slots from unauthorized use. Techniques to enforce such protection rules are treated in detail in Chapter 7.

Although mailboxes are convenient for message passing, they do not provide an easy method for critical section synchronization. Synchronization can be effected by putting a special process in charge of allowing access to the critical section. A process sends a message to the special process when it wants to enter the critical section. It may proceed as soon as it receives an acknowledgment. The special process is careful to allow only one process to be in the critical section at a time. This "special process solution" to synchronization leads us to the concept of monitors.

2.6.2   Hoare's Monitor

A *monitor* is a collection of procedures and data structures which is shared among processes, but can only be used by one process at a time [Hoare and Perrot, 1972; Dijkstra, 1971]. The concept of a monitor is analogous to that of a room for which there is a single key. If a process shows up to use the room and the key is hanging on the door, the process may unlock the room, enter, and use one of the monitor's procedures. If the key is not hanging up, then the process must wait until the current user has left the room and relinquished the key. Furthermore, no one is allowed to stay in the room forever.

Consider, for instance, a resource which is allocated by a scheduler program. Each time a process wants to acquire some units of the resource, it has to call the scheduler. The scheduler procedure is shared by all the processes; any process may want to invoke the scheduler at any time. However, the scheduler is capable of serving only one process at a time. This scheduler, then, is an example of a monitor.

It is sometimes necessary for a monitor to delay its caller. For instance, if a process requests the monitor to grant it a resource which is already in use, the monitor should block that process until the resource becomes available. Processes are blocked and unblocked using the *wait* and *signal* operations. When a monitor blocks a process with a wait command, it must also specify the *condition* under which the process may resume execution, such as "resource-is-not-busy." When the condition becomes true, the monitor issues a signal command for that condition. If there are any processes waiting for the condition, one of them is awakened and allowed to continue its execution; the next instruction it executes is the one directly after the wait command which blocked it. If there are no callers waiting on that condition, then the signal has no effect.

A monitor contains one or more reentrant procedures with static global data structures. The first time the monitor is invoked, it initializes its

```
binarysemaphore : monitor ;
    begin integer s;
        condition semaphorepositive ;
        procedure P ;
            begin if s < 1 then semaphorepositive.wait ;
                s := -1
            end ;
        procedure V ;
            begin s := s + 1 ;
                    if s = 1    then semaphorepositive.signal
            end ;
        s := 1
end
```

FIG. 2–8   Implementing P and V using Hoare's monitor.

variables. All subsequent calls use the values of the variables remaining from the previous call. It should be emphasized that a monitor is a passive object, like a room. It is not a process. The monitor becomes alive only when a process chooses to use its services. The unique feature of a monitor's code is that only one process can execute the code at a time.

The use of the monitor is illustrated in Fig. 2–8, by implementing the P and V operations on a semaphore S. The notation condition-name.wait and conditionname.signal refers to the wait and signal operations for the condition "conditionname." The operations P and V are invoked by the notation binarysemaphore.P and binarysemaphore.V. The condition "semaphorepositive" indicates when it is safe for a blocked process to continue. In Fig. 2–9 two processes are mutually excluded from a critical section by using the monitor binarysemaphore. This monitor could be modified to handle several semaphores by adding a parameter to the monitor call that specifies which semaphore is desired.

If there is at least one process waiting on a condition, the semantics of the monitor guarantees that no other caller can intervene between the signal of that condition and the continuation of exactly one of the waiting processes. Therefore, in Fig. 2–8 S does not have to be retested after the wait operation in P. The signal implies that S = 1, and no other process can modify S before one of the processes is released. Also, since there may be more than one process waiting, a queue of waiting processes is associated with each condition. A simple queuing discipline of releasing the process that has been waiting longest ensures that no caller is postponed indefinitely from continuing.

Using the monitor as the basic synchronization and communication mechanism, processes no longer need to share data explicitly. Rather, shared variables are always accessed within the body of a monitor.

```
Begin
    parbegin
        P1 :  begin
                do while (true) ;
                    call binarysemaphore.P ;
                        critical section for P1 ;
                    call binarysemaphore.V ;
                        remainder of P1
                end
              end ;
        P2 :  begin
                do while (true) ;
                    call binarysemaphore.P ;
                        critical section for P2 ;
                    call binarysemaphore.V ;
                        remainder of P2
                end
              end
    parend
end
```

FIG. 2–9   Mutual exclusion using monitor calls.

With this restriction, critical sections are automatically eliminated. Since only one process can use the monitor at a time, shared variables are never accessed by two processes simultaneously. Furthermore, the inability to share variables within the processes themselves allows the system to locate illegal sharing when the system is compiled.

Although monitors do not exhibit increased computational power over semaphores, they do have several advantages over the more primitive synchronization mechanisms. First, monitors are very flexible. In addition to semaphores, numerous other synchronization commands can be implemented as monitors. For example, the mailbox scheme in the last section is easily coded as a monitor. Also, by localizing all shared variables within the monitor body, obscure constructions in synchronizing processes are avoided. Complex process interactions can be synchronized in an understandable manner. Monitors also enable processes to share critical section code. If several processes each access a shared resource in exactly the same way, then only one monitor procedure is required. This is in contrast with semaphores, where each process has its own copy of the critical section. In all, monitors appear to represent a significant improvement over semaphores in complexity and understandability, with only a minor loss in efficiency.

A modified version of Hoare's monitor, called a *facility,* has been implemented as the synchronization mechanism in the SUE System.

A facility is a process that functions as a monitor. Although somewhat more flexible than the monitor, the facility is less efficient, since it requires all the extra data structures associated with processes. Facilities are discussed in detail in the SUE System description in Chapter 10.

The communication primitives discussed in this chapter are a small sampling of the many existing mechanisms. The choice of a primitive for a particular system is likely to be influenced considerably by properties of the hardware which affect efficiency. Most synchronization mechanisms, though, are conceptually quite similar to either semaphores, mailboxes, or monitors.

2.7 Deadlocks

Several methods of process synchronization that allow processes to cooperate successfully have been introduced. Using communication primitives, such as semaphores, processes can block and unblock each other to synchronize their operation. If synchronization primitives are not used with care, however, unexpected problems can arise. For example, let P1 and P2 be two parallel processes (Fig. 2–10). READER and PRINTER are binary semaphores initialized to one. If P1 executes $P(READER)$ while P2 executes $P(PRINTER)$, both processes are then blocked on their second P operations. Furthermore, they will be blocked forever, since neither process has any hope of passing its second P operation. Such a situation, where processes wait for each other indefinitely, is called a *deadlock*.

The notion of deadlock has been formalized in terms of a simple model similar to that presented in Section 2.2 [Holt, 1972]. Let a system be a set of *states* and a set of *processes*, where each process is a function that maps states into states. A process is *blocked* in a state if it cannot execute when in that state. A process is *deadlocked* in a state if it is blocked in that state and in all future states which the system can reach. A state is *safe* if no process can map that state into a deadlock state.

In a system with many different kinds of resources, deadlock is a difficult problem. Careful resource management is required to avoid the situation of two processes holding each other's resource requirement and being unwilling to relinquish it, as in Fig. 2–10. Whether explicitly defined or not, every system has some policy with respect to deadlock. There are basically three such policies: prevention, automatic detection, and operator detection.

The prevention scheme takes the view that the system should not be allowed to reach an unsafe state. Therefore, when a process makes

P1 :   P2 :

⋮   ⋮

P (READER) ;   P (PRINTER) ;
P (PRINTER) ;   P (READER) ;

⋮   ⋮

FIG. 2–10

a request that can lead to deadlock, the system takes action to avoid the unsafe state: either the request is not granted, or a resource is preempted from another process to avoid the possible deadlock. This method has the advantage of always averting deadlock. However, resources are frequently left idle, since requests for available resources will occasionally be rejected to prevent reaching unsafe states. Also, the prevention algorithm itself can present a great deal of overhead.

An automatic detection policy allows deadlock states to be reached, but a program detects them when they do occur. The system can then preempt some processes' resources to get other processes going again. In the preceding reader–printer example, the system would allow the deadlock state to be reached. However, the system could then deallocate P2's printer and assign it to P1. P2 will still be blocked, but the two processes are no longer deadlocked. Deadlock recovery can either be automated or be put under operator control. The automatic detection policy in general allows a higher resource utilization than the prevention policy, since the former assigns a resource even if the assignment leads to an unsafe state. If deadlock is sufficiently infrequent, the increase in resource utilization more than compensates for the expense involved in deadlock recovery.

The third policy takes the view that deadlock happens so infrequently that it is not worth worrying about. When deadlock does occur and the operator detects it, then the system is merely restarted. The expense of a deadlock detection algorithm is avoided. However, when deadlock does occur, it is more costly. The operator may not notice the deadlock for some time. When he does notice, the system restart is usually quite expensive in terms of lost time.

Of the three policies, the problem of prevention has probably received the most attention. An example of a prevention algorithm is presented in the next section.

2.7.1   A Deadlock Prevention Algorithm

Consider a system where processes compete for the use of tape drives. A process will execute for only a finite period of time, provided that

(a)

Process name	Maximum demand	Allocation	Claim
A	4	2	2
B	6	3	3
C	8	2	6

(b)

Process name	Maximum demand	Allocation	Claim
A	4	2	2
B	6	3	3
C	8	4	4

FIG. 2–11

the tape drives it needs are put at its disposal. Each process, before it can request any tape drives, must specify the maximum number it will ever need simultaneously. The tape drive manager should grant tape drive requests as long as the requested allocation cannot lead to a deadlock. That is, there must be an execution sequence which permits every process to complete. For example, let the system consist of three processes and ten tape drives. Associated with each process is a maximum demand, the current number of tape drives allocated to it, and its remaining claim. A typical state of the system is described in Fig. 2–11a. The worst possible case in terms of deadlock is for each process to request all of its remaining claim. If all processes can complete in this circumstance, then the system is safe in this state. In particular, a safe state is described in Fig. 2–11a. Now, assume process C requests two more tape drives. If C's request is granted, and if all processes request their remaining claims (Fig. 2–11b), then the system is deadlocked. Therefore, it is not safe to grant C's request.

In general, it is possible to detect algorithmically whether the granting of a request leads to an unsafe state. One detection procedure, called "the banker's algorithm," works on the principle described in the preceding paragraph [Dijkstra, 1968a]. The new state is safe if and only if every process can still complete. It is this latter condition that the banker's algorithm checks.

The algorithm (Fig. 2–12) is analogous to a decision procedure for deciding if a bank can safely issue a loan. Each process is identified by an integer i, $1 \leq i \leq N$. Associated with process i are its maximum demand (maxdemand[i]), the number of units currently allocated to it (allocated[i]), its remaining claim (claim[i]), and a flag (maynotfinish[i]). The system maintains a global variable, totalunits, specifying the total number of units that exist in the system. Initially, it is not known whether any processes can finish (maynotfinish[i] = true for all i). Every time a claim can be filled from the remaining unused

```
unusedunits := totalunits ;
for i := 1 step 1 until N do
    begin       unusedunits := unusedunits − allocated [i] ;
                maynotfinish[i] := true ;
                claim[i] := maxdemand[i] − allocated[i]
    end ;
flag := true ;
do while (flag) ;
    flag := false ;
    for i := 1 step 1 until N do
        begin if maynotfinish[i] and claim[i] ⩽ unusedunits
            then    begin maynotfinish[i] := false ;
                          unusedunits := unusedunits + allocated[i] ;
                          flag := true
                    end
        end
    end
end ;
if unusedunits = totalunits then   system is safe
                            else   system is unsafe
```

FIG. 2–12   Banker's algorithm.

units, the process is assumed to run to completion and its units are released. If all the units are eventually released, then all the processes can complete and the system is safe. If the system is not safe, then the request is not granted.

2.7.2   Final Remarks

Although the banker's algorithm is simple, its implementation can be quite expensive, since it must be invoked every time there is a request for a new unit of the resource. A simpler method is for each process to request its maximum demand at once. In order to increase its allocation, a process must first relinquish its current allotment. Although such a scheme forces some processes to request resources long before they actually need them, the implementation is far simpler than the banker's algorithm, since the system is always in a safe state. It is a frequently used scheme for resource allocation in operating systems.

Deadlock is an important and interesting problem. It is among the easier operating system problems to formalize. Consequently, extensive work has been done in the area (for example, Coffman *et al.* [1971], Habermann [1969], Holt [1972], Hebalkar [1970]). In particular, the graph theoretic model by Holt has been included in Appendix II. However, despite the elaborate analytic treatment of deadlocks, simple schemes are still common. The overhead of deadlock prevention in a production system is generally too costly relative to the expense of an occasional system failure.

Problems

2.1 What is the difference between explicit parallelism, such as characterizes the ILLIAC IV machine organization, and implicit parallelism, such as is characteristic of the IBM 370/195 machine organization? Which organization has the greater potential for machine performance? Which machine is easier to program? Why?

2.2 Consider the program of Fig. 2–4, implementing Dekker's algorithm. Define the internal states of the program and the transitions among the states which describe the algorithm's progress during computation.

2.3 Consider a set of eight partially ordered tasks $\{A, B, C, D, E, F, G, H\}$. Task A must precede tasks C, B, and E. Tasks E and D must precede task F. Tasks C and B must precede task D. Task F must precede tasks G and H.

(a) Express the operation of this sequence of tasks as a program using the parbegin and parend primitives, exploiting parallelism among tasks wherever possible.

(b) Now assume that the additional constraint that task E must precede task C is added. Can you still find a "maximally parallel" expression using parbegin and parend?

(c) If semaphore operations were also permitted, how would your answers to (a) and (b) be altered?

2.4 Consider the process definition given in Section 2.2. Define a set of variables and a set of actions that will compute the cross product of two $n \times n$ matrices. Do you make maximal use of the permitted parallelism?

2.5 Provide mutual exclusion among n processes, each having a single critical section, using memory interlock.

2.6 Outline how a producer–consumer relationship can be implemented using memory interlock. Use Dekker's algorithm as a macro to provide mutual exclusion.

2.7 The Sleeping Barber Problem [Dijkstra, 1968a] A barbershop consists of a waiting room W and a room B containing the barber chairs. There are sliding doors D which allow communication from B to W and from W to outside. If the barber inspects W and does not find anybody, he goes to sleep. If a customer enters the barbershop and finds the barber asleep, he should wake him up. There are a finite number n of chairs in the waiting room. Program the Barber and the Customers as processes. Use message communication for their synchronization. What if there were two barbers? Express the operation of the barbershop using Petri nets, as outlined in Section 12.2.

2.8 Consider a dinner table with five chairs and five settings. There is a fork in between each setting. For a guest to eat his spaghetti he must use *both* the forks that are adjacent to his setting. Assume there are five guests at the table who alternately eat spaghetti and discuss politics (no forks are required to discuss politics). Program the guests as a set of processes, using semaphores for their communication. Make sure that there is no possibility of deadlock among the guests [Dijkstra, 1971].

2.9 Consider a very simple operating system consisting of a main process M running on a CPU, a reader process R running on a reader channel, and a printer process P running on a printer channel. Program the three processes such that R reads data in and passes them to M, which performs a transformation and passes them to P for output. Program M, R, and P with

(a) two buffer pools, each of size K,

(b) only one buffer pool of size K.

2.10 There is sometimes a need in a system for a process to send a rather long message, such as a file, to another process. The standard mailbox mechanism is clearly inefficient, since it requires extensive copying of messages within memory. Outline a method for sending long messages, given that one has the ability to send short messages.

2.11 Consider an operating system where processes communicate via message passing. When a process A sends a message, it expects a response. Sometimes, though, something goes wrong in the responding process and the response is never sent. If A puts itself to sleep with a RECEIVE command, it will never be awakened. One method of avoiding this problem is for A to set an "alarm clock," which will wake A up if it does not get a response within a prespecified time interval. Design a special process which, using a hardware timer, issues alarms to processes requesting them.

2.12 Processes and the process communication mechanism can generate considerable overhead in an operating system. Design a process descriptor and a process communication facility that is very simple and efficient. Generality and flexibility may be sacrificed where necessary.

2.13 Consider a set of processes where each process is identified by a unique integer. Each process has a constrained region which can be entered only if the sum of all integers associated with the processes currently executing in their constrained region is divisible by three. Outline an implementation of constrained regions using semaphores. Outline another implementation using Hoare's monitor. Compare the two solutions. Is it possible for a process to be locked out of its constrained region forever in your implementations?

2.14 In a message-passing environment, memory space is needed for the messages. One approach is to have the sender provide the space out of its working space. Another approach is to have a pool of buffers managed by the system for this purpose. Discuss the relative merits of the two approaches.

2.15 Use a monitor to implement a producer–consumer relationship between two processes.

2.16 Consider a network of computers. Outline a process communication mechanism that can be used between processes operating on different nodes of the network.

2.17 Prepare a survey of deadlock models and algorithms for deadlock prevention and detection.

2.18 Prepare a survey of models for parallel computation similar to the example presented in Section 12.2. Outline the different theoretical results obtained from these models.

2.19 Prepare an essay on Petri nets and related theoretical results.

2.20 Suppose there are two classes of processes, called "readers" and "writers," which can access a critical resource, such as a file. Writers must have exclusive access to the resource. Any number of readers can access the resource, providing that no writer is accessing it. Assume that a reader will be refused access only if there is a writer currently accessing the resource. Program the readers and writers as concurrent processes using semaphores for synchronization [Courtois *et al.*, 1971].

3

PROCESSOR ALLOCATION

3.1 Introduction

The processor has traditionally been the most important resource in the system to be allocated. Despite the increasing importance of memory and I/O devices, processor allocation still plays a central role. It is obvious that a process cannot progress through its computation without the processor. With today's high-speed machines, every second represents millions of instruction executions. Even a small amount of wasted processing time represents a great deal of lost computing power. Consequently, most system designers put a considerable amount of attention into efficient use of the processor.

In this chapter a *job* is defined to be a unit of computation consisting of a set of one or more modules. Each module contains a machine-language program and/or some data. It is the task of the system to efficiently schedule user jobs.

The chapter begins by outlining a progression of processor allocation schemes in order of increasing complexity [Rosin, 1969]. More modern environments, such as multiprogramming, are then discussed. The chapter concludes by presenting various classes of scheduling disciplines and their implementations.

3.1.1 Dedicated Machine

In the early days, the computer was allocated to one user at a time. Small machines are frequently operated in this way today. This situation has become especially common with the proliferation of minicomputers. The user mounts his tapes and disk packs, then sits at the console and runs his program. The operation is not too difficult, since the system is usually simple and slow, and there is time to think. The user's program may get some system support, such as standard I/O and utility routines. However, the system does not protect the user from his own mistakes. The program has to synchronize itself to wait for any I/O. It must verify tape and disk labels, send messages to the console, and alert the user to abnormal program conditions, such as overflow. The operating system is either nonexistent or of very little use in helping in these matters. The user is really on his own.

The throughput of a dedicated machine operation is often quite small. A lot of time is lost while the programmer mounts tapes, loads cards, etc. Also, the machine itself wastes time, since the processor is generally idle while I/O commands are serviced. With faster and more powerful machines, such an operation becomes prohibitively expensive. Therefore, for large systems more efficient modes of operation are needed.

3.1.2 Batching: Job File at a Time

As the cost of computer installations increases, long idle periods become less tolerable. To reduce idle time, a batch system collects a number of jobs on an input tape. Jobs are read into a small "satellite" machine, which prepares the input tape. Then the main processor executes the programs from the input tape, one at a time, and writes the output onto an output tape. In the meantime, the satellite machine can create the next input tape and print the previous output tape. A typical batch system is IBSYS for IBM 7090 with an IBM 1401 as a satellite computer.

The jobs on the input tape are serviced first-come–first-served. Therefore, if the computer spends 1 hour processing an input tape, the average turnaround time for a job is probably around 2–3 hours, depending on the speed of the satellite machine. In this method, short jobs receive no special treatment. A 15-minute job has the same turnaround time as a 15-second one. Thus, there is no incentive, other than processing charges, for keeping down the length of program execution.

Batching is a simple operation. It yields good throughput, certainly an improvement over the dedicated machine. However, debugging may be more difficult, because there is no direct interaction between the programmer and his program. Batching works best, therefore, in a production system where long jobs are executed according to a periodic schedule.

3.1.3 Direct Coupled Machines

In a direct coupled system two (or more) computers are connected by means of memory-to-memory communication. The slower machine, called the *master* computer, is in charge of scheduling jobs for the faster machine, called the *slave*. The master computer reads jobs from the card reader and queues them onto a disk. When the slave machine finishes executing a job, it sends a request to the master machine for more work. Scheduling, accounting, and I/O are controlled by the master computer. The slave machine is responsible only for raw computing power on user jobs. It relinquishes control over the executive tasks to devote all its time to productive labor.

The scheduling of jobs can be very complicated and depends largely on the service that the installation wants to provide. The discussion of scheduling disciplines is deferred until Section 3.3.

3.2 Multiprogramming

In a multiprogrammed system several jobs are partially executed at a time. Usually, the jobs are resident in main memory, and the central processor spends some of its time executing each one of them. The primary reason for multiprogramming is to compensate for the discrepancy of speeds between processing and I/O operation. I/O operations are slow relative to instruction speeds. When a job issues a read command to a channel, it must wait until the channel has completed the read. Instead of allowing the main processor to idle during the I/O operation, in a multiprogrammed system the processor can be switched to execute a different user job. A job currently doing I/O regains control of the processor sometime after the I/O is complete. Since there are several jobs residing in main memory concurrently, the processor will be idle only if all of them are waiting for channel completions.

A job is *active* if it is in core and can execute. The number of active jobs can be bounded or it can vary. It is desirable to keep as many active jobs as possible, so that the processor will rarely be idle. However, jobs need main memory to be active, which creates serious contention among them to get memory space. Therefore, it is important that memory strategies be able to pack memory efficiently.

The set of active jobs in a system is called the *job mix*. Choosing the job mix is a critical decision in a multiprogrammed system. It is usually desirable to have at least one "compute bound" active job, that is, a job which spends most of its time computing and does very little I/O. Even if all other jobs are doing I/O, the compute bound job can be trusted to keep the processor busy. Since it is desirable to have many jobs in core simultaneously, jobs with small memory requirements are quite useful. "Small jobs" can be implemented artificially by keeping only part of a job's code and data resident in core. The remainder of the job resides on drum or disk. When code or data are needed, the job is temporarily suspended (that is, made inactive) and the additional information is brought in from the peripheral device. This type of memory management allows more jobs to be active, since only part of the job is ever in core.

Although processor idle time should be minimized, there are other system goals. Peripheral devices should also be utilized as efficiently as possible. The system should choose active jobs which keep the tape drives, disk drives, card readers, and line printers running. The system is obviously unbalanced if all the active jobs use disks, but none of them use tapes. Prior knowledge of resource requirements for a job is clearly quite helpful. However, *balancing* the system, that is, keeping all the resources occupied, is an extremely difficult problem for which optimal solutions are known only for very simple cases. Methods of choosing a job mix are therefore based more on intuition and experience than on any provable mathematical properties of the resource balancing problem.

3.2.1 Time Sharing

A *time-sharing* system interacts with many users, giving each of them fast individual attention. Multiprogramming is the usual mode for implementing such an operation. Fast processing of many user requests is rarely accomplished without storing many jobs in main memory concurrently. The speed of system response permits a significant improvement in man–machine communications. Time sharing combines the close user contact of a dedicated machine with the efficiency of the batch system. Similar user environments are sometimes referred to as *real-time* in process control and *on-line* for business applications.

3.2.2 Time Slicing

In a multiprogrammed environment it is necessary to share the processor among the active jobs. To effect sharing, the processor's time is divided into intervals and each job allocated an interval every so often. Each interval is called a *time slice* or *quantum*. For example, if there are five user jobs in core, each may be allocated a 1-second time slice every 5 seconds. Time slices, though, are not necessarily of equal length for all jobs. Factors such as a job's priority and processor requirements generally influence the size of a job's time slices and the frequency with which it receives them.

Time slicing is particularly important in a time-sharing system, where each user expects continuous attention. Short time slices give each user the illusion that the machine is executing only his job. The system may give each user a 0.1-second time slice every second. The user merely sees his job executing on a machine which appears to move a tenth as fast as the actual hardware.

There are numerous algorithms for time slicing among several jobs. In the remainder of this chapter a number of popular methods of multiprogramming scheduling are discussed.

3.3   Multiprogramming Scheduling Methods

In a multiprogrammed system a number of active jobs compete for processor time. Assume that each user job executes as a process within the system. In addition to user processes, there are system processes which also share the use of the processor. All active processes which are waiting to obtain control of the processor are stored on the *ready queue*. Processes which are blocked (for example, waiting for an I/O completion or for a semaphore to go positive) are stored on separate *blocked queues*. Figure 3–1 is a schematic representation of these queues: R is a system of one or more ready queues and P is the processor. Corresponding to these queues, a process can be in one of the following states: ready, blocked, or running. A process from the ready queues is given a time slice on the processor. It executes until either its quantum runs out, it becomes blocked (for an I/O operation, for example), it terminates, or it is preempted by another process, which is now given control of the processor. After finishing its time slice for one of the four reasons just stated, the process is returned to the ready queue, put on a blocked queue, or released from the system. A process on a blocked queue is moved to the ready queue when it becomes unblocked. A *scheduling discipline* for this system of queues is a method for choosing a ready process from R and assigning it a quantum size.

Associated with each process in the ready queue is an integer-valued *priority* which specifies the importance of the process. The calculation

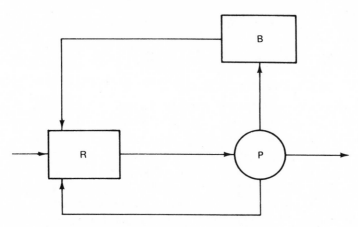

FIG. 3–1 Schematic diagram of processor scheduling (R, ready queue(s); B, blocked queue(s); P, processor).

of priority is based on both static and dynamic characteristics of the process. Static characteristics include the size, estimated execution time, and estimated amount of I/O activity of the process. If the process is a user job, the rate scale chosen by the user, usually by a priority number on the front of the job deck called the *external priority,* may also be one of its static components. Priority is also influenced by dynamic behavior of the process within the system. A process's current resource allotment, total waiting time, amount of recent processing time, amount of recent I/O interaction, and total time in the system may be considered in calculating priority. Since these characteristics change with time, priorities may be recalculated a number of times during the life of the process.

In most systems the external priority plays a minor role in the priority calculation for the ready queue. External priority is mainly useful in initially getting the job into an active state and, once it has completed execution, getting it printed quickly. Since most job execution times are very short relative to the time spent waiting to be loaded into core and waiting to be printed, the incremental gain by external priority on ready queue priority would have a minimal effect on a job's turnaround time and could have disastrous effects on the balance of the job mix.

Many system processes execute as if they were user jobs. Accounting calculations and routine monitoring and maintenance fall in this category. Some system processes, however, need special privileges. A device manager, for example, should not be delayed when it is ready to use the processor. Until it is given control, its associated channel is probably idle, waiting for a start command to be issued. To avoid idle time on peripheral devices, some processes enjoy a privileged status which allows them to take control of the processor more easily than user processes. Although no special mention of these processes will be made when discussing specific scheduling algorithms, it should be realized that virtually all scheduling disciplines must be capable of handling privileged processes. For example, in a highest-priority-first algorithm privileged processes are generally given infinite priority.

In scheduling the ready queue, the system has numerous performance measures to consider, such as good resource utilization, low processor idle time, high throughput, and reasonable waiting times for user jobs. There is the additional constraint that no job within the system be required to wait forever. Sometimes, goals conflict. For instance, in improving average response time, some long jobs may have to wait a long time before executing. One way of evaluating a scheduling rule is in terms of a loss function. A *loss function* expresses the value of completing a job as a function of how long it is delayed. Relevant parameters to a loss function include waiting time, total time in system, and deadlines. The system tries to schedule in a way that minimizes the average loss or bounds the maximum loss over all jobs. However, minimizing loss may not be in line with good system utilization. For example, minimizing average waiting time may postpone long jobs from executing. If a long job is using a nonsharable resource, then that resource can be used more effectively by executing the long job quickly. Choosing whether or not to run the long job depends on which performance measure is considered to be more important. In general, scheduling rules for real systems attempt to yield reasonable performance across a number of goals. Although no single goal is optimized, good overall performance is obtained.

In this section three classes of scheduling rules are discussed: highest priority first, round robin, and feedback queues [Coffman and Kleinrock, 1968]. First-come–first-served (FCFS) is occasionally mentioned for comparison purposes. The three basic rules cover most processor scheduling problems and generalize to a number of other resource allocation problems.

3.3.1 Highest Priority First

One simple method for scheduling the ready queue is to assign the processor to the process which has the highest priority (HPF). In the nonpreemptive case the highest priority process executes until it either finishes or blocks itself. If a process arrives with higher priority than the running process, it must wait until the running process relinquishes the processor. When preemption is permitted, a higher priority arrival interrupts the running process's execution and takes control itself. The preempted process is returned to the ready queue. In the highest priority first (HPF) discipline, the components of priority, the use of preemption, and the organization of the ready queue are free parameters in the implementation.

Every time the processor is free, the highest priority job must be removed from the ready queue. If the queue is sorted, then it is a simple matter to remove the top element. However, insertions into the queue are time consuming; on the average, half the queue will be searched for each arrival, assuming doubly linked elements with pointers to the top and bottom of the queue. If the queue is kept unsorted, then it must be searched every time a new process is needed. Insertions, though, are trivial. Compromise strategies are also possible. For example, the queue may be sorted every T time units. When a process arrives, it is added to the top of the queue. However, the pointer, P, to the top of the sorted part of the list is retained. To choose the highest priority process, the search begins at P and continues through the top of the queue. The number of elements which have to be searched is smaller than the unsorted cases and the sort time is reduced from the strictly sorted case. For the sake of simplicity, though, systems generally use a sorted ready queue.

The primary decision when choosing a HPF discipline is on what characteristics to base the priority. One of the most frequently cited HPF strategies schedules the shortest job first (SJF). That is, priority is inversely proportional to processing time. Since exact execution time for a process is rarely known in advance, an estimate is usually used to determine the priority. It is clearly advantageous for a process to have a low estimated execution time. Users can lie about their estimates to increase their priority. This type of behavior can be defeated by punishing a user who overruns his time estimate. For example, processing charges can be increased for a process which exceeds its estimate.

The SJF discipline can be implemented with or without preemption. In the nonpreemptive case processes always run until they finish or are blocked. In the preemptive case if a process arrives with an estimated time smaller than that of the running process, then the running process is preempted and the new process takes over. The preemptive strategy is better for short processes than the nonpreemptive one. With preemption, long processes find it more difficult to hold on to the processor.

Although preemption improves service for short processes, there are costs involved. The time required to preempt delays all the processes in the ready queue. Therefore, if the running process is nearly finished, it is probably not worth preempting it.

Typical execution time distributions have a preponderance of "short" processes. In this type of environment the SJF rule works quite well, since it heavily favors short jobs. Long processes, though, do not get good service. If the system is heavily loaded, long processes do particularly badly, especially when preemption is permitted. However, when the system approaches saturation no scheduling rule works particularly well.

Since advance information about execution time is usually very inaccurate, many scheduling rules attempt to base decisions on information gained about the process while it is in the system. One class of rules uses linearly increasing priority [Kleinrock, 1970]. Each process is assigned a priority upon entering the system. The priority increases at a rate a while it is waiting on the ready queue and at a rate b while it is being processed. Depending on how a and b are chosen, different scheduling rules result. For instance, if $0 < a \leq b$, then the rule schedules first-come–first-served (FCFS). When $0 > b \geq a$, then last-come–first-served (LCFS) results. In his original description of this class Kleinrock describes all possible rules which can be obtained by varying the parameters a and b. In the next section one algorithm from this class is discussed.

Many variations on the linear increasing priority scheme can be devised, although very few of them have been analyzed. For example, the rates a and b can be based on the process's external priority, that is, how much money it is willing to spend. Also, nonlinear functions can be chosen. Priority may be allowed to decrease linearly with time. When a maximum time is reached, the priority jumps to some high value. This favors short processes with the proviso that no process has to wait too long to get service. A similar rule can be appended to SJF, so that long processes start gaining priority after having been in the system for a while. Nuances in the type of processes which the system handles will greatly influence the type of priority scheme which is chosen.

One important goal of scheduling rules is to keep peripheral units busy. Toward this end, processes may be given high priority during periods of heavy I/O activity. Such activity is easily monitored, since the process generally goes to a blocked queue after invoking an I/O command. Specifically, a process may have a priority inversely proportional to the length of time since its last I/O command. There is experimental evidence which shows that programs tend to do their I/O in concentrated spurts. Using a HPF strategy based on I/O activity, peripheral devices will be kept busy a high proportion of the time, since those processes doing the most I/O have the best chance of gaining control of the processor.

Clearly, the number of different priority rules is virtually limitless. Despite the efficiency of HPF disciplines in giving good service to most processes, HPF has the side effect of keeping low priority processes waiting for a long time. In some system organizations this behavior is unacceptable. In a time-sharing system, for example, a user would much rather have 1 second of execution time every 5 seconds than a 12-minute interval of execution time every hour. HPF cannot guarantee this kind of service. Thus, we are led to a second major class of scheduling rules, round robin.

3.3.2 Round Robin

The simple *round robin* (RR) scheduling rule uses no static or dynamic priority information. The top process in the ready queue is given a time slice of q seconds and then is sent back to the end of the ready queue, providing it did not block itself. If there are K processes in the ready queue, then each process gets q seconds out of every Kq seconds of processor time. Consequently, each process has the illusion that it is running on a processor with a speed $1/K$ of the physical processor's speed. The size of the ready queue is therefore an important parameter in determining how fast processes progress.

The quantum size, q, affects how evenly the processor is distributed over short periods of time. If q is infinite, then RR reduces to FCFS. Since processes are typically entering and leaving the ready queue all the time, a large (finite) quantum size may randomly favor some processes. For instance, if four new processes arrive just as a process is finishing its quantum, its next quantum will be delayed by $4q$. On the other hand, a process can get lucky and find many of the processes which are ahead of it getting blocked, thus reducing its waiting time on the next round. Such random effects are reduced as q decreases, since the probability of an arrival or blockage in any single quantum becomes small.

As q decreases, service for smaller processes improves. When q is very small, all ready processes get equivalent service, and waiting time is directly proportional to the amount of service required. However, q can be chosen too small. For "reasonable-sized" quanta, the time required to switch execution from one process to another is negligible. When q is on the same order of magnitude as process switching time, then the delay in switching is noticeable. In fact, if q is too small, the system can spend more time switching processes than executing them. Therefore, the size of the time slice in RR must be chosen at an intermediate value so that intolerable switching overhead is not incurred.

RR is frequently used in a time-shared system with numerous users. Such systems must generally guarantee reasonable response times to each process. That is, independent of the quantum size, users expect to be serviced at least once every certain number of seconds. If q is constant and there are K processes in the queue, the response time is approximately Kq. For large K, this may be too long. The response time can be guaranteed if a cycle-oriented RR rule is used. In this discipline a cycle time for the ready queue is chosen which is equal to the minimally acceptable response time. At the beginning of each round through the ready queue, the quantum size is calculated by dividing the cycle length by the number of processes in the queue. Arrivals during a cycle are held up until the completion of the cycle before being added to the ready queue. If the queue is too full, switching loss may be noticeable, since q will be quite small. One can compensate for this problem by specifying a minimum time slice. Under a heavy load, response time suffers, but at least switching overhead stays at a low level.

There are a number of other variations on the RR discipline. One rule, called *biased RR*, assigns a quantum to each process based on its external priority. Each process has its own quantum length, so a process progresses at a speed proportional to its priority. Similar rules can be devised based on other priority factors, such as resource allocation. I/O activity, and estimated service time. Another RR discipline is obtained from Kleinrock's linearly increasing priority schemes (Section 3.3.1). If the parameters a and b are such that $0 \leq b < a$, then a scheduling rule called *selfish RR* results. On entering the system, a process waits until its priority reaches the value of the running processes. It then executes in RR with other running processes. Since executing processes increase their priority with a rate $b < a$, waiting processes must eventually catch up. Selfish RR and RR both favor short processes over FCFS, simply because short processes receive a larger proportion of their total execution time on each quantum. In fact, when $b = 0$, selfish RR reduces to the simple RR rule.

By using more than one ready queue, the system can take advantage of the distribution of execution times. For instance, suppose it is known that if a process does not complete in three time slices, then there is an 85% chance that it will not complete before receiving 12 time slices. This property of execution time can be exploited by using two ready queues, a foreground and a background queue. Each process goes through three quanta in the foreground queue. After its third quantum, it is dropped into the background queue. The processor spends most of its time executing foreground processes, thus giving excellent service to short processes. In one cycle-oriented discipline, processes in the foreground queue are given a fixed quantum. If there is still time left in the cycle after all the foreground processes have executed, then that time is used to execute background processes. This two-queue system can be generalized to multiple level feedback queues.

3.3.2 Feedback Queues

The basic *feedback* (FB) discipline uses n ready queues, each of which is serviced FCFS. An arriving process enters the system in the first queue. After receiving one quantum, it drops back to the second queue. After each succeeding quantum is received, it goes to the next higher queue. The processor is scheduled so that it services the lowest-numbered nonempty queue. In the FB discipline a new arrival implicitly receives a high priority and executes for as many time slices as the least number run by any process in the system. The FB rule gives better service than RR for short processes, without requiring advanced information about execution times. However, maintaining multiple queues can require a lot of overhead in header space, especially if the quantum size is small.

One way of reducing the number of queues needed is an extension of the cycle-oriented foreground–background case. Instead of changing queues after each quantum, allow processes to cycle a fixed number of times within each FB queue before falling into the next lower priority. The FB queues are now serviced RR within queue, applying the same processor allocation rule among queues. Although the discrimination among different-sized processes is no longer as good, the overhead in queue maintenance is reduced.

Users can exploit the FB rule by breaking up their jobs into short processes. The overall service is significantly improved over submitting the same job as a single long process.

The main advantage of FB and RR over HPF is that the former do not need advance information about process execution time to give good service to short requests. On the other hand, when priority is a function of a process's resource allotment, it is often desirable to favor high priority processes for resource utilization reasons. If it is desirable to consider priority information, then composite rules, such as biased RR, can be used which balance the use of both dynamic and static data.

3.4 Multilevel Scheduling

In previous sections a variety of processor scheduling schemes were discussed. Most of these disciplines require queue manipulation, process switching, and sometimes priority and quantum calculations. In this section a general method for implementing scheduling rules is presented which efficiently organizes calculations while maintaining sufficient flexibility in scheduling decisions.

3.4.1 Implementing a Processor Scheduler

In most systems processors communicate via interrupts. The main processor may experience an interrupt when an interval timer expires, when a channel completes, or when a running program attempts to do I/O. When an interrupt occurs, control of the main processor is passed to the supervisor or kernel. The supervisor performs some action, such as initiating a channel, unblocking a process, or creating a process, and then returns control of the processor to a process on the ready queue. Since interrupts occur frequently, it is inefficient to execute very many instructions each time a process on the ready queue is assigned the processor. However, it is important to save information regarding the current state of the processor, as well as to perform a number of calculations regarding priority and quantum size. One goal, then, is to devise a method for managing the ready queue which requires these calculations to be made only infrequently.

The key principle behind the method is that operations which occur frequently should be less time consuming than those which occur infrequently. This principle, which is pervasive in the design of operating systems, is specifically applicable to scheduling algorithms by separating operations into levels based on frequency of execution. The *multilevel scheduling* method considered here is a three-level system consisting of a *dispatcher,* a *short-term scheduler,* and a *long-term scheduler.* The dispatcher is invoked after the handling of an interrupt has been completed. It chooses the next process to be executed from the ready queue. Since the dispatcher is executed very frequently, it should be quite short. In the best case, it should only have to take the top process off the ready queue and assign the processor to it. The short-term scheduler is invoked to insert a process into the ready queue [Brinch Hansen, 1971]. Although this scheduler may have to examine the state of the process, priority adjustments should be kept to a bare minimum at this level. Processes get inserted into the ready queue frequently, perhaps every few milliseconds. Hence, any complex modification of process state should be left to the long-term scheduler. Long-term adjustments, which are made infrequently, can be more complex. Process state information, such as resource allotment, may be used to recalculate priority. Since the long-term scheduler is invoked only once every few seconds, it can afford to spend several milliseconds in execution.

This three-level organization has the advantage of localizing scheduling overhead. When approximate frequency of invocation is known in advance, then the constraints on how much computation is permissible at each level is also predictable. Any feasible scheduling rule must be able to satisfy the time constraints of each level.

3.4.2 An Example of Multilevel Scheduling

In Section 3.3.2 the notion of process speed was discussed in the context of a RR discipline. It was shown that process speeds could be varied by adjusting the size of the quantum for each process. The speed of a process is then calculated by dividing its quantum size by the time required to cycle once through the ready queue. Although this scheme permits adequate control over process speeds, it does not guarantee how often a process will get control. Consider a system which runs both batch and time-sharing services. The batch system wants 75% of the processor time, but does not care when it gets it. The time sharing needs only 25% of the processor, but it must have control at least once every second. Furthermore, there are multiple processes running under both subsystems, and each of those processes must satisfy the timing constraints of its parent. That is, no time-sharing process can be locked out of the processor for more than 1 second. Cycle-oriented disciplines can guarantee a deadline, namely, the cycle time. However, this deadline must be the same for all processes. If "real-time" services were also being provided, and the real-time processes must receive 20 microseconds every 10 milliseconds, then the cycle time for the RR queue would have to be 10 milliseconds. This is clearly infeasible, since process switching costs would become prohibitively high. A solution to this problem, proposed by J. J. Horning for Project SUE involves the use of a multilevel scheduler.

In the proposed scheduling system each process $P(i)$ is given a quantum length $q(i)$ and a *time frame* $f(i)$. The time frame specifies how often the process must receive its quantum. Process $P(i)$ has to receive $q(i)$ seconds of processor time within $f(i)$ seconds after entering the ready queue. The process's speed, defined as $s(i) = q(i)/f(i)$, represents the fraction of the processor it receives, when it is unblocked. For example, in the simple cycle-oriented RR rule, $f(i) = f$ is the cycle time for the queue, and each process receives a quantum f/K if there are K processes altogether.

After entering the ready queue, a process $P(i)$ has a *deadline* $T(i)$, by which time it has to have received its quantum. If $P(i)$ enters the queue at time $t(i)$, then $T(i) = t(i) + f(i)$. The ready queue, then, is ordered by deadline. The top process on the queue is run for its quantum, or until it blocks itself. If it is unblocked at the completion of its quantum, it is returned to the ready queue and a new deadline is calculated.

The amount of code required for this three-level scheduler is consistent with the timing constraints of each level. The dispatcher need only take the top element off the queue. The short-term scheduler must recalculate the deadline and insert the process in the queue. Long-term schedulers can adjust $f(i)$, $q(i)$, and $s(i)$ for each process. In addition, this simple three-level system can be adjusted to approximate many of the scheduling algorithms previously mentioned. For example, an RR rule is implemented by setting $q(i) = q$ and $f(i) = f$ for all processes. If $q(i)$ exceeds each process's processor requirement, the algorithm reduces to FCFS. Other rules can be obtained in a similar manner.

The SUE algorithm, although elegant, does have some serious limitations. It was designed under the assumption that all processes are in core memory. While this may be true in a multiprogrammed batch environment, it is generally not true in a time-sharing system. Most time-sharing systems have core space for several processes. As users communicate via their terminals, processes are brought into core from peripherals, and other processes are swapped out of core to disk. The problem is how to stop an executing process so that another can be put in its place. Clearly, some other process must do the stopping; however, it may be delayed in getting the processor, since it must be initiated by a long-term scheduler. As long as all the processes are in core, things go smoothly. As soon as processes start moving in and out of core, alternative scheduling mechanisms must be devised.

3.5   Final Remarks

The scheduling algorithms presented in this chapter constitute a range of techniques to efficiently allocate a processor to a queue of processes. These rules are also applicable to some other resource allocation problems in operating systems. The multilevel scheduling approach provides an example within which scheduling disciplines can be implemented with limited overhead. Despite these known techniques, optimal scheduling is still beyond the state of the art for most systems.

Whatever disciplines are implemented, there should be a way to validate the effectiveness of the discipline or to locate the sources of performance failure. This may be accomplished by analyzing the system or by monitoring the system after it is implemented. A survey of techniques for evaluating system performance is deferred until Chapter 9.

Problems

3.1 Consider a highest priority first scheduling algorithm with preemption, where the priority of each process changes with respect to time. The rate of change is proportional to a constant a when the process is idle and to a constant b when a process is executing. If there is more than one highest priority process, then all the highest priority processes are serviced in a time-shared fashion with very small quantum size. Assume preemption is free. Investigate the behavior of the algorithm for the entire range of values of a and b [Kleinrock, 1970].

3.2 Describe the process scheduling algorithm of a particular system in detail. Is memory allocation related in any way to the scheduling algorithm?

3.3 How much cost does 10% of CPU idle time represent in your own installation? Compare this cost with other major expenditures in a computer installation.

3.4 Assume you have a machine with a single processor which allows no preemption. Devise a scheduling algorithm which will minimize average waiting time when processor time requirements are known in advance. Devise another algorithm which will minimize maximum waiting time. If preemption were allowed for free, how would your algorithms be affected?

3.5 In a multiprocessing system, would you let one of the processors schedule all the others or would you route the jobs to the different processors, which then in turn can do their own scheduling? Discuss the advantages and disadvantages of each scheme.

3.6 Many theoretical papers make the assumption that the length of time between job arrivals is exponentially distributed. Perform an experiment in your installation to verify this hypothesis.

3.7 The load in a computer system is not uniform throughout the day. Perform an experiment to determine the load variation for a day in your installation and graph the results. Outline a set of measures which may help smooth the peaks of the load.

3.8 Most analytic models for scheduling make many assumptions. For example, the scheduling model of Sevcik [1971] assumes that:

1. work is scheduled on a single processor,
2. the scheduling objective is to maximize service rendered,
3. a loss function associated with each request reflects the decline in utility caused by its delayed completion,
4. each request is associated with a request class for which the distribution of service times is known,
5. the process by which new requests arrive is known for each request class,
6. preemption of a request not yet completed requires a fixed amount of processor time.

Criticize or validate each assumption from a practical viewpoint. What kinds of experiments would be necessary before the results of an analysis based on these assumptions could be applied?

3.9 Design a scheduling algorithm which controls the load and job mix based on the current status of the system. Investigate its dynamic properties by simulation. Do you think that the algorithm can correct the imbalance in the system faster than the environment changes due to jobs being submitted? Justify your answer.

3.10 Consider a set of processes with mutual exclusion implemented using semaphores. If a process P loses control of the processor while executing a critical section, then all the other processes will be blocked until P regains control. Outline a way that the scheduler can avoid stopping processes in critical sections. Consider the same problem using other communication mechanisms, such as message passing or monitors.

4

MEMORY MANAGEMENT

4.1 Memory Management Functions

Memory management may be thought of as three functions [Denning *et al.*, 1971] (see Fig. 4–1):

1. *naming function* ($\mathfrak{N}$) maps each user-defined name into the unique identifier of the information to which it refers;
2. *memory function* ($\mathfrak{M}$) maps unique identifiers (that is, program addresses) into the real memory locations (that is, memory addresses) where they are located [Denning, 1970];
3. *contents function* ($\mathfrak{C}$) maps each memory address into the value which it contains.

Each of these three maps is time dependent; that is, it may change throughout the time that a job is being handled by the system. For example, $\mathfrak{N}$ is usually not fixed until the job is "linked" to the system modules and files which it references. The $\mathfrak{M}$ function can be fixed

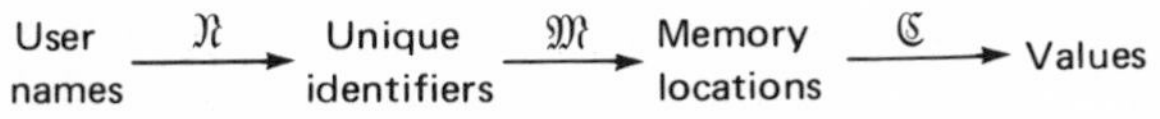

User names $\xrightarrow{\ \mathfrak{N}\ }$ Unique identifiers $\xrightarrow{\ \mathfrak{M}\ }$ Memory locations $\xrightarrow{\ \mathfrak{C}\ }$ Values

FIG. 4–1 Memory maps ($\mathfrak{N}$, naming function; $\mathfrak{M}$, memory function; $\mathfrak{C}$, contents function).

when the job is loaded. However, under some allocation strategies $\mathfrak{M}$ changes during the entire time that a job is in core. Clearly, the outcome of the function $\mathfrak{C}$ changes every time a "store" instruction is executed.

4.1.1 Binding

The act of fixing one of these maps is called *binding*. The time at which a map f is bound is called the *binding time of f*. Binding may occur when the job is coded, or it may occur while the job is in the system, for example, during compilation or loading. Sometimes, a map is bound so frequently that it is more natural to consider it as not being bound at all. The contents function $\mathfrak{C}$ is such a map. Since $\mathfrak{C}$ is completely specified by the user, it is not particularly interesting from the system viewpoint. However, both $\mathfrak{N}$ and $\mathfrak{M}$ are under system control, and the choice of their binding times is an important issue for the system. Take the memory function $\mathfrak{M}$, for example. A late binding time of $\mathfrak{M}$ is desirable for flexibility, since it allows the system to move a job around in core to maximize memory utilization. Unfortunately, the structure of some machines makes it expensive to implement. Early binding time of $\mathfrak{M}$, although easy to implement, puts severe restrictions on the ability to balance memory use. Similar considerations apply to the naming function. In the succeeding discussion, the reader should keep in mind the trade-off between flexibility and expense in each implementation strategy.

4.1.2 Naming

A given name may refer to different objects, depending on the context in which it is used. The problem of matching names with their corresponding objects is pervasive in software systems. For example, in block-structured programming languages (such as ALGOL) a given name can refer to several different variables, depending on the block in which it is used. In operating systems the context with which one is generally concerned is that of the user program. Several users may have the same names for different files or procedures. It is the job of the operating system to associate the correct object with every name within each user context.

In general, it is desirable to allow different programs to refer to a single object by different names. This is frequently helpful in the case of files, where different users may refer to system files by different names. It is also important that if one given name is used to refer to a single object in several places, then each instance of the name must be linked to that object. The former problem, that of using multiple names for one file, is discussed in Chapter 6. The latter problem, binding names to the objects to which they are meant to refer, is the subject of the next section.

4.1.3 The General Linkage Problem

Consider a program which consists of a group of procedures and data structures, some of which are user defined (such as FORTRAN and PL/1 programs) and others of which are system defined (such as the FORTRAN compiler and utility routines). Each separately compiled (or assembled) procedure or data structure, called an *object module,* is coded relative to address zero. Modules cooperate, so that one module can call a procedure or can access data in another module. These calls and accesses are called *external references.* For example, a procedure PROC1 in one module may wish to call a procedure PROC2 in another module. Since the modules are compiled separately, PROC1 cannot "know" the address of PROC2. PROC1 can only know the procedure PROC2 by its name. Thus, before the entire program can be loaded into core, the reference must be *resolved;* that is, PROC1 must find out the address of PROC2 within its module. This process of resolving references, called *linking,* can be done in one of three ways:

1. the programmer may supply a set of procedures, which are linked during compilation;
2. previously compiled routines are linked either before or while they are being loaded into core;
3. linkage is postponed until execution, at which time it is done automatically by the system.

Most high-level languages implement method 1 by allowing a user to define many procedures which can call each other within a single program. Thus, the procedures (such as PROC1 and PROC2) are linked by the compiler. The object module generated by the compiler can then be either moved into core directly or first linked to other system routines. If the module must first be linked to system routines, then linking can be considered to be a hybrid of methods 1 and 2.

In method 2 linking is accomplished as a separate step between compilation and loading. Although the linking and loading steps can be performed separately, the one-step *linking loader* has become increasingly popular. In addition to resolving external references, the linking loader modifies all zero-origin relative addresses to align them with the address at which the modules are loaded. This operation is called *relocation*.

Method 3, that of execution time linking, is useful when the names of some of the constituent procedures are not known before execution time. This situation arises whenever the data has an effect on the type of calculation to be performed. Rather than linking all routines which may be needed, routines are linked only as they are called. Since this method is closely allied with an allocation scheme presented in Section 4.6, its description is deferred until the end of this chapter.

4.2. Linking Methods

The complexity of linking methods is highly hardware dependent. In this section a simple hardware structure is assumed. Each group of object modules is linked into a single *linked module* which is coded relative to address zero. Since the linked module is coded independently of the location where it will be loaded, the module is said to be *relocatable*. When the module is loaded into main memory, the absolute address of its first word is stored in a *relocation* (or *base*) *register*. All address references are then calculated by adding the (relative) address of the reference to the contents of the relocation register to obtain the absolute address of the word in memory. In later sections linking will be discussed in the context of other addressing mechanisms.

4.2.1 Linking Loader

The linking loader is a one-pass routine which links object modules, relocates addresses, and physically loads the program into main memory. In addition to the actual program text and its length, each object module must provide the loader with

1. those names which are declared in the module and which can be referenced from other modules;
2. those names which are referenced in the module but are not declared within the module (that is, external references);
3. those addresses which must be recomputed based on where the module is loaded in the linked module (for example, those addresses coded relative to the origin of the object module).

The loader works by constructing a name table containing all names which can be referenced external to a module. Associated with each name in the table is an entry which can have one of two possible interpretations. If the name is declared in a module which has already been loaded, then the table entry contains the address of the name relative to the beginning of the linked module. If the object module in which the name is defined has not yet been loaded, then the table entry points to a linked list of address fields which will eventually contain the name's address. When the name is finally encountered, the linked list is traced through and the address in each element of the list is filled in. Each module is successively loaded into contiguous locations of main memory. Address references are no longer relative to address zero, and consequently have to be displaced by the sum of the lengths of the modules which were previously loaded. Then the name table is updated and each external reference within the module is either resolved or linked to the list associated with that name. Once the entire program has been loaded, the name table can be either discarded or saved for debugging purposes.

Additional information on linking loaders can be found in the books of Gear [1969] and Donovan [1972].

4.2.2 Linkage Editor

The resolution of external references among modules and the relocation of absolute addresses can be separated into a function which is independent of loading. The former operations, called the *linkage editor,* merge the object modules into a single module, called a *load module.* The load module contains the program text and a section which assists in relocation. The relocation and loading processes are then implemented by another routine, called the *loader.*

4.2.3 Comparison of Linking Methods

There are several advantages to the two-step operation. First, the linkage editing need not be done every time a program is run, saving some execution overhead. The second advantage relates to core requirements. Since the loader is less complex than the linking loader, it is also smaller. Thus, the execution step, which needs the loader in core to initiate, requires less core in the two-step case. A third advantage is that linkage editors can implement "overlaying," which is discussed in Section 4.4.

The main problem with two-step linking and loading is I/O. The linkage editor has to output the load module, which is then read in again for the loader. Most of the user's code requires little, if any, modification before loading. Thus, the reading and writing, which are frequently the most expensive parts of the operation, are largely redundant.

The big saving in the two-step case is that linking need only be done once, provided the program does not change. However, for user jobs which will run very few times or which will be changed frequently, the gain in not having to link in later runs is minimal compared to the expense of the two-step operation during debugging. Thus, for jobs which are run only once or which are changed often, the linking loader is usually the cheaper method.

In the remainder of this chapter it will be assumed that the job has been linked and exists as a zero-origin relocatable load module. The relocation method depends on the type of allocation scheme which is used. In most allocation schemes, such as the one discussed in this section, relocation is quite straightforward. Thus, our attention can be concentrated on how the linked module is stored in main memory.

4.3. Storage Allocation

A technique which assigns storage to a job is called a *storage allocation strategy*. A program can execute only when its instructions and data are in main memory. The simplest allocation strategy is to load the job in its entirety into contiguous core locations. However, since only a small portion of the job is executing at a given time, memory can be conserved by storing in core just that portion of the job which is currently active. The rest of the job is kept on a peripheral device, such as a drum, until it is needed. In the latter strategy memory is used more efficiently, but there is overhead in moving parts of the job in and out of core when they are needed. In succeeding sections several allocation strategies are investigated which, under certain conditions, improve average memory utilization without incurring a large overhead.

4.3.1   Binding the Memory Map

The memory function $\mathfrak{M}$ assigns actual storage locations to the relocatable load module. In *static allocation* schemes the storage locations are bound either before loading by the programmer or compiler or at loading by the loader. A third strategy is to not bind $\mathfrak{M}$ at all, allowing the job to be moved around in main memory during execution. This strategy, called *dynamic storage allocation,* enables the system to pack memory in an efficient manner. As blocks of information are moved in and out of core, spaces appear between jobs which are often too small to be of use. When a large number of such gaps exist, memory is said to be *fragmented.* If $\mathfrak{M}$ can be rebound after loading, then by moving jobs around in core, these spaces can be merged into areas which are large enough for storing jobs. Thus, dynamic storage allocation gives the system flexibility in reducing fragmentation.

The binding times of the memory map for static and dynamic allocation schemes correspond to [Denning *et al.*, 1971]:

1. *absolute address programming*   the programmer specifies the machine addresses when the program is written;
2. *symbolic programming*   the compiler or assembler produces memory addresses from symbolic names during the translation process. These memory addresses may then be allocated as follows:
(a) the memory addresses produced are fixed absolute addresses;
(b) the memory addresses are relocatable and are assigned absolute values by the loader for the entire execution period of the module;
(c) the memory addresses are relocatable and are assigned absolute values at each reference.

Methods 1, 2a, and 2b are static in the sense that the memory map is bound before or while the job is loaded into core. Method 1 is an example of combining the maps $\mathfrak{M}$ and $\mathfrak{N}$ once and for all. This technique is quite common in small machines where only one job runs at a time. Method 2 separates the binding of $\mathfrak{M}$ and $\mathfrak{N}$. In method 2a $\mathfrak{M}$ is bound immediately after $\mathfrak{N}$. Fast compilers frequently use this approach; the compile and load steps are sped up at the expense of execution efficiency. By storing instructions as they are generated directly into executable locations, most of the overhead in linking and loading is eliminated. Method 2b, which is used in most models of the IBM/360 series, binds $\mathfrak{M}$ at load time. In this scheme, load modules are relocatable; they can execute anywhere in core, but are generally not moved after initial loading. The implementation of all three strategies is straightforward.

Method 2c is truly dynamic, since $\mathfrak{M}$ is never bound. Techniques which use this approach are discussed later in the chapter.

If relocation of information is to be done, properties of rotating devices make it best to move the information in blocks in order to minimize overhead. As noted in Section 1.1, when a record is retrieved from a disk or drum, the *seek time* is crucial. That is, the time required to find the record is generally much greater than the time required to move it into core, making the length of the block relatively unimportant. Thus, it is more efficient to move information in large blocks. The reduction of the number of seek operations more than compensates for the added time in moving longer blocks.

Exactly how a job is broken up into blocks depends upon the allocation strategy. Blocks may correspond to logical subgroups, such as procedures, or to a physical device attribute, such as drum track size. In the remainder of this chapter block sizes are assumed to be arbitrary, unless specified explicitly, and all jobs are assumed to be relocatable.

4.4   Overlaying

It is possible to store two program modules in the same memory locations, provided that they do not both have to be core resident at the same time and that proper precautions are taken for saving values [Pankhurst, 1968]. That is, the memory map $\mathfrak{M}$ is bound at load time, but several program addresses are permitted to be mapped into the same memory address. For instance, let C be a main procedure which first calls procedure A, then at some later time calls procedure B. As shown in Fig. 4–2, A and B can be allowed to occupy the same memory space.

In systems which use a single relocation register for the linked module, it is usually the responsibility of the linkage editor and loader to ensure that the correct procedure is in core locations 40K–70K when procedure C executes a CALL. The input to the linkage editor includes the program modules and an *overlay map* (Fig. 4–2d) that specifies which procedures share main memory space. The linkage editor then constructs special commands which invoke the loader whenever one of the overlaid routines is called. The loader brings the called module into main memory, if it is not already loaded. Thus, program modules are dynamically moved into and out of main memory during execution as they are needed.

The amount of main memory required by the program can be reduced considerably by overlaying modules. In a system which allows overlaying, even programs whose overall length exceeds the size of main storage are able to be processed. For example, consider a system which has 80K of core and uses a loader which requires 10K to operate. This system can run the job of Fig. 4–2, even though the total size of the job is larger than core. Hence, by constructing a more complex linkage editor and loader which permit overlaying, one gains flexibility in allocating memory.

However, there are still two memory management problems which overlaying does not solve. Recall the original assumption that the overlaid modules do not need to be core resident at the same time. For certain kinds of dynamic program behavior, such as data-dependent procedure calls and recursive procedures, it is impossible to predict

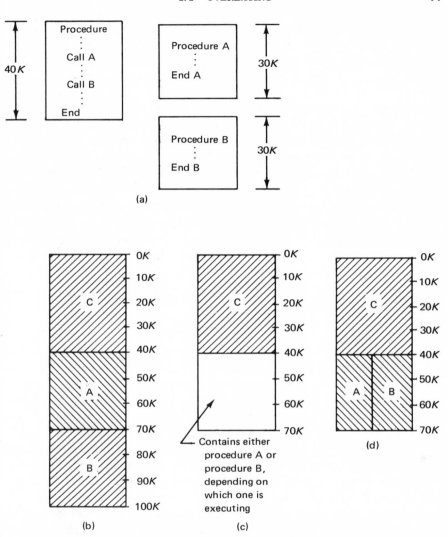

FIG. 4–2 Example of memory overlay. (a) A set of procedures which call each other. (b) Procedures stored contiguously. (c) Procedures stored with procedure A and procedure B overlaid in 40K–70K. (d) "Overlay map" showing procedure A and procedure B occupying the same memory space, 40K–70K.

whether two procedures can be overlaid. That is, the programmer may not know whether two precedures will call each other, making it impossible for him to construct an overlay map. Since it is the programmer's responsibility to specify the overlay structure to the linkage editor, unpredictable program behavior makes overlaying infeasible.

Until now, it has been assumed that the amount of main memory space available to the job is known in advance. That the amount of available memory may vary dynamically during execution leads to the second major problem of overlaying. As system load increases, memory becomes more crowded. Under reduced space allotment, a job's overlay structure may no longer fit into its portion of memory. However, there may be procedures belonging to other jobs which can be overlaid by the first user. The programmer has no way to know this in advance. Conversely, when the machine load is light, the extra overhead incurred by dynamic overlaying may be unnecessary, since there is plenty of memory available. The point is that the program should manage memory differently depending on the state of the system in which it is run. Furthermore, the system should be allowed to optimize memory allocation globally among jobs. Since a single user cannot anticipate the system load or the behavior of other programs, the dynamic overlaying strategy is of limited help in improving overall memory usage.

4.5. Job Swapping

In an overlaying scheme, once a job is allocated a memory area and loaded, it executes in that area until it completes. That is, the memory map $\mathfrak{M}$ is bound at loading time. In addition to the problems of anticipating both a job's maximum storage requirements and the amount of available main memory, this assumption has two undesirable effects. The first relates to memory utilization. Assume a multiprogramming environment where memory is packed as in Fig. 4–3a. If JOB3 is the first to complete, the new memory map will appear as Fig. 4–3b. The system will now be unable to fulfill a new request for a contiguous 150K block since memory is fragmented, even though 150K of free storage is available. The obvious solution is to move JOB2 down 50K, so that it is contiguous with JOB1. However, this requires rebinding the memory map after loading.

The second undesirable effect relates to the utilization of resources other than memory. Again, assume that there are three active jobs in memory, as in Fig. 4–3a. Say that JOB2 is the only job currently using the disk drives. When JOB2 completes its execution, it relinquishes control of these disks and leaves core. Clearly, the disk drives will be idle until a new job that uses a disk is brought into core. Assume that the only job which is waiting to run and has need of a disk (call it JOB4) is 250K long. Unfortunately, there is only 150K of free space, not enough

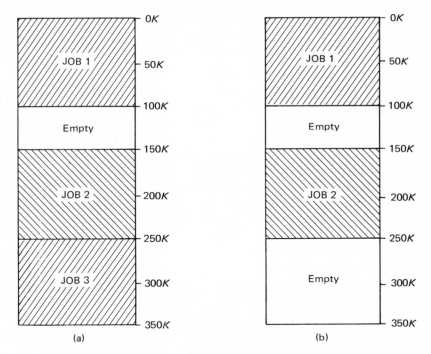

FIG. 4–3   Example of memory fragmentation. (a) Original state of memory.
(b) State of memory after JOB3 has left.

for JOB4. To prevent the disk from remaining idle until enough space
is freed, it may be desirable to move one of the still active jobs, namely,
JOB1 or JOB3, out of main memory to make room for JOB4. Moving
JOB4 into core quickly improves disk utilization (that is, reduces total
idle time). However, as in the case of poor distribution of memory,
this requires moving a job after loading, thus rebinding the memory
map.

One solution to the foregoing difficulties is to permit the system to
move entire jobs in and out of core after their initial loading. This
strategy, called *swapping* or *roll-in–roll-out*, can be implemented by using
a relocation register. As previously noted, all jobs are assumed to be
coded relative to location zero. If the machine is designed so that addresses are calculated by adding the contents of a relocation register
to each address referenced by the job, jobs can be moved to new locations in core without upsetting their addressing scheme: when a job
is resident in memory beginning at location A, the value A is stored
in the relocation register.

The ability to relocate programs after initial loading assists the management of memory and the balancing of resource utilization. First, memory can be repacked when fragmentation reduces the length of contiguous storage areas, as exemplified in Fig. 4–3. Second, better use can be made of the rest of the system, since the system has more control over which jobs are currently in core. For example, if all of the core-resident jobs are I/O bound, then one of them may be swapped out in favor of a compute bound job, in order to balance the load. Care must be taken, though, to make sure that the savings due to swapping are not negated by the overhead incurred from moving jobs around.

Swapping programs in and out of memory is clearly a time-consuming operation. One method of reducing overhead in swapping is the use of reentrant code. If a large program that several jobs may wish to use at the same time, such as a compiler, is written as a pure procedure with a completely separate data segment, then only one copy of it need be in core at a time. Several jobs can use the one copy of the procedure with their own local data areas. Only the local data area needs to be swapped for any job that uses this procedure. Reentrant code is an important concept which is useful for other storage schemes as well. However, it significantly reduces swapping overhead only if a specific block of code is frequently shared among a number of jobs.

The key difficulty in swapping is that the entire job must be moved out of core. This is usually a more drastic measure than is actually required. If a job is executing one of its procedures, then most of its other procedures are not needed in core, at least temporarily. Thus, additional room can be made without discarding the whole job, and without disturbing its execution. The idea behind overlaying is to roll out part of the job. The problem with overlaying is that the programmer must anticipate what code is safe to move out. A better solution is to combine the dynamic quality of swapping with the option of only swapping part of a job at a time. Strategies that accomplish this aim are the subject of the remainder of the chapter.

4.6 Segmentation

Most programs are composed of a number of logical units, such as procedures, data areas, and program blocks. *Segmentation* is a scheme by which the program's addressing structure reflects the logical program divisions. In segmentation each program's address space is split into a number of variable-sized blocks, called *segments,* which generally reflect logical divisions of the program. For example, a segment may be a procedure or a data area. A word within the program is identified by a two-part address which specifies the name of the segment and the location of the word within the segment, called the *displacement*. Since program segments are referenced by name, the memory allocation mechanism can store segments in noncontiguous locations of main memory. In fact, not all of the program's segments need be in main memory at one time; some of them can reside on a peripheral device. If a program tries to reference a segment which is not in main memory, the system intervenes and brings the segment in from secondary storage. Although a segmented program address space is considerably more flexible than a nonsegmented one, implementing the two-part address can be quite expensive without special hardware. Therefore, most systems which use segmentation have hardware assistance for address calculation.

4.6.1 Implementing Segmentation

Each address reference within the system is a pair $[s, d]$ where s is the segment name and d is the displacement. Associated with each job or process is a core-resident *segment table* which contains one entry for each segment of the job. The table, which is used by the system to map program addresses into real memory locations, is pointed to by a hardware register called the *segment table register*. Stored at the sth entry of the segment table is

1. a *flag* (or *presence bit*) to indicate whether or not the sth segment is currently in core;
2. the *base address* of the sth segment;
3. the *limit* which indicates the number of locations occupied by the segment;
4. protection bits to check the mode of access (optional).

To access a word $[s, d]$, the segment table is entered, using the segment table register (see Fig. 4–4). The sth entry of the table points to the location of segment s in storage. The dth location of this segment is the desired word, $[s, d]$. Two memory accesses are required to obtain the word $[s, d]$, one access for the segment table and one access for the word within the segment. Since segments vary in size, there is no fixed upper limit for d. Therefore, the limit information is needed to prevent a job's accessing past the end of the segment. In many systems, such as the Burroughs B5700, the foregoing address calculation and limit check is hardware assisted [Organick, 1973].

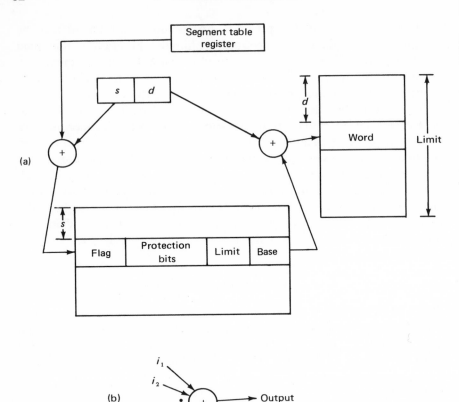

FIG. 4–4 Address calculation in segmentation. (The symbol in (b) denotes an adder where output $= i_1 + i_2 + \cdots + i_n$. Let $\mathfrak{C}(X)$ be the contents of word X. Then $\mathfrak{C}(\text{word}) = \mathfrak{C}(\mathfrak{C}(\mathfrak{C}(\text{segment table register}) + s) + d).$)

Before the address calculation can take place, the flag is checked by the hardware to see if the segment is in core. If so, then the memory address can be automatically calculated as described in the preceding paragraph. If the segment is not in core, then a *segment fault* is said to have occurred, and the hardware generates an interrupt which invokes a supervisor routine called the *segment fault handler*. The segment fault handler finds the desired segment on secondary storage and moves it into main memory. If there is no room in main memory for the new segment, then the system may make room by moving a core-resident segment onto a peripheral device.

If at any time the system wishes to switch its attention to another program, it merely changes the value of the segment table register to point to a new segment table, and $[s, d]$ references are interpreted through the new table.

4.6.2 Advantages of Segmentation

A segmented program address space offers numerous advantages over the conventional absolute addressing scheme. First, overlaying is now accomplished by the system without any prespecification by the programmer. If there is not enough room in core for all of the program's segments, then some segments will temporarily be moved to secondary storage. Unlike overlaying, segmentation allows programs to overlay each other's memory areas. If a program needs a new segment brought into main memory, the system can move any segment in main memory onto secondary storage. The replaced segment need not belong to the program whose new segment is being moved into core. As long as the flag in the appropriate segment table is turned off when the segment is moved onto secondary storage, it does not matter with which segment table the segment is associated.

A second advantage of segmentation relates to linking. In a segmented address space, object modules can be coded as segments. Resolving external references is considerably simplified, since the linkage routine need not be concerned with absolute addresses. In fact, the linking operation is reduced to a table lookup to find the $[s, d]$ address corresponding to the external reference. Loading now entails no special problems other than initializing the segment table to point to each segment. Furthermore, special loaders and linkage editors are no longer needed for overlaying, since overlaying is now done by the system.

Segmentation also facilitates the sharing of reentrant code. A reentrant procedure which occupies a separate segment can be shared by storing its location in several segment tables. Special care must be taken in updating all the tables when the segment is moved to a new location in core or secondary storage. An example of sharing segments appears in a later section.

If the hardware supports a segmented address space, then most of the foregoing advantages are "free" from the user's viewpoint. The complexity of the addressing references is taken care of by the system; the user is unaware that his segments are not contiguous or even necessarily core resident. However, segmentation does carry with it the problem of handling storage so that the flow of segments through core and peripheral devices is managed efficiently. A discussion of techniques for managing segments is deferred until Chapter 5.

4.7   Paging

Paging is a memory management technique in which memory address space is split into fixed-length blocks. In paging, the core memory space is divided into physical sections of equal size called *page frames*. Programs and data are divided into logical units, called *pages*, of the same size as the core page frames. Thus, one page of information can be loaded into one page frame.

4.7.1   Paging Implementation

Address references in a paged memory space are similar to those in a segmented program address space. Each reference consists of a pair $[p, d]$, where p is the name of the page and d is the displacement within the page p.

Associated with each job is a *page table* which contains a list of those pages that together compose that job (called the *page set*). Each entry in the page table, which corresponds to a page of the job, contains

1. a flag which indicates whether or not the page is in core;
2. the location of the page (in core or on secondary storage);
3. protection bits to check the mode of access (optional).

In addition, there is a special register, called the *page table register*, which contains the core location of the page table associated with the job that is currently running.

In the following discussion of address calculation, the reader is referred to Fig. 4–5. When an address $[p, d]$ is encountered during execution, the page table is entered, using the page table register. The pth entry of the page table contains a pointer to the desired page. By counting d locations down that page, the desired word is found. Therefore, two memory accesses are required to obtain a word, one access for the page table and one access for the page itself. As in segmentation, it is possible to include special hardware for the page table to cut down on the delay this causes (for example, MULTICS system [Organick, 1972]).

Associated with each pointer to a page there is a flag which indicates whether or not the page is already in core. Before the address calculation is made, the flag is checked by the hardware. If it is on, then the page is in core and address is automatically calculated. If not, then an inter-

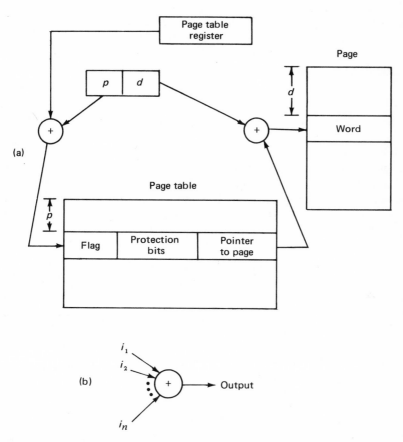

FIG. 4–5 Address calculation in paging. (The symbol in (b) denotes an adder where output $= i_1 + i_2 + \cdots + i_n$. $\mathfrak{C}$ (word) $= \mathfrak{C}(\mathfrak{C}(\mathfrak{C}$ (page table register) $+ p) + d).$)

rupt is generated by the hardware to notify the supervisor that a page must be brought into core. This is called a *page fault*. There also may be protection bits along with the pointer and flag. These bits ensure that the mode of access being requested (for example, read or write) is allowable. As in address calculation, the check of protection bits can be hardware assisted.

Every paging system must adopt a *fetch policy* and a strategy for *page replacement*. The former policy refers to the method of choosing a page from auxiliary storage to be moved into core. The latter refers to the method of choosing a page to be overlaid, given that another page is ready to be moved into core. *Page traffic*, that is, the movement of pages into and out of core, is a function of the fetch policy and the replacement strategy. Fetch and replacement policy are equally important for segmented address space, where segments must be moved from secondary storage into main memory. Methods for fetching and replacing pages and segments are discussed and analyzed in Chapter 5.

4.7.2   Advantages of Paging

Many of the advantages of a segmented program address space are also present in paged memory address space. Previous remarks regarding overlaying in segmentation apply equally well to paging. As in segmentation, hardware-assisted address calculation makes addressing complexities transparent to the user. However, the fixed-size pages lead to important differences between the two techniques.

Since pages are of fixed size, a page may not be large enough to contain a whole logical subdivision of a program. Therefore, linking in a paged address space is not as simple as in a segmented one. However, the fixed-size pages simplify memory allocation considerably. Since all pages are of equal size, bringing a new page into core is easier than bringing in a new segment. The page may either be placed in an empty page frame or another page may be replaced to make room for the new page. In either case no pages need be rearranged in core in order to make room for the new page.

4.7.3   Fragmentation

The term fragmentation refers to the existence of gaps in memory. *External fragmentation* occurs when the empty spaces appear between memory blocks, while *internal fragmentation* occurs when there are empty spaces within the blocks themselves. With fixed-length blocks (that is, paging) there is no external fragmentation, since each time a block is removed, it is replaced with one of the same size. Thus, there are no unusable gaps between blocks. However, there is internal fragmentation, since a logical grouping of information may not be evenly divisible by the page size; one grouping, for example, may occupy three and a half blocks, leaving half a block empty. In general, the length of a job will not be evenly divisible by the block size. Therefore, if one adopts the rule that a page cannot contain data or code from more than one job, then at least one block in each job will be only partly full. Conversely, with variable-length blocks the internal fragmentation problem is solved, since the block size can be tailored to fit the length of the information. Unfortunately, this creates external fragmentation, since after removing a block from memory, it may not be possible to replace it with one of the same size. Thus, holes develop as blocks are moved in and out of core. The problem of fragmentation is illustrated in Figs. 4–6 and 4–7.

If the operating system is in a paged environment, then page traffic and internal fragmentation have to be taken into account when deciding what size to make the pages. Up to a limit, it is desirable to have large pages, since it is more efficient to move one large block than several smaller ones. A large page size implies that only a few pages are needed to store a job. A small number of pages in the system implies low page traffic, since for a given memory size there are not many pages to move in and out of core. However, large pages generate a great deal of internal fragmentation. For example, consider a job of 1545 words (see Fig. 4–6). If pages are 1500 words long, two pages will be required, but 1455 words will be wasted on the second page. If pages are 500 words long, then four pages are needed; the expected page traffic is increased, but only 455 words will be left blank. In other words, there is a balance between the overhead in handling page traffic and internal fragmentation. The goal is to find a compromise page size which minimizes both factors as much as possible. Currently popular page sizes range from approximately 256 to 1024 words.

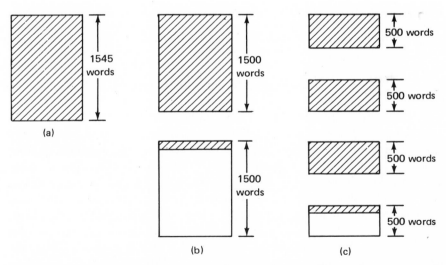

FIG. 4–6   Internal fragmentation. (a) Entire job. (b) Job split into 1500-word pages; 1455 words are wasted. (c) Job with 500-word pages; 455 words are wasted. (In splitting up a job into pages, some space is wasted. In general, the smaller the page size, the less the internal fragmentation.)

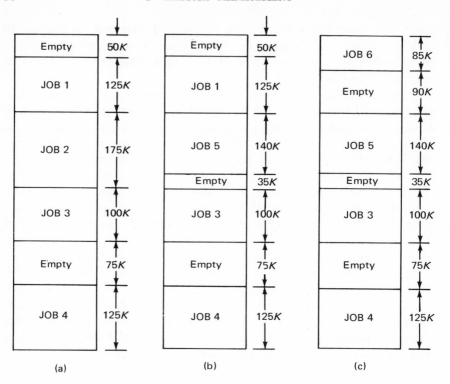

FIG. 4–7 External fragmentation. (a) Original state of memory. (b) JOB2 leaves and JOB5 arrives. (c) JOB1 leaves and JOB6 arrives. (As variable-length jobs arrive and leave, gaps appear and disappear in memory.)

4.8   Segmentation with Paging

Segmentation and paging may be unified such that each segment is paged by using its own page table. In this scheme addresses have three components, $[s, p, d]$. The first component gives the segment number s (see Fig. 4–8). The segment table is entered via the segment table register; the sth location of the segment table contains the base address and length (that is, limit) of the page table for that segment. The second component of the address, p, locates the entry of the page table which points to the pth page of segment s. The displacement d is now added to the base address of the page to find the word. Thus, the address $[s, p, d]$ may be interpreted as the dth word of the pth page of the sth segment of the job which is defined by the contents of the segment table register.

For such a three-component reference three memory cycles are re-

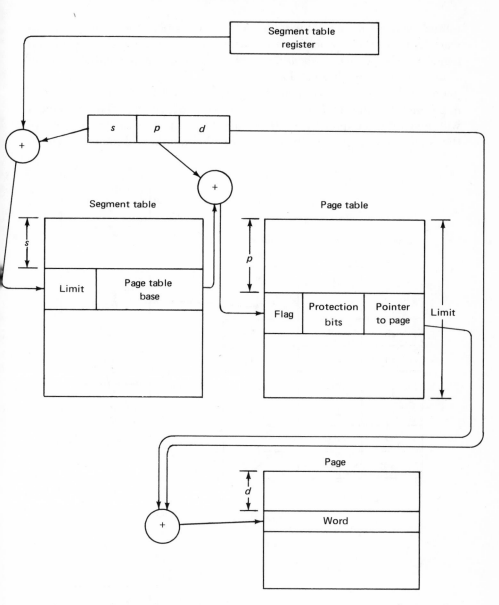

FIG. 4–8   Address calculation in segmentation with paging.   ($\mathfrak{C}$(word) = $\mathfrak{C}$(d + $\mathfrak{C}$(p + $\mathfrak{C}$(s + $\mathfrak{C}$(segment table register))))).)

quired, generating an intolerable delay even when addressing is hardware assisted. This problem is circumvented by adding a group of fast memory cells, called *associative registers*, which map combinations of *s* and *p* into the physical locations of the pages (see Fig. 4–9). The main attribute of the associative registers is that they can be searched in parallel. Given a memory reference to $[s, p, d]$, the associative memory will generate the pointer to the page $[s, p]$ if it is stored in one of the associative registers, thus reducing the number of memory cycles

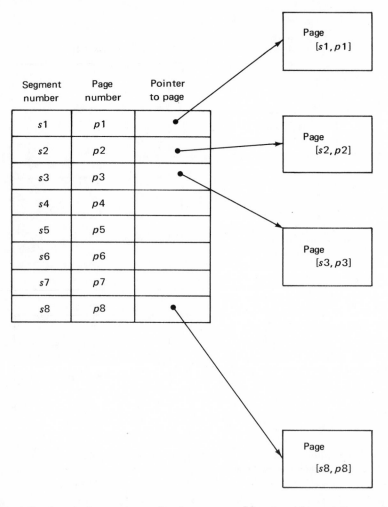

FIG. 4–9 Associative registers for fast page addressing. (Associative registers can be searched in parallel to obtain the page address from an $[s, p]$ pair in one instruction cycle.)

needed by two. If the combination $[s, p]$ is not in an associative register, then an interrupt is raised, and the supervisor replaces one of the $[s, p]$ associative register entries with the new reference $[s, p]$. Since memory references are observed to cluster in a few heavily accessed pages, most page address references will find the appropriate $[s, p]$ combinations in the associative registers.

A segmentation–paging scheme has all the advantages of both segmentation and paging. Since the program address space is segmented, sharing and linking are quite straightforward. Since memory address space is paged, memory allocation is simplified over the simple segmentation strategy. Also, external fragmentation is eliminated. The price for all of this flexibility is the three-component address reference. However, with appropriate associative hardware, the cost of extra memory references can be kept within reasonable bounds.

4.9. Linking Using Segmentation with Paging

4.9.1 Static Linking

As noted in earlier sections, reentrant procedures can be shared among several jobs. However, the linking of these procedures is often quite cumbersome. Segmentation with paging provides a convenient mechanism for managing such shared blocks. Consider a segmented–paged system and a shared procedure P which is stored in its own segment. If a user wishes to use P (that is, call P as a subroutine), the external reference to P within the user program is resolved by adding an entry in the segment table associated with the user program and assigning to that entry a pointer to P's page table. A private data area for P is also added to the user's segment table. This segment table update is sometimes done by the linkage editor before loading. However, as shown in the next section, it can be delayed until execution time.

4.9.2 Dynamic Linking

Using segmentation, it is possible to postpone linking of shared segments until execution time. Thus, the modules which are actually linked may be data dependent. In this section one possible implementation of dynamic linking using a segmented–paged system is discussed (refer to Fig. 4–10).

At compilation time, a section called the *linkage segment* is stored in memory along with each object module (that is, segment) of the job. This linkage segment contains a subsection associated with every

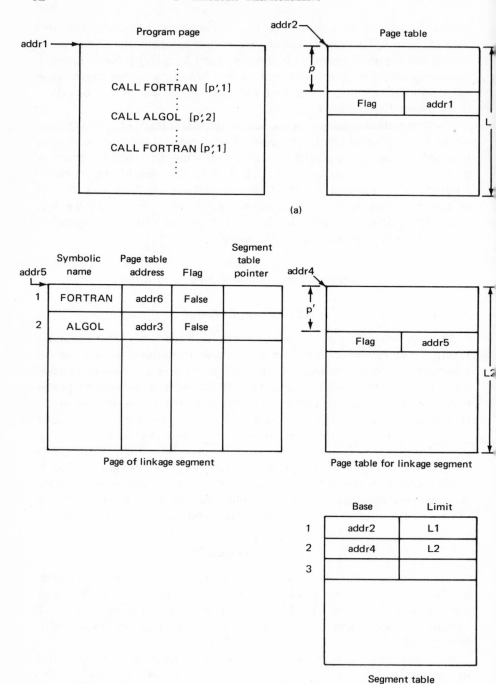

(a)

Page of linkage segment

Page table for linkage segment

Segment table

(b)

FIG. 4–10a,b

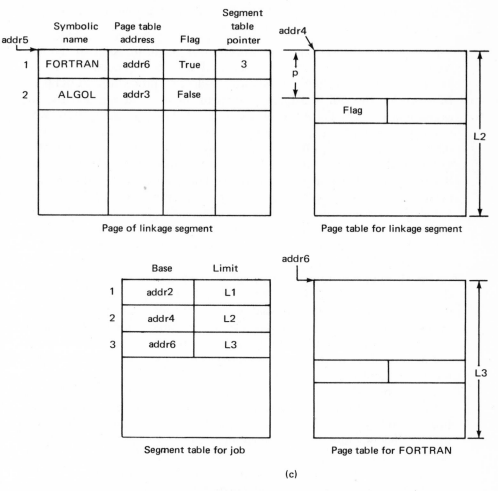

(c)

FIG. 4–10c

FIG. 4–10 Dynamic linking. (a) Program page and page table of segment which calls the shared segments FORTRAN and ALGOL. (b) Segment table for the job, page table for the linkage segment, and a page of the linkage segment before linking FORTRAN or ALGOL. (c) Segment table for the job, page table for the linkage segment, page of the linkage segment, and page table of FORTRAN *after* FORTRAN has been linked.

procedure referenced in that module. For a given referenced procedure, the associated subsection of the linkage segment contains

1. the symbolic name of the referenced procedure;
2. the page table location for that procedure;
3. a flag to indicate whether the routine has been linked yet or not (initially false);

4. a pointer (which is set at the first call of the routine encountered during execution).

Each external reference to a procedure is made to point to the subsection of the linkage segment associated with that procedure. Assume job A, which is currently executing, calls the procedure FORTRAN. In executing the call, the linkage segment for A is entered and the flag associated with FORTRAN is checked. If it is false, meaning FORTRAN is not yet linked to A, an interrupt is raised by the hardware to inform the operating system to link the procedure. When invoked, the operating system makes a new entry in the segment table of A, which contains the page table location of FORTRAN. The pointer in the linkage segment is made to point to A's segment table entry for FORTRAN, and the flag is set to true. Subsequent calls of the procedure will access its linkage segment and be directed by it to the correct segment table entry. This entire operation, which constitutes the linking of FORTRAN to A, is illustrated in Fig. 4–10.

One distinct advantage of dynamic linking is that the location of the shared procedure (say, FORTRAN) may be changed at any time without altering the linkage information. The linkage segment is only concerned with the location of FORTRAN's page table, which in this scheme must be locked in at the time it is linked. Its pages are moved in and out of core like any other paged routine. Similar schemes can be devised for use without paging, and without locking the shared procedure's page table in core.

Note also that static and dynamic linking techniques can be combined. For example, user-defined modules may be statically linked before loading. Shared modules, such as compilers and system routines, may then be linked dynamically when needed. The MULTICS system [Organick, 1972], which uses a segmented–paged addressing scheme, is capable of dynamic linking similar to that shown in Fig. 4–10.

Problems

4.1 A single procedure may be overlaid into different locations of main memory during a process's execution. Describe linkage problems this overlaying creates if the procedure is shared among many processes. How might these problems be solved?

4.2 What advantages are there to segmentation over dynamic overlaying? Are there situations where a user might prefer an overlaying structure to a segmentation one?

4.3 Describe the memory allocation scheme of a machine which uses pure segmentation, such as the Burroughs B5500.

4.4 In some machines, words of memory can be addressed. In other machines, bytes of memory can be addressed in addition to words. In still other machines, individual bits or arbitrary sequences of bits in memory can be addressed. Discuss the advantages and disadvantages of each addressing scheme.

4.5 In some systems pages which were not altered when they were core resident are not rewritten back onto the paging drum when they are replaced. Outline a software technique to implement such a decision mechanism.

4.6 Assume you are given a machine which does its addressing relative to a base register which is specified in the instruction format. You are also given an assembler which produces machine code which executes in absolute locations. Outline a series of steps which will bootstrap the environment to the point that independently compiled modules run together in a relocatable mode.

4.7 In the paging–segmentation scheme described in Section 4.8, is it necessary that the page table for each segment be core resident? If not, briefly outline an implementation where it is unnecessary. Why is it necessary for the segment table to be core resident?

4.8 Design a dynamic linking mechanism for a paging–segmentation environment where the shared procedure's page table need not be locked in core. What are the advantages to this scheme?

4.9 Write a detailed description of the MULTICS virtual memory hardware. Explain how linking is accomplished in MULTICS.

4.10 Suppose you want to allocate a large sparse matrix with the property that the probability of either reading or writing the element (i, j) is $\frac{1}{2}**\max(i, j)$. Find a method of efficiently allocating the matrix in a linear memory space for each of the following cases. Try to minimize the space requirements.

1. The items are fixed length and small.
2. The items are fixed length and large.
3. The items are variable length.

5

VIRTUAL MEMORY

5.1 Introduction

Most of the information in a system is not kept in main memory. Rather, it is stored on large-capacity peripheral devices, such as drums or disks. However, an active process is only able to access directly information which is stored in main memory. Thus, a process might be expected to have to initiate I/O in order to maintain its activity.

In a virtual memory system each process has the illusion that all of its information is in core. The system maintains this illusion by keeping some of the unused sections of a process's data and code on a peripheral device. If the process tries to access information which is not resident in core, a condition is automatically raised to alert the supervisor. The supervisor moves the needed information from a peripheral device into core, so that the process can access it. This latter activity is transparent to the process, since its execution is suspended by the supervisor until the transfer is completed. After completion of the transfer, the process resumes execution, and, as far as it "knew," the information it wanted was in core all the time. That its information physically resides on one or more peripheral devices is invisible to the process.

In this chapter the design and analysis of allocation methods for virtual memory are examined. The chapter is divided into three sections. Section

5.2 contains a description of special hardware devices and memory organizations which are available to a system designer. In Section 5.3 allocation strategies are discussed for two methods of implementing virtual memory: segmentation and paging. The problems involved in these two techniques are briefly compared. Section 5.4 presents several models for program and system behavior in a virtual memory system. In addition, the analysis of allocation mechanisms and the balancing of overall system performance against local strategies are considered.

5.2 Hardware Devices for Virtual Memory

There are many well-known hardware devices for information storage and retrieval, including registers, core, drum, fixed-head disk, movable-head disk, magnetic tape, punched paper tape, and cards. It is assumed that the reader has a basic knowledge of each of these media. In addition, there are hardware mechanisms especially adapted for virtual memory. In particular, multilevel memory and the paging drum have significantly improved the economic feasibility of virtual memory over conventional hardware design. In this section the properties of these two memory organizations are investigated.

5.2.1 Multilevel Memory

The most common type of storage organization consists of two levels (see Fig. 5–1). Level 1 is a large electronic store, such as core, which is directly addressable from the central processing unit. Level 2 consists of one or more high-capacity peripheral electromechanical devices, such as drum, disk, and tape. If information which is needed is not located in core (in a paging system, this situation corresponds to a page fault), then that information must be brought into core from a peripheral device before it can be accessed. This scheme was used in nearly all early paging and segmentation designs and is still found in a majority of small and medium-sized machines. However, large high-speed machines with instruction cycle times on the order of 100 nanoseconds find the basic two-level organization inadequate.

When a fast CPU operates on a core memory which is too slow, it spends a large portion of its time waiting for fetch and store operations from memory. The obvious solution, that of a very fast, large, integrated circuit memory, is not economically feasible under the current technology, although there are indications that large monolithic memories might be economically feasible in the near future. Not only is such memory expensive, but a fast CPU would generally need one or two million

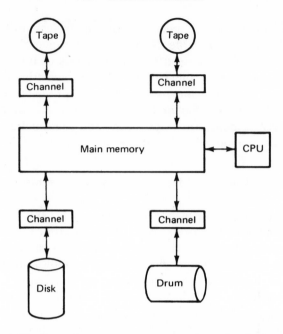

FIG. 5–1   Common organization of two-level store.

words of it to run efficiently. The solution to this problem has been the development of multilevel main storage [Kuck and Lawrie, 1970].

Figure 5–2 is a schematic diagram of an N-level storage system [Mattson *et al.*, 1970]. Memory device $M(N)$ is an electromechanical device. All other memory levels are main stores of varying speeds. In general, for $i < j$, $M(i)$ is faster, smaller, and more expensive (per word) than $M(j)$. In the following discussion of multilevel memory it is assumed that memory is paged (that is, all transfers are with fixed-sized blocks).

A page which is stored at level i is also stored at all levels higher than i. If the CPU tries to access a word which is not in level 1, then the system starts searching higher-numbered levels for the page containing the desired word. When the page is found, the CPU is allowed to access the word, and the page is brought into the faster memory levels until it finally reaches level 1. In bringing a page from a higher level into a lower (faster) one, an old page is replaced. The replaced page is usually the one which was least recently accessed. The idea is that those pages which are currently being accessed most frequently are residing in the faster end of memory.

This organization has been implemented in several large machines, including the IBM 370/168 and IBM 370/195 [Liptay, 1968]. In the IBM implementation, level 1 (called *cache*) contains between *16K* and

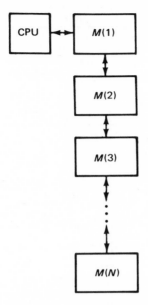

FIG. 5–2 Multilevel store.

$32K$ of 100-nanosecond silicon register memory, level 2 contains about one million words of 1-microsecond core, and level 3, the outer level, is a paging drum. The interface between silicon register memory and core is all in the hardware, so that storage levels are invisible to the user. The resulting average access time for the three-level memory is observed to be quite close to that of level 1.

5.2.2 Paging Drum

Special hardware devices can be adopted which speed up the transfer rate from secondary to primary storage. One such device, the paging drum, provides a considerable increase in efficiency over the standard track-oriented drum organization.

The paging drum is logically divided into n sectors and m tracks, as shown in Fig. 5–3. Associated with each logical track is a set of read–write heads; one logical track can be the width of several physical tracks. The list of waiting drum requests is stored by sector number, so there are n waiting lists altogether. The connection of these lists to the drum control unit is such that the ith waiting list is connected to the drum just as the ith sector comes under the read–write heads. The result of this organization is that the drum will rarely have to wait some fraction of a revolution to begin its next transfer. That is, the utilization of the drum channel becomes quite high. The classical

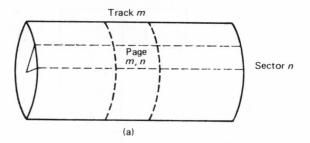

(a)

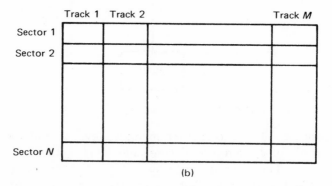

(b)

FIG. 5–3   Paging drum. (a) Physical drum layout. (b) Drum surface laid flat.

design of a nonsectored drum serviced by a single first-come–first-served queue has been shown to be far less efficient than the sectored multiple-list design. The principle of the paging drum has also been applied to fixed-head disks with one head per track. A complete analysis of the paging drum can be found in the article by Weingarten [1966]

5.3.   Allocation Strategies in Segmentation and Paging

From a conceptual viewpoint, segmentation and paging are logical and physical schemes applied to program address space and memory address space. In a real implementation, the conceptual framework is reduced to problems of storing logical segments in physical memory and of breaking up programs into fixed-sized pages. Therefore, from the implementor's viewpoint, the main difference between paging and segmentation is merely that the former uses fixed-size blocks and the latter uses variable-size blocks. Hence, although paging and segmentation are very different concepts, problems in implementing the two schemes are so similar that it is appropriate to discuss them together.

In implementing segmentation or paging, there are three basic problems to consider:

1. how to allocate space at each level of memory;
2. what criteria to use in deciding when to move a page or segment from secondary storage into main storage;
3. when moving a page or segment from secondary storage into main storage, what criteria to use in deciding which old pages or segments should be displaced to make room for the new one being moved in.

Problem 1 is really no problem at all in paging. Memory is divided into fixed-size page frames, and the system maintains a table of pages and their page frame locations. The allocation of free space is just a matter of knowing which frames are not being used at any given time.

When variable-size segments are used, the problem is more difficult. When a storage request is encountered, there are several reasonable strategies for allocating the space. In Section 5.3.1 these strategies are described and compared.

The second problem, that of choosing a page to move from secondary store, is known as *fetch policy* or *pull policy*. Moving a page from secondary store before it is actually referenced in the computation is called *prepaging;* moving pages into core only when a reference results in a page fault is called *demand paging*. The question whether to use prepaging or demand paging is treated in Section 5.3.2.

Given that a specific page must be moved from secondary into primary storage, which page should be replaced to make room for the new one? Numerous *replacement policies* have been suggested, including one which is guaranteed to be optimal (although impossible to implement!). In Section 5.3.3 a number of well-known replacement rules are introduced. These rules are evaluated in Section 5.4 with respect to certain principles of program and system behavior.

5.3.1 Allocation Strategies for Variable-Size Segments

Assume main memory is being allocated in blocks of K words, where K typically ranges from 8 to 2000. Memory requests are always for contiguous blocks. For example, in a system where all memory blocks are 1024 words, a job needing $100K$ words of storage requests 100 contiguous blocks. The goal is to find an allocation strategy which permits high memory utilization with low overhead in the allocation algorithms.

5.3.1.1 LINKED LIST OF AVAILABLE SPACE

One of the simplest methods of storage management uses a linked list of free storage areas, called the EMPTY LIST, sorted by increasing address. Each free storage area on the list contains a POINTER to the next area and a LENGTH field specifying how many blocks the area contains (see Fig. 5–4). When a formerly allocated area is freed by its owner, it can conveniently be added to the EMPTY LIST. The elements of the EMPTY list are searched sequentially; the newly freed area is merged into the list to preserve increasing address order. If the previous or succeeding area (or both) on the EMPTY LIST is contiguous with the newly freed area, then it can be merged with the newly freed area into a single empty area.

There are two well-known strategies for allocating storage from an EMPTY LIST: *first-fit* and *best-fit*. Assume there is a request for an area of length K blocks. In both strategies an area of the appropriate size is found, the first K blocks are reserved for the requesting process, and the remainder of the area is returned to the EMPTY LIST. In the first-fit method the EMPTY LIST is traced from the top, and the

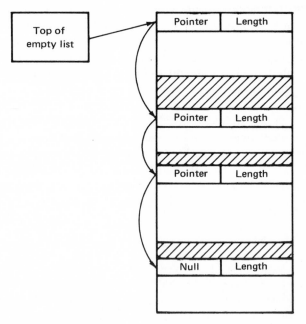

FIG. 5–4 Memory management using an empty list. (Shaded areas are nonempty.)

first free area with LENGTH $\geq K$ is used. In the best-fit method it is the smallest area with LENGTH $\geq K$ that is used. Unless there happens to be a free area of exactly K blocks, the best-fit method involves tracing the entire EMPTY LIST on every request. Therefore, on most requests, the best-fit algorithm is slower than first-fit. Also, in a series of simulations it has been found that first-fit packs memory tighter than best-fit in most cases [Knuth, 1968]. Note that using either method, if there are no areas of size at least K, the request will fail. Emergency measures for such cases are discussed in the next section.

An alternative organization for the EMPTY LIST is to sort the list by increasing LENGTH rather than by increasing address. Now, first-fit and best-fit are the same algorithm. Additional time can be saved in the allocation by having pointers into this list, $\{P1, P2, \ldots, Pi, \ldots, Pm\}$. The pointer Pi points to the first area on the list which has between $i*c$ and $(i + 1)*c$ number of blocks, where c is a constant depending on the implementation. Such a set of pointers can speed up the search, but maintenance of the pointers can be expensive. The key problem with this scheme is that merging newly freed blocks back into the EMPTY LIST is difficult and time consuming.

A third list strategy, called the *buddy system,* allocates storage areas in blocks of size $2**K$. If memory is of size $2**S$, then the system maintains $S + 1$ lists, where LIST(K) holds blocks of length $2**K$. Initially, all lists are empty, except for LIST(S), which points to the first word of memory. To allocate a block of size $2**K$, one begins by searching LIST(K). If it is nonempty, then one of its blocks is allocated. Otherwise, LIST($K + 1$) is checked. If it is nonempty, then one of its blocks is split into two halves, allocating one and putting the other on LIST(K). If LIST ($K + 1$) is empty, the process is repeated until a nonempty list is found. If LIST(J) is empty for all J, $S \leq J \leq K$, then the request fails.

The allocation scheme guarantees that every block of size $2**K$ has an address which is an exact multiple of $2**K$. Hence, for every block of $2**K$, it is easy to find the address of the block (of length $2**(K + 1)$) from which it was split. Whenever two matched blocks of length $2**K$ (that is, "buddies") which were split from the same $2**(K + 1)$ block are found to be free, then they are merged. Merging is a simple operation, since buddies are uniquely identified by the addresses of their first words. In simulation experiments this method was found to be slightly faster than the first-fit method. However, if requests are uniformly distributed between 1 and $2**S$, the buddy system needs about a third more memory space than first-fit because of internal fragmentation [Knuth, 1968].

5.3.1.2 COMPACTION

As memory fills up, it becomes more and more difficult to satisfy large storage requests. When a request is received for an area whose size exceeds the largest empty area, there are three possible courses of action. One is simply to reject the request. Alternatively, a segment currently in storage can be preempted; that is, its storage is taken away and assigned to the new request. The third possibility is to reorganize memory to merge some of the small areas into a single block which is large enough to meet the request. This last method is called *compaction* (see Fig. 5–5).

Using a first-fit algorithm in a system with random-sized storage requests, compaction generally does not become necessary until storage is nearly full. Since memory space is about to run out anyway, the computing overhead of redistributing most of the storage usually does not pay. However, when storage requests are large, one can easily imagine situations where a third of storage is not being used due to external fragmentation (see Fig. 4–3). In such situations compaction is an economically feasible approach.

Compaction may also be profitable if the processor is not being kept busy by the active jobs. The idle time of the processor can be used to compact memory in order to make room for an additional active

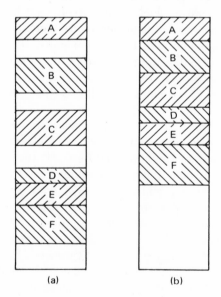

(a)   (b)

FIG. 5–5 Compacting memory (a) before compaction and (b) after compaction.

job. The new active job will then help to keep the processor busy. Since the processor would have been idle if it had not been engaged in compaction, the operation of compaction can in this case be considered to be free.

Knuth has shown that using first-fit allocation in a system where the number of available areas tends to stabilize at an equilibrium position, then the number of unavailable areas is approximately twice the number of available ones. However, the available areas tend to be small in size, making fragmentation a less serious problem than one would expect.

Additional information on dynamic storage allocation can be found in the book by Knuth [1968].

5.3.2 Fetch Policy

In the last section the allocation of segments in memory was discussed. It was noted that page allocation is a trivial operation, since all memory blocks are of equal size. The next problem to consider is how to choose information to move from secondary storage. The case of paging is treated first and is subsequently generalized to the case of segmentation.

In deciding which pages to move from secondary into primary storage, there are two cases to consider: prepaging and demand paging. If one can anticipate program behavior by discovering which pages will be needed in the near future, then clearly prepaging will save page faults. The savings in eliminating a page fault is the difference between the processing overhead in servicing the interrupt and the processing overhead in choosing the page to be prepaged. The effort required to bring in the new page from drum is not a saving, since it is necessary to bring the page into main memory whether or not it is prepaged. If a page is brought into core prematurely, that is, it is prepaged but never referenced, then a certain loss is incurred for the unnecessary operations. This loss includes the processor time in choosing a page, the channel time in transferring it to core, and the cost of taking up a page of core temporarily. From the preceding discussion it is clear that the loss in prematurely prepaging one page is much greater than the gain in correctly prepaging one page. Therefore, if prepaging is to pay off, prepaged pages must be referenced with a very high probability. The prepaging algorithm must be confident that the information it prepages will be referenced before that information is overlaid by another incoming page.

Unfortunately, future program references are difficult to predict. Thus, in most cases demand paging is the better strategy. In fact, under certain cost assumptions, it has been shown that prepaging will never gain over demand paging [Aho *et al.*, 1971]. Still, there are anomalous conditions which lend themselves to prepaging techniques. For example, it may be known that every program needs a certain set of system tables and its initialization code to begin execution. In such a case, it makes sense to load these pages right away, instead of waiting for the program to request them via page faults [Oppenheimer and Weizer, 1968]. In a segmented–paged scheme, similar considerations apply. Whenever a segment is newly entered, some of its pages will be referenced with a very high probability. Again, prepaging can save page faults. In most circumstances, however, prepaging is a losing strategy where wrong guesses cost far more than right guesses save.

Nondemand paging is rare. Nondemand segmentation is rarer still. Prepaging is useful mainly when some logical connection between pages is known. However, since most segments are already complete logical units, much of the motivation for predicting reference behavior is lost. Therefore, segment fetching should almost always be done on a demand basis. In the remainder of this chapter it will be assumed that paging and segmentation are being done on a demand basis.

5.3.3   Page Replacement Rules

Given that a certain page must be moved into core, the question is where to put it. If an unused page frame exists, then there is no problem. In most cases, though, every frame has a page in it, and it must be decided which page should be replaced. A *replacement rule* is a policy which makes such a decision. Although these rules apply equally well to both segment and page replacement, the vocabulary of paging will be used for uniformity in the following discussion.

Replacement rules are judged on how well they minimize the expected amount of future page traffic. The idea is not to replace "useful" pages. Thus, pages which are not expected to be referenced are generally better choices for replacement than those which are expected to be referenced. A given strategy, which consists of either a single rule or several rules used in conjunction with each other, can be applied locally or globally. When a replacement rule is used locally, memory is partitioned into work spaces, with one work space for each running job. Within each work space, the given rule is applied with complete indifference to the other work spaces. Global application treats the entire memory as one unit, applying the replacement rule to the whole memory space, regardless of which job is making the demand.

In this section some of the more common replacement rules are discussed. The behavior of some of the rules is analyzed later in the chapter.

5.3.3.1 RANDOM SELECTION

In this strategy the page to be discarded is chosen at random. It is very simple to implement, of course; but clearly, useful pages are frequently removed.

5.3.3.2 FIRST-IN–FIRST-OUT (FIFO)

Here, the "oldest" page is retired, oldest meaning the one which has been in core for the longest time. FIFO can be used either as a local strategy within each process's storage area or as a global strategy among all the pages in core. It is quite simple to implement. The page frames in memory (assume there are K of them) are ordered in a contiguous list of K elements with a pointer to the newest page. Each time a page is brought in, the pointer is incremented by 1 mod K, and the page then pointed to is removed.

The disadvantage to this procedure is that it works very badly when the system is under a moderate to heavy load, since a great many useful pages are removed. Clearly, the oldest page is not necessarily the least useful. In addition, while there is experimental evidence confirming the existence of sequential instruction fetch patterns in programs, data references are not entirely sequential. If they were, this strategy would be ideal. Although the simplicity of the implementation is appealing, FIFO has serious performance limitations.

5.3.3.3 BIASED FIRST-IN–FIRST-OUT (BIFO)†

This is a local strategy. Each active job i is allocated a set of $n(i)$ pages, where in general $n(i) \neq n(j)$ for $i \neq j$. Within each group of $n(i)$ pages FIFO is applied. Every t time units, $n(i)$ is changed for all i, so that a user's set may grow or shrink. Therefore, at any given time one or more users are favored. By changing the $n(i)$'s, the favoritism is distributed around. The parameters $n(i)$ and t are chosen based on both system and job characteristics.

5.3.3.4 LEAST RECENTLY USED (LRU)

In this strategy the page which has not been referenced for the longest time is discarded. LRU replacement is rather difficult to implement. The most common software implementation uses 1 bit associated with

† Belady and Kuehner [1969].

each page. The system maintains a table where for each page in core, there is an entry in the table which contains the number of time intervals since the last reference to the page. When a page is referenced, the bit associated with it is turned on. After each fixed interval of time, the bits are sampled to see what pages were not referenced in that interval. These page numbers are then recorded in a table; the associated nonreference count for each of these pages is incremented by one. When a new page is brought in, the table is consulted. That page which has not been referenced for the largest number of intervals is replaced.

Empirically, LRU is known to perform well in most cases. Its main disadvantage is the expense in implementation. Hardware assistance can improve the economic feasibility of the rule. For example, the hardware can set the reference bit every time a page is accessed. In multilevel memory, page replacement is usually LRU implemented in the hardware. Overall, LRU is probably the most popular strategy for page replacement.

5.3.3.5   PREDEFINED PRIORITIES

In this method the programmer or compiler supplies special directives which tell the system which pages are to be given high priority in the near future. If the programming language is highly structured, the compiler may be able to detect reference patterns which will aid in page replacement decisions. Using the predetermined priorities, the system can judge which pages are least likely to be referenced in the near future.

5.3.3.6   SYSTEM-DEFINED PRIORITIES

In a similar way, the replacement algorithm can be related to the priorities assigned to each job for scheduling purposes. The jobs currently in the system are ordered in a queue according to their priorities. When a page fault occurs, the queue is scanned for the job which has lowest priority and has pages in core. Ties can be arbitrated by another rule, such as the length of time in system. The system selects one of this job's pages to replace according to some rule, for instance, LRU. If the program which page faulted has lowest priority, then it must replace one of its own pages. If a job's last page is swapped out, it must wait until another job finishes and frees some page frames.

The disadvantage to this algorithm is that the jobs with highest priority often accumulate a large number of pages which are referenced once and never again. These useless pages remain in core until the program finishes executing, since no other program is permitted to steal page frames from it.

5.3.3.7 OPTIMAL REPLACEMENT

Finally, there is an algorithm called *OPT* given by Belady [1966] and proven to be optimal by Mattson *et al.* [1970]. It generates the fewest number of page faults relative to the number of references. OPT replaces the page whose next reference is farthest in the future, that is, the page which will not be referenced for the longest time. Although this is an optimal algorithm, it has one rather severe drawback—it is impossible to implement, since at any given moment one does not have complete knowledge of future references. However, OPT does serve as a useful standard of comparison for other, implementable algorithms.

5.3.3.8 COMPOSITE METHODS

Although the foregoing methods have nice, concise definitions, many composite and common-sense rules work equally well. For example, in the Spectra 70/46 Time-Sharing Operating System (RCA Corp.), there is a list of choices for page replacement which is ordered by decreasing desirability [Oppenheimer and Weizer, 1968]:

1. an accessed-only page from an inactive task;
2. a written-into page from an inactive task;
3. a control program page not accessed in the previous half second;
4. a page from an active task awaiting I/O;
5. a page from another active task.

A list of pages is maintained for each subgroup. When replacement is necessary, a page is chosen from the most desirable nonempty list.

In general, page replacement strategy is a difficult design choice. Some of the methods which are known to work well, like LRU, are difficult to implement without assistance from the hardware. However, many of the simpler algorithms remove a great many useful pages. In the next section, several analytic techniques for comparison of replacement rules are discussed which hopefully help a designer in making an intelligent choice.

5.4. Analysis of Paging Systems

In the previous discussion rules for fetching and replacing pages were introduced. Making reasonable choices among these alternative system designs requires a good understanding of program and system behavior under paging. The working set [Denning, 1968] is one attempt to model this behavior.

5.4.1   Working Set Model and Locality

In a paged virtual memory environment a program generally has only a fraction of its total page set in core at one time. If those core-resident pages are the ones being referenced frequently, then there will not be many page faults, implying low page traffic. Informally, the working set of a process is that set of pages which is required to be core resident in order to obtain a "reasonable" amount of processor time before a page fault occurs [Denning, 1968; Denning and Schwartz, 1972]. It is the responsibility of the system to determine, by observing the page reference pattern, which pages are in the working set.

The *working set* $W(t, T)$ of a process at time t is defined to be the set of pages referenced in the process time interval $(t - T, t)$, where process time consists of the time that a process has a processor assigned to it. Thus, the working set is precisely the set of those pages which were referenced in the last T seconds of process time.

Let e be the fraction of a process's instructions which generates page faults, and let p be the fraction of a process's pages which is core resident. If it is assumed that all address references within the process are random (that is, every reference has an equal probability of being directed toward every page), then $e = 1 - p$. However, programs are known to have nonrandom reference patterns. References tend to cluster around a subset of the whole program, namely, that subset which contains the code and data which are being accessed. This property of programs, that references tend to be grouped together, is called *locality*. In view of program locality, if a good subset of a program's pages is in core (for example, the working set of the program), the addition of extra pages into core is not likely to make a substantial improvement on the fault rate e.

In Fig. 5–6 the effects of random versus clustered referencing patterns under the fault rate are compared. Notice that on the LOC curve, after about a third of the process's pages are allowed to be in core, increasing p does not effect an appreciable decrease in e.

There is a key assumption made in this graph. For each p, it has been assumed that the "best" p of the pages are core resident. That is, the p most heavily referenced pages are in core. Furthermore, it is assumed that as the program executes, the system will service page faults in such a way that the most frequently referenced pages are always those that are core resident. These assumptions are clearly a function of the replacement rule which is used. For example, OPT satisfies these assumptions, whereas LRU does not.

Denning has proposed a replacement rule based on the working set

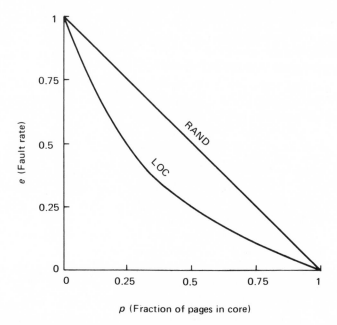

FIG. 5–6   Effects of referencing pattern on fault rate. (RAND, random referencing pattern; LOC, reference pattern of programs which exhibit locality.)

to help optimize the LOC curve. There are other methods, though, of improving paging performance. By careful arrangement of program and data within pages, page references can be clustered, thus increasing the locality of the process. Several of these methods are discussed in Section 5.4.3.

5.4.2   Anomalies in Paging Behavior

5.4.2.1   THRASHING

When either memory or one job's work space within memory is over-committed, a serious degradation of system performance can occur due to increased page traffic. This phenomenon is called *thrashing.*

In the local strategy where the replacement rule operates within each job's work space, if a job is not given enough page frames, every page fault is likely to force the replacement of a useful page. A large fraction of address references generate page faults, bringing page traffic to a critically high level. The global case yields similar results. If memory demand is too high, every page fault again forces the replacement of a useful page, perhaps belonging to another job. Page traffic increases and performance is degraded accordingly. The result is that most of the computing time is spent servicing page faults; while the machine is operating at full speed, useful computing comes to a standstill.

Although virtual memory usually produces excellent results when about a third of each active job fits into core, it must be remembered that nothing is a substitute for real memory. Large programs need lots of core under any memory management system.

5.4.2.2 BELADY'S ANOMALY

In determining the efficiency of a particular paging strategy, it is essential to have some objective means of evaluation. Common sense or intuition are all too often misleading. For instance, one would probably assume that as the number of page frames allocated to a program is increased, the number of page faults generated is decreased. While this is certainly true on the average, there are occasions when precisely the opposite occurs [Belady *et al.*, 1969]. Consider a five-page program where each page is named by a numeral between 1 and 5. Under FIFO, it has been observed that a five-page program with reference pattern 1-2-3-4-1-2-5-1-2-3-4-5 will generate ten page faults when given four page frames, but only nine faults when given three!

Although the anomaly seems to be unique to FIFO replacement algorithms, it is not completely artificial. Real programs have been found which perform in this way. It remains as a warning that lack of careful analysis can lead to surprising and often undesired results.

5.4.3 Effects of Paging on Program Design

It was noted earlier that good locality limits the number of page frames required for a low fault rate. By careful program organization, a significant improvement in locality can be obtained.

5.4.3.1 PAGINATION

The way a program is split up into pages, called *pagination,* can have a significant effect on locality. Experiments have been performed where changing the distribution of program modules has had a dramatic effect on paging behavior [Comeau, 1967]. Programming style is also known to affect the performance of a particular pagination scheme. Recent work in the area of structured programming has suggested a uniformity of style [Weinberg, 1971]. By clearly defining a good programming style, one may be able to construct compilers which paginate more effectively, since knowledge of reference patterns is known at translation time. However, the development of efficient, automatic pagination methods is still in its beginning stages.

5.4.3.2 ATLAS PAGE OPTIMIZATION

The ATLAS system, an early example of a demand-paged system, tried to contain each program loop within the same page. The goal of this strategy is to keep referencing the same page(s) over and over. This is basically a method of trying to optimize locality through clever pagination. Although quite efficient for loops, it does not do well for more random reference patterns. In addition, implementation can be very costly.

5.4.3.3 MATRIX OPTIMIZATION

For calculations involving large matrices in a paged system, poor locality of references can seriously degrade performance. McKellar and Coffman [1969] have shown that careful sequencing of matrix operations can save an enormous number of page faults. However, indexing the array elements is complicated, making address calculation somewhat expensive. Nevertheless, the gain in reducing the fault rate appears to be greater than the loss in the additional computation of element subscripts. Also, in solving large systems of equations by forward elimination using partial pivoting (that is, Gaussian elimination), the fault rate can be significantly improved for large matrices by storing them as a group of submatrices.

This type of analysis of program behavior is useful in the design of compilers for paging. By applying these techniques, language translators and subroutine packages may be designed to optimize program performance in a paging environment.

5.4.4 Problems of Designing Paging Systems

In paged computer systems there are numerous free parameters which can be adjusted to obtain good designs. To name a few, one can choose from various replacement rules, core sizes, job partition organizations, scheduling strategies, and page sizes. In this section several analytical results relating to system design decisions are discussed. They are intended to be only a sampling of the papers published on the analysis of paged systems.

5.4.4.1 COMPARISON OF REPLACEMENT RULES

Among the replacement rules presented in Section 5.3.3, OPT [Belady, 1966; Mattson et al., 1970] is known to be optimal. Although unrealizable in real systems, OPT can be simulated. Replacement rule simulations generally involve running several test programs, making a record of each new page reference during execution. This page reference sequence can then be used as input to the simulation, which determines fault behavior under different replacement strategies and memory sizes. Note that OPT can now be implemented, since there is complete knowledge of future references. This provides us with a basis for comparison to other rules.

Coffman and Varian [1968] selected four test programs in order to obtain sample reference strings: a SNOBOL compiler, a WATFOR compiler, a program for Fourier transforms, and a differential equations solver. The results of testing these programs under LRU and OPT are summarized in Fig. 5–7. It was found that in all cases the difference between LRU and OPT was bounded by 30–40 percent. In addition to observing the expected increase in page faults when the allotment of core page frames was reduced, Coffman and Varian also found that increasing the number of pages in core was of greater benefit than increasing page size (see also Section 5.4.4.2).

Belady and Kuehner [1969] compared the fault rates of FIFO and BIFO. Programs which demonstrate a reasonable locality of references have a distribution of time between page faults (called *interfault time*) versus page frame allotment as shown in Fig. 5–8. Most paging schemes give each job a fixed allotment of pages, say A. By applying a mathematical model, Belady and Kuehner found that a longer average inter-

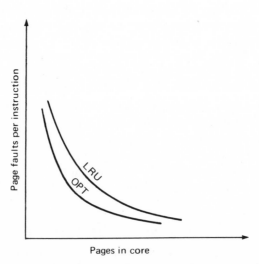

FIG. 5–7 LRU versus OPT replacement rules.

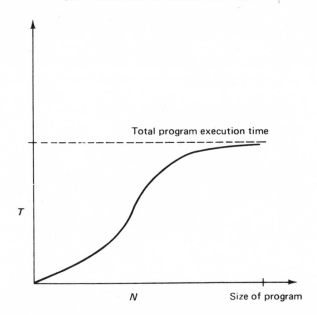

FIG. 5–8 Interfault time versus work space size. (T, time between page faults; N, number of pages in core.)

fault time could be obtained by operating a job half the time with $A - k$ page frames and half the time with $A + k$ page frames, where k is a small integer constant. Using BIFO as a representative of this biased scheme, experiments have shown BIFO realizes a 10–15 percent gain in interfault time over an unbiased FIFO rule.

In the preceding examples simulation and mathematical analysis were used to compare page replacement rules. However, many systems use *ad hoc* rules (such as Spectra 70/46) which are difficult to analyze. Also, the nuances of each system make simulation results difficult to generalize. Thus, it is not surprising that despite the many existing studies of replacement rules, there is no real consensus among designers as to which is the "right" one to implement.

5.4.4.2 DETERMINING PAGE SIZE

There are several factors which affect the optimization of page size. To reduce internal fragmentation, page sizes should be kept small. However, the number of pages required for a large program increases as page size decreases. Consequently, each program's page table grows in length. When only internal fragmentation and page table length are considered, page size should be about 45 words for average program sizes [Denning, 1970]. Unfortunately, small page size increases page traffic, complicating things considerably. Since it is the seek time which is crucial in page fetches from secondary store, increasing the number of page transfers degrades system performance significantly. Hence, relatively large pages must be used to cut down on page traffic. Page sizes typically range from about 256 to 1024 words, in order to balance fragmentation and page table length against page traffic.

5.4.4.3   OTHER RESULTS

A number of interesting problems relating to paging have been formulated and solved. Coffman and Randell [1971] have shown that for a certain class of replacement algorithms, one can predict fault rate performance for a system if additional memory has been added to it. The only information needed for such a prediction is a record of page replacements, which can easily be obtained from sample runs in the system before memory is extended. In this way, the improvement in system behavior can be determined before actually buying the extra memory.

Denning [1968] has proposed a model in which memory and processor demands can be balanced. By predicting both processor and memory demands by mathematical functions, jobs can be chosen which maintain a balance of the two resources. While this approach does help maximize resource usage, it may not be in line with reducing the waiting time for individual users.

Belady and Kuehner [1969] have studied the effect of limiting space allocation for large jobs. Their results show that an allocation strategy which limits core allotments actually increases system load by preventing other processes from using this storage for long periods of time. They conclude that a process which requires a considerable amount of storage should be given it, so that it will leave the system as quickly as possible.

Coffman and Ryan [1972] have investigated fixed and dynamically varying partition sizes. Their results show that for working sets which have small variation in size, fixed partitions appear to be acceptable. They also quantify the saving in using dynamic partitioning for working sets whose size varies widely with time.

Rice and van Dam [1971] have investigated the problem of choosing paging parameters for the particular case of a text-editing system. In particular, they consider page size, replacement rules, pagination, and working space size. Paging and segmentation are also compared. They conclude that both methods seem to work well in text editors, and that ease of implementation is likely to be the deciding factor in choosing a scheme.

There exists a plethora of material on the analysis of paging systems. This is partly due to both the increasing importance of virtual memory and the ease with which paging problems can be formulated. The reader interested in pursuing these analytic techniques is directed to the Annotated References.

5.5   Final Remarks

Although the bias in this chapter has been toward paging in virtual memory systems, there have been very successful pure segmentation systems (notably, the Burroughs systems). In general, though, variable-sized segment transfers are difficult to implement. Still, the natural fragmentation lines of programs and data into variable-sized segments makes the approach intuitively appealing. The obvious compromise, that of a paged–segmented system (see Section 4.8), uses the best properties of both strategies. However, it also contains many of the disadvantages of each. Its implementation in MULTICS has demonstrated its feasibility. Whether, in fact, its complicated addressing scheme is justifiable in terms of the added convenience remains an open question.

Problems

5.1   There are some exceptions to the strict storage hierarchy concept discussed in Section 5.2.1. For example, information can move from tape to disk only by going through main memory. Another example is some CDC machines where the information can only move from disk to slow core by going through fast core. Can you give a reason for these discrepancies?

5.2   Outline a computer system where one processor does storage management and another processor performs only user computations.

5.3   Most theoretical models of virtual memory deal with demand paging. On the other hand, many systems do some form of prepaging when a job is initiated. Why does this apparent discrepancy exist?

5.4   Outline a formal notion of locality of programs. How would you define locality for a data structure shared by many processes? Do program modules and data modules have the same locality? Justify your answer.

5.5   Identify some programming language features which might lead to bad locality of programs. Propose a set of informal rules for programming which when followed will improve the locality of programs written [Weinberg, 1971].

5.6   Assume processes are scheduled highest-priority first. Outline a page replacement algorithm that favors jobs which are about to receive the processor. Why is it inadequate to always replace the lowest priority job's pages?

5.7   The FIFO page replacement algorithm is among the easiest and least expensive to implement. However, FIFO page replacement can result in thrashing, especially if applied globally over all pages in core. Propose a simple implementation change which would avoid the thrashing problem while changing the FIFO discipline only slightly. Can you evaluate the performance of your algorithm relative to LRU or OPT?

5.8   Consider several of the page replacement algorithms in the chapter. Describe the characteristics of programs which perform best under each algorithm.

5.9   The way in which a compiler lays out compiled code into pages can have a significant effect on page fault behavior (for example, McKellar and Coffman [1969]). An "intelligent" compiler might be able to predict referencing patterns by examining the source code. Can you isolate some good *ad hoc* rules for a compiler to follow in paginating the code? How might you verify that the rules are effective?

5.10   Outline a program whose working set varies very widely over time. What replacement algorithms perform particularly badly for such a program? Which ones perform particularly well?

5.11   Suppose that an operating system performs management of free storage using the buddy system, as described in Section 5.3.1.1. If a job in the system accidently (or maliciously) returns the same memory area twice, the system would eventually crash. Redesign the buddy system so that it becomes totally foolproof. (Assume that the computer has no memory protection hardware.) Compare your foolproof buddy system with the first-fit algorithm.

5.12   The following page replacement algorithm (slightly simplified here) was suggested for the ATLAS computer [Kilburn *et al.*, 1962]:

For every (resident and nonresident) page, the system records t, the time since the page was last referenced, and T, the time interval between the previous two references to that page. All times are measured as number of instructions executed. When a page needs to be replaced, the system selects a page for which

1. $t \geq T + 1$

or if none exists,

2. $T - t$ is a maximum and $t \neq 0$.

What is the rationale behind this algorithm? How sensitive is it to programming style? Suggest reasons why this algorithm does not work as well as LRU in practice.

5.13 In a virtual memory system, core memory should be allocated effectively. That is, it is unacceptable to give to a program more page frames than it actually needs. How would you detect this situation, which is exactly the opposite of thrashing? Assume that programs are given a private core area and that page replacement is done locally within the private area. In this case, what measures are needed to ensure that each program receives no more pages than its working set?

5.14 Outline a scheme for charging for main memory usage in a paging environment. Should the user pay for such internal problems as page fault behavior and large working set size?

PART II

TECHNIQUES

The material covered in Part I of this book has had a conceptual nature. An operating system was viewed as a set of processes cooperating in the use of the main resources of the system. The concepts presented are basic and well understood, for example, processes and memory management.

In addition, operating systems have some aspects which are present for historical reasons, as well as many new aspects which are not well understood. File systems exemplify the former, while the problem of design exemplifies the latter. One could adopt the purist's point of view and avoid these subjects altogether. The value of discussing these topics is to expose the material to greater attention. Perhaps a few new concepts will be discovered which will enable the subject to be unified and distilled into a few basic ideas. The topic of protection seems to be in just such a position. The material covered in the last five chapters of this book may seem *ad hoc* and ill structured. Our inability to describe it properly, however, should not reflect on its importance. It is hard to explain ideas which are currently evolving. On the other hand, it is unfair to ignore them, since they directly relate to the core of the subject referred to as operating systems.

6

I/O AND FILES

6.1 Introduction

Files provide one more technique for managing names and relocating data in a manner which is transparent to the user. A *file* is a physical representation of information about a collection of objects. A file usually consists of smaller units, called *records,* each of which contains information about a specific object. The attributes of the object are encoded as values of the *fields* of the record. For example, consider a personnel file. For each employee, there is one record which describes him. The fields within each record might be name, address, spouse, children, department, manager, job history, salary, etc.

A *file system* is that part of an operating system which implements files. There are seven characteristics which should, ideally, be incorporated in a file system:

1. the ability to allocate secondary storage effectively;
2. flexibility and versatility of access;
3. a mechanism which is, as much as possible, invisible to the user;
4. machine and device independence to as great a degree as possible;
5. the ability to share common files;
6. security and integrity of the information stored in files; and
7. an efficient implementation of file manipulation commands.

File systems have two basically different functions. First, they are responsible for manipulating data on storage devices in an efficient manner. Second, file systems give the user the ability to create his own name space and to store and retrieve data from it in a flexible manner. Unfortunately, the physical and the logical properties of file systems are sometimes confused. This situation has hindered the development of consistent file system concepts. In this chapter the problems of organizing data on secondary storage devices are discussed with an eye to collecting these problems into easy to understand groups.

Files are generally stored on peripheral devices, such as disk and tape drives. The first problem a file system must solve is to allocate storage on these devices efficiently. Usually, the physical space on a peripheral device is allocated in *blocks*, which can be of fixed or variable size. If the system is paged, it is important that the size of the blocks have some relation to the size of the pages, to avoid fragmentation. The block size may or may not be related to the size of records in the file.

Each file is essentially a collection of blocks. Blocks can be linked together by forming linked lists; each block has an area set aside for a pointer to the next block in the list. Alternatively, a table, called a *storage map*, can be maintained. For each block there is an entry in the map which specifies the location of the block in the file. This second method is preferable because it allows the blocks to be manipulated without necessarily being accessed. (Since disk accesses are a thousand times slower than core accesses, chasing pointers on disk is prohibitively expensive.)

When the system is initialized, all available storage is in the *free pool*, that is, the collection of blocks not yet allocated to any file. As files are created and expanded, blocks are removed from the free pool and assigned to the various files. When a file is contracted or deleted, its blocks are returned to the free pool. Allocation strategies for core were discussed in Chapter 5. Similar approachs apply here.

The second major problem a file system attempts to solve is naming. Users want to create their own name space. When users share files, they prefer to call the files with their own private mnemonic names. In such an environment a single name can refer to different files and different names can refer to a single file. The context within which a name is used must resolve any naming conflicts.

Files are essentially named memory segments [Organick, 1972]. A file name used in a certain context defines a function mapping addresses into objects within the file. Files give the user more flexibility than named memory segments for structuring name space. The records are the units of the name space, and references to them can be effected according to different rules. That is, name space has structure by virtue of the relation between names. For instance, the user can view the records of the file in sequential order, in a tree fashion, or in any other way that fits his application. File systems also extend the name–addressing relationship as discussed in Chapter 4 and 5 to more devices than just the main memory–paging drum pair. Unfortunately, since file systems arose historically before there was a well-understood theory of memory management, they are seldom described using the terminology of segmentation and address transformations, as presented in Chapter 4.

The file system establishes a name within a context by constructing *directories*. A user refers to a specific file by a symbolic name. For each symbolic name in a given context there is a directory entry which translates the symbolic name into the actual location where the file resides. This translation may be effected by going through more than one level of directories. In addition, directories contain information pertaining to the usage of the file. For instance, a directory entry for a file may contain

1. the symbolic name which the user associates with the file;
2. the actual location of the file;
3. a unique identifier for the file which is the same for all users of that file;
4. the type of access permitted to users;
5. when the file was last accessed; and
6. how often it has been accessed.

As an example, consider a personnel file shared by many users. Assume a user wants to access a particular record in the file. The user can specify the record either by its position within the file (for example, the seventh record) or by some values of the record fields which together uniquely identify the record (for example, name and social security number). (Positional referencing makes the program highly dependent on the file structure and discourages some kinds of file sharing.)

To service a request, the file system must locate the named file. The file name supplied by the user is used in the context defined by the user's directory to obtain the file's unique identifier. The physical medium on which information is stored, such as a tape reel or a disk pack, is called a *volume*. After obtaining the unique identifier, the file system tries to locate the particular volume(s) associated with this identifier. If the volume(s) on which the file is stored is not mounted, the file system should request that the operator mount the volume on some free drive. When this has been done, the file system can access the file. The position of the required record(s) is either given explicitly as an address; or given indirectly, for example, through a computation based on field values; or located through searching based on the file's known organization. The file system then has to generate the appropriate commands to the I/O hardware which transfers the desired record(s) of the file between main memory and the peripheral device storing the file. Buffering is sometimes necessary if more than one record is requested.

It should be clear from the preceding discussion that the file system has to perform many diverse operations to service even a single request. Some operations performed by the file system are logical in nature, such as identifying the unique file name from the user's local name. Other operations are very close to the hardware, such as transferring blocks of information between the main memory and a particular device. These various functions of a file system can be described by a series of levels of software [Madnick and Alsop, 1969]. Starting close to the hardware, these levels can be made to correspond to five basic subsystems within the file system (see Fig. 6–1). Each level implements some more flexible facilities based on the facilities of the previous levels. The first levels deal mainly with the physical aspects of the file system; the last levels deal mainly with the logical user-oriented aspects of the file system.

6.1.1   I/O System

The operation of the physical devices is coordinated by this first level of software. The processes comprising this system operate close to the hardware. They manipulate volumes and read in or write out blocks of information between specified addresses of main and secondary storage.

6.1.2   Basic File System

This system is responsible for converting the unique identifier of a file into an object called a *file descriptor*. The file descriptor provides the physical address of the file, as well as its length. If the file consists of multiple blocks, the file descriptor points to the different blocks that make up the file. The basic file system also provides commands for breaking up (or *subsetting*) files into smaller subfiles.

6.1.3   Logical File System

The function of the logical file system is to determine the unique identifier associated with the symbolic name given by the user. The

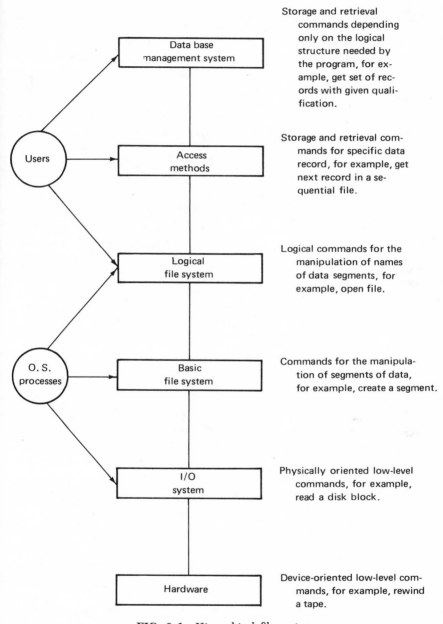

Storage and retrieval
   commands depending
   only on the logical
   structure needed by
   the program, for ex-
   ample, get set of rec-
   ords with given quali-
   fication.

Storage and retrieval commands for specific data
   record, for example, get
   next record in a se-
   quential file.

Logical commands for the
   manipulation of names
   of data segments, for
   example, open file.

Commands for the manipulation of segments of data,
   for example, create a segment.

Physically oriented low-level
   commands, for example,
   read a disk block.

Device-oriented low-level commands, for example, rewind
   a tape.

FIG. 6–1 Hierarchical file system.

symbolic name is interpreted in the context of the user's directory to obtain the unique identifier associated with the file, which corresponds to a particular descriptor at a lower level. The function of the logical file system is not related to physical properties of the devices on which the files are stored. The users who request services from this system do so in a device-independent fashion.

6.1.4   Access Methods

This system provides logical methods of accessing data which can be completely different from the way the data is physically stored. Users sometimes wish to access records in an order not directly represented by the way the file is physically allocated on the volume. For example, assume the records of a personnel file are sorted as a sequential list ordered by social security number. A sequential access method merely accesses the records in the order in which they are stored. Some user, though, may want to access records based on the value of a field, such as income. This is accomplished by mapping the user's access method (that is, ordered by income) into the physical structure of the file.

6.1.5   Data Base Management System

Although not really part of a file system, data base management systems are nevertheless a natural extension. Different programs may expect a different logical structure from the files on which they work. On the other hand, it is uneconomical to keep separate files for each structure when the information contained in each is the same. A data base management system provides a flexible user program interface by allowing a single physical file to be accessed according to various logical structures. This organization allows sharing of the same information between programs which require different logical structures of the data.

In the following sections each of the levels will be described in greater detail. The facilities provided by the various levels of the file system vary from detailed low-level commands to high-level user-oriented commands. This separation of facilities into levels not only groups activities into more easily managed blocks, but it also enables the file system to support the needs of both the operating system and the operating system's users. Although these two separate functions may be combined in one file system, generally the part of the file system supporting system processes is too complicated for casual users and is hidden from such users.

6.2   I/O System

The I/O hardware of computers normally consists of a hierarchy of channels, control units, and devices. An instruction to start I/O generally indicates the device and the address in main storage of a stored program (called the *channel program*) which governs the I/O operation. The channel executes the channel program instructions to effect the desired data transfer. Completion of an operation or an abnormal condition is signaled with an interrupt. When an I/O interrupt is taken by the processor, information is stored which indicates the status of the I/O operation. If an error has occurred, additional information concerning the component status can be made available by issuing instructions to interrogate the status of the component.

The I/O system consists of software processes corresponding to and governing each element of the I/O hardware. This permits the standard communication mechanisms of the system as described in Chapter 2 to be used in the I/O system. The communication paths are then an internal image of the hardware connections. One of the functions of the I/O system is to convert the interaction between the processor and the I/O hardware into the standard communication format. The system can then view devices as cooperating processes.

This approach has three major advantages. First, the software is organized so that asynchronous activity in the hardware is managed by independent cooperating processes. This makes design and implementation of the rest of the system much easier conceptually, since the differences among device speeds are no longer visible to the system. Second, special conditions, such as channel errors, are corrected by the lowest level of the file system. That is, these problems are resolved by the software which is best equipped to handle them, and are transparent to other levels of software. Third, all device-dependent activity is localized at the innermost level of the file system. Nuances of device communication need not concern other processes which want to do I/O operations.

The following is a possible organization of the major parts of an I/O system [Atwood *et al.*, 1972]. The organization is heavily influenced by the characteristics of IBM hardware, since it is nearly impossible to discuss I/O systems in a machine-independent manner.

6.2.1   Channel I/O System

This subsystem consists of processes called *channel managers,* one channel manager associated with each hardware channel. Logically, each channel manager initiates I/O on its channel by sending a message to the channel telling it to execute a channel program. The channel manager receives notification that the I/O is complete by receiving a message from the channel specifying a complete operation or an abnormal condition. The channel managers can be written using exactly the same communication logic as is used by all processes. Processes communicating with a channel manager behave as though they are sending messages directly to a control unit and are receiving answers from it. Therefore, it is the channel manager's job to sort out the interrupts it receives, acting on those applying only to channel conditions, and passing others down to the relevant control unit managers.

6.2.2   Disk I/O System

The disk I/O system consists of one process for each disk control unit and one process for each disk drive. The channel managers are used to operate the (logical) disks. Each disk accepts high-level commands, which it translates to appropriate commands for a channel manager. Commands include

1. format a disk in blocks according to the standard specification of the system;
2. read or write a volume label uniquely identifying a volume on a disk drive;
3. write a block of information from memory to disk;
4. read a block of information from disk to memory.

The same organization can be used for other rotating devices, such as drums.

6.2.3   Terminal I/O System

This subsystem supports interactive terminals in an environment similar to a telephone answering and switching service. All typewriter-like devices (including the processor's master console) can be treated as if they were dial-up devices. Thus, each terminal acts as a telephone which can dial up the system and then can disconnect from the system. During the time that the terminal is connected with the system, it can transmit and/or receive messages.

The channel manager constructs two message paths, a control path and a communication path, to support the terminal I/O system. The control path is primarily used to inform the system when a terminal dials up or disconnects. The communication path is used to send lines of data to a terminal.

The terminal system examines the first line transmitted by a terminal (following dial up) and decides which subsystem(s) (if any) should converse with the terminal. If exactly one such subsystem is found, then the communication path is connected directly to that subsystem. After the connection is established, the messages from the terminal are sent directly to the subsystem. If many subsystems are involved, the terminal system determines from the terminal how the messages intended for each subsystem are to be distinguished and relayed to the proper subsystem.

6.2.4   Peripheral I/O System

The peripheral I/O system manages all hardware devices except the disks, drums, and the typewriter-like devices, which are managed by their own subsystems. Peripheral devices need separate handling because of their widely varying operational characteristics. The peripheral I/O system uses the channel managers to support the following peripheral devices.

1. *Printers* which accept commands of the form: *print n lines from memory;*
2. *Card readers* which accept commands of the form: *read n cards into memory;*
3. *Card punches* which accept commands of the form: *punch n cards from memory;*
4. *Magnetic tape drives* which accept commands of the form:
    (a) *advance* or *rewind;*
    (b) *read n blocks from tape to memory;*
    (c) *write n blocks from memory to tape.*

Each component has a process to manage it.

The I/O system organization given is by no means complete. Most of the details, and there are many details in an I/O system, are not discussed. It is important for the reader to understand what an I/O system provides. How it does this can only be discussed after dwelling in detail on specific hardware features. Some of these features will change considerably in future hardware designs. Consequently, it is not appropriate that these features be discussed in depth in a book about principles of operating systems.

6.3 Basic File System

The I/O system enables the rest of the system to send and receive data from physical devices. A main storage address and a physical address on the device need to be specified before data can be moved. To specify a physical address, the *basic file system* manages file descriptors which provide the required physical addresses of the blocks belonging to a file. In addition, it supervises the mounting of volumes through communication with the operator and can be used to define subsets of a file or to expand the storage area of a file.

A *file descriptor* is a small data structure which uniquely identifies the file. It generally contains the physical address of each block belonging to the file and control information about the manner by which the descriptor can be passed around and manipulated.

File descriptors can be created and manipulated using separate commands to the basic file system.

1. CREATE DESCRIPTOR (*Allocation*)

Create a new file descriptor associated with the region specified by *Allocation*. Instead of explicitly defining a CREATE DESCRIPTOR command, a file descriptor for an entire volume can be given automatically to the process which owns the volume. The descriptor can then be further subsetted into file descriptors corresponding to regions within the volume using the following commands.

2. SUBSET (*File Descriptor, Subset*)

Generate another file descriptor corresponding to a *Subset* of the file which can be specified (say) by the *Subset*'s first and last word. After the command has been executed, the new *File Descriptor* can be used to reference the *subset* of the original file.

3. ALLOCATE (*File Descriptor, Allocation*)

Generate a new file descriptor corresponding to the combined space of the file specified by *File Descriptor* and another region specified by *Allocation*.

4. DEALLOCATE (*File Descriptor, Allocation*)

Return part of the file specified by *File Descriptor* to the free area. The particular part which is released is specified by *Allocation*.

The basic file system also manages the volumes of secondary storage. Therefore, it must establish a communication path to the operator's console in order to issue mounting instructions. It can instruct the operator either to mount a volume on a specific drive or to mount it on any available drive. In the latter case, the basic file system would expect an operator response describing which drive was chosen.

The basic file system maintains a volume table which contains the current status of all volumes in the system. The entry for a volume may contain

1. volume name and a unique volume identifier;
2. the name of a logical drive if the volume is mounted or a flag if the volume is not mounted;
3. a count of currently active files in the volume;
4. a pointer to a table which describes the layout of the volume;
5. protection information about the volume (for example, owner and legal users); and
6. the date of creation.

To manage volumes, the basic file system implements commands such as the following.

1. REQUEST (*Volume Name*)
The calling process requests that the system introduce a new volume entry in the volume table. The basic file system checks ownership, accounting, and protection information and creates a file descriptor for the volume. *Volume Name* can be a local name of the volume for mounting information. It need not necessarily coincide with the volume's unique identifier.

2. RELEASE (*Volume Name*)
The basic file system releases the volume called *Volume Name* from active use and modifies the accounting information concerning the volume's owner. The process issuing this command should be required to demonstrate ownership of the volume.

3. ATTACH (*Volume Name*)
The basic file system connects the volume specified by *Volume Name* to a drive. The ownership of a drive or the ability to request a drive should be indicated by the process. The volume table is updated to indicate the change of the volume's status. Communication with the operator will be necessary if the volume is not mounted.

4. DETACH (*Volume Name*)
After consulting with its volume table, the basic file system disconnects

the volume specified by *Volume Name* from its drive. It then notifies
the operator that the drive is available.

The previously listed commands enable the basic file system to provide
two important services. First, it manages regions (basic files) of the
volumes as represented by file descriptors. Second, it provides volume
management which permits the connection and disconnection of volumes
and the introduction of new volumes into the system.

With a basic file system, the operating system can manipulate file
descriptors in response to higher-level commands. This enables the file
system to generate proper commands to the I/O system upon receiving
(say) a READ command. Sometimes higher-level users also need to
refer to a particular space on a volume or otherwise manipulate information regarding such an area. The manipulation of file descriptors by
users presents a real design choice. Sometimes users need this facility;
other times they do not. For instance, users may prefer mnemonic symbolic names over explicit file descriptors, in which case they would need
a logical file system, as described in the next section.

6.4   Logical File System

The logical file system provides the name transformation from user-
oriented local names to system-oriented unique identifiers (that is, the
$\mathfrak{N}$ function in Section 4.1). In addition, it prepares a file for read and
write operations by issuing commands to the basic file system.

Each user of the logical file system is identified with an entity called
a *sponsor*. A sponsor is a permanent unit residing on secondary storage
which contains information about a particular user account, including
a list of the account's files. When a user logs on, the system obtains
information from the sign-on procedure which identifies the user's sponsor. When a user logs off, permanent information about his environment,
such as newly created files, is transcribed to his sponsor.

Sponsors can be used to provide the context for interpreting a user-
oriented mnemonic name given to a file. For instance, a separate directory can be associated with every sponsor, as in Fig. 6–2. The directory
has an entry for every user-oriented name which can refer to one of
the sponsor's files. Information about a file can be obtained in two steps.
First, the local name is used to find the appropriate entry in the sponsor's
directory. The sponsor's directory specifies a file identifier which points
to a unique entry of a master directory of all files in the system. In
this manner, each user has the flexibility of using local mnemonic names

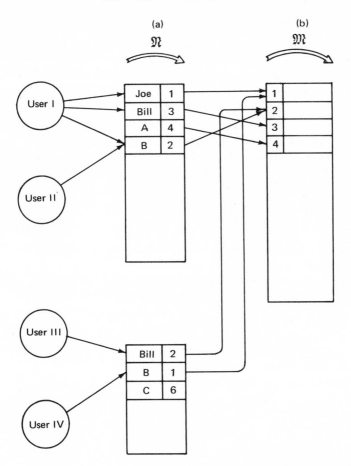

FIG. 6–2 Two-level directory structure. (a) Sponsor directories; (b) master directory.

for files which can be shared by others. The search to find the corresponding unique identifier is also local to the sponsor and therefore
rather efficient. Sharing of files is important for any flexible operating
system environment, in order to eliminate unnecessary duplication of
data. In this chapter the mechanism for allowing easy sharing is emphasized. In Chapter 7 methods will be discussed which constrain sharing
according to security guidelines.

In this two-level approach to directories a unique entry is incorporated
in the master directory for every file. The entry contains a system-wide
unique name identifying the file, the owner's identification, the date
of creation, a count or linked list of active users, and the file descriptor

of the area belonging to the file. In Section 6.7 an example of a file system is outlined which uses the idea of local and master directories.

The logical file system implements commands which enable a user to create, read, and write on a file. The logical file system also requires a user to notify the file system about his intention for acting on the file. This notification is done with an "open" command. As a result of an open command, the file system locates the file in the directories and gets prepared to receive the read or write commands. The units of data which are read and written usually refer to a number of blocks of the file. The blocks do not necessarily correspond to records. Rather, they are physical blocks used for the allocation of secondary storage. The following are examples of commands implemented by the logical file system.

1. CREATE (*File Name, Size, Volume Name* [optional])
A request is made to create a new file, *File Name*. If *Volume Name* is specified, the file should be on that particular volume. Protection and accounting information should be specified.

2. DELETE (*File Name*)
A request is made for the deletion of the file *File Name*.

3. OPEN (*File Name*)
A request is made to open the file *File Name*.

4. CLOSE (*File Name*)
A request is made to close and disconnect the user from the file *File Name*.

5. READ (*File Name, Nfile, Mprocess, Count*)
A request is made to read *Count* number of blocks starting from the *Nfile* block of the file *File Name*. The blocks are deposited in a contiguous memory area beginning at the address *Mprocess*.

6. WRITE (*File Name, Nfile, Mprocess, Count*)
A request is made to write *Count* number of blocks on the file specified by *File Name*. Writing begins from the *Nfile* block in the file. The data in main memory are in contiguous locations beginning at the address *Mprocess*.

Each command can have many outcomes. For example, the CREATE command may have one of the following results.

1. The file *File Name* has been created according to specifications. The user can subsequently refer to this file.

2. The name *File Name* is in conflict with another name known to the sponsor. The system cannot create another file with the same name.

3. *Volume Name* cannot be found, or is not mounted, or is full. The user has to specify another volume for his file.

The user's process must have logic to deal with these different outcomes, or else the condition will have to be treated as an unexpected error.

6.5 Access Methods

In the previous sections a file was discussed as a set of blocks of information without any concern for the nature or structure of the information which it contains. Each group of users needs the information structured in its own particular way. Users frequently need to access specific records within the file which are identified by some of the records' data fields. The system can provide this mechanism through *access methods*.

There are several methods of identifying the particular record or set of records in a specific file in which a user is interested. The simplest way is to use the position of the record within the file. If the logical file has an implicit order of records, then it is meaningful to address the ith record of a file. (The logical order of records can be independent of the properties of the physical device on which the file is stored.) In the same manner, if a pointer points at a particular record, "next," "previous," and "current" are meaningful attributes of that record. These attributes correspond to simple relations, since the size of the records does not play any role. A more flexible way to refer to records is by using some of the data fields as *keys;* the value of a key uniquely identifies a record within the file. For instance, in a personnel file the social security number can serve as a key. A *partial key* is a data field whose value corresponds to zero, one, or more records. For instance, the salary field in a personnel file is a partial key, since the number of employees who have a salary of $10,000 can be zero, one, or more. Therefore, any data field can be used as a partial key. Specific data fields within records are often singled out as keys or partial keys to allow the file to be accessed with respect to the values of the fields. For instance, if employee records are retrieved according to their social security number, then the latter should be declared as a key.

A *query* is a language construct which enables the user to specify a request for retrieving data. If a query is written in terms of the keys used to organize a set of data, then the system can use these keys to retrieve particular records more quickly than if the keys were not used. There are many approaches for implementation of the qualification of a record to a query.

In the first approach, the system scans the records sequentially until it finds all the records which contain the correct values of the keys. This operation can be expensive due to a large number of disk accesses, since the entire file must be scanned. On the other hand, it is very simple to program. It is also appropriate for small files.

In the second approach, for each value of the key the system establishes an element with pointers to all records which match the key. The set of all these elements, which is itself a file, is called an *inverted file* or an *index table*. For instance, assume that a personnel file uses "department" as a partial key. For every department a set of pointers in the "department" inverted file points to all employees in this department. In this case, the department inverted file is composed of the set of all groups of pointers, each group corresponding to a department. Certain special queries can now be retrieved faster than by the sequential access method, specifically, those queries which use the keys established with inverted files. However, the inverted files themselves take a considerable amount of storage and need to be searched for the appropriate departments. Furthermore, inverted files require extensive maintenance, especially in the presence of many update operations on the keyed fields.

In the third approach, the system establishes a chain (or *multilist*) of all records which have the same value of a particular partial key. For instance, the first employee record of a personnel file in department X has a pointer to the next employee record in department X and so on until the last record. The chain, which can be arbitrarily linked, is transparent to the user. These pointers are established by the system in order to service queries faster. For instance, if a user asks for all employee records in department X, then the system can pick the first one either with a dictionary or by searching and then use the pointers to retrieve the rest. This operation is again rather fast for certain queries. On the other hand, all the pointers mentioned take space, and they need to be very carefully manipulated and updated when keyed data fields change in records.

It may be very difficult to choose between the three approaches previously discussed for an existing environment. The performance of the system is highly dependent on the type and frequency of the queries serviced. Analytical tools, simulation, and monitoring must be used to evaluate different solutions. However, except for very well-defined applications, the initial choice of features to implement may be little better than a guess.

Operating systems usually provide some standardized access methods. They enable the user to identify and retrieve records from a file using simple commands which invoke searching or indexing mechanisms in the file system. The actual implementation of the mechanisms is transparent to the user.

The access methods provided by operating systems have two basic characteristics. They can be *basic* or *queued,* and can be *sequential* or *direct.* A *basic* access method is one in which the user has to do his own buffering of records retrieved from the file, for example, IBM's BSAM. In this respect the user has flexibility to devise his own buffering mechanism to suit his own application. In a *queued* access method the system has a standard buffering scheme, for example, IBM's QSAM. The user is freed from the burden of buffering his data, but he has to abide by the conventions of the mechanism provided by the system. A *sequential* access method organizes the records of the logical file in a sequential order. The user can only retrieve and store data in the file records by accessing them sequentially, for example, IBM's BSAM, QSAM. A *direct* access method enables the user to access records in a random fashion within the file, for example, IBM's BDAM. The user references the desired record(s) directly without concern for the record's position in the file; the system has the necessary mechanisms to locate and access the record(s).

A direct access method does not preclude the possibility of sequential access. Sequential access is usually allowed, but it may be not as efficient as when a sequential access method is used. In some cases, a sequential access method can be augmented through the use of indices to provide some direct access in the file, for example, IBM's ISAM.

The attributes of access methods (that is, basic, queued, sequential, or direct) are conceptually unrelated to their detailed implementation or the physical devices on which the files reside. They are logical attributes of the facilities which the access methods present to the users. Of course, it is a fact of real life that direct access methods are implemented for files on random access devices, such as disks and drums. Sequential access methods generally allocate the records sequentially in storage devices, but they do not have to. At any rate, the internal mechanisms of the access method should be of little concern to the user. Unfortunately, access methods are often presented with too much emphasis on the peculiarities of individual implementations.

A great number of access methods are documented and implemented in existing systems. Most application programs interface at this level with the operating system. Access methods have traditionally been considered important for commercial applications.

There is much duplication of functions provided even within the same operating system. Some recent access methods try to reorganize and consolidate the facilities of their predecessors (for example, IBM VSAM). Future hardware might in fact directly provide some of the facilities of access methods.

6.6 Data Base Management Systems

Different user programs generally make different assumptions about the structure and format of the files which they manipulate. Until recently, this has necessitated the existence of many files, even when the information content of the files was the same. In addition, users' programs had to be modified each time there was a format change on the corresponding files. To achieve a certain degree of program independence from the file and to enable many different programs to share the same information from a single copy, a facility called a *data base management system* has been developed.

A data base management system is an application system which superimposes several logical structures on some information according to the needs of users' programs. Consider once again a personnel file. Different programs view the personnel file in different ways. For example, a salary update program accesses the file in a different manner than a management reporting program. Some time after a file is designed, new information requirements may arise. Either the file must be modified, or another file must be generated. If the file changes drastically, the old programs will not run. A data base management system concentrates in one part of the system all the assumptions that a program has to make about the structure of the file on which it operates. In view of changing requirements and multiple requests, the data base system provides a flexible interface to the application programs. Each program can work on the "logical" file it expects through the use of the data base system.

Data base systems use inverted files, indices, keys, and multilists to implement the various logical structures required by users. Typically, data base systems are rather large and complex. Some of them provide completely independent query languages and data manipulation facilities (for example, IBM's system GIS). Others are implemented as a set of calls from a host language, such as PL/I, COBOL, or assembler (for example, GE/Honeywell IDS and IBM IMS). In addition, they may provide a teleprocessing facility, allowing many users to access the data base simultaneously. Such an environment is sometimes called a *management information system*.

6.7 Example of a Simple File System

In this section a file system is described which is appropriate for a minicomputer with a disk. The file system bears some resemblance to the UNIX System [Thompson and Ritchie, 1973]. The I/O system is not discussed in order to present a design which is as machine independent as possible. What appears in the example essentially corresponds to the combination of a very simple basic file system environment and a simple access method based on a logical file system.

Each user corresponds to a single sponsor and has his own directory of files. The entries in the sponsor's directories are pointers directed at a *master directory* where physical addresses of the files are stored. A user program accesses a file using the sponsor's directory. A directory entry contains (see Fig. 6–3)

1. the user program's symbolic name for the file;
2. a number i which points to the ith entry on the master directory;
3. a Read pointer; and
4. a Write pointer.

The master directory consists of control blocks for the files. Each control block (organized as in Fig. 6–3) contains

1. the unique file identifier;
2. a *count* indicating the number of user programs which currently have the file open;
3. the identification of the owner;
4. the mode of access permitted to owner and other users; and
5. a group of pointers, each referencing either a block of memory containing information or a block of memory containing pointers, each of which references a block of information. A bit is included with each pointer indicating whether pointers are indirect or not.

Suppose memory blocks are 64 words in length, and there are up to 8 pointers in the group of pointers. Within these constraints regular files can be constructed ranging in size from 64 to 8*64 words, and *long files* may contain up to $8*64*64 = 32K$ words.

The file system enables the user to reference words of information within his file by pointing with his Read/Write pointers. The directory structure allows users to have mnemonic names in their directories referring to common files which are shared through the master directory. The facilities are offered in the form of the following commands.

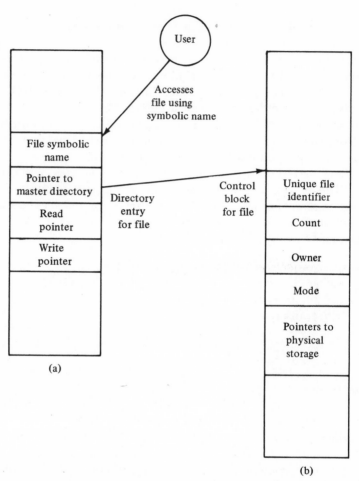

FIG. 6–3 Example of the file system structure. (a) Sponsor directory; (b) master directory.

1. $K := \text{CREATE}(Joe, mode)$

This command serves to create a file. The argument *Joe* is the symbolic name with which the user program will refer to the file. The system finds the first empty block in the master directory and creates a control block. *Count,* in the control block, is set to one. A unique file identifier is entered, as well as owner and *mode.* The unique file identifier is assigned to the variable K. The system also creates an entry in the sponsor's directory with the file name *Joe* (CREATE also implies

OPEN) where the Read and Write pointers are initialized to the beginning of the file.

2. *Bill* := OPEN (*K,Read/Write*)

The master directory is searched for an occurrence of a file identifier matching the one assigned to the variable *K*. When it is found, a check is made of *Read/Write* against the mode given in the control block. If the access requested is permitted, an entry is made in the sponsor's directory with file name *Bill*, and *count* is increased by one. This user program may now refer to this file as *Bill*. The appropriate pointer is initialized. For instance, the Read pointer is set to the beginning of the file and the Write pointer to the end.

3. CLOSE (*Joe*)

The entry with name *Joe* in the sponsor's directory is deleted, and count is decreased by 1 in the control block corresponding to *Joe*. If *count* is 0, the control block is deleted. Note that the last close command serves as a delete command. A separate *delete* command can also be implemented if necessary.

4. *nread* := READ (*Joe,buffer,readcount*)

The purpose of this command is to read information from the file which a user's program has opened and identified with the name *Joe*. The parameter *readcount* gives the maximum number of words to be read, while *buffer* designates the buffer into which the words are to be moved. Reading begins from the current position of the Read pointer and ends after *readcount* words or when it hits the end of the file. A number n of words (not exceeding *readcount*) are read from the file, *nread* takes on the value n, and the Read pointer is then increased by n.

5. *nwrite* := WRITE (*Joe,buffer,writecount*)

This is the analogous command for writing into a file. *Writecount* is the maximum number of words written from *buffer* into the file *Joe*. The actual number of words written is assigned to *nwrite*, and the Write pointer is increased by this amount. Unless previously adjusted by a seek command, the Write pointer points at the end of the file. Thus, when writing takes place, the file grows and nothing is overwritten.

6. SEEK (*Joe, offset, flag*)

This command serves to adjust the Read or Write pointer by the value *offset*. The parameter *flag* may assume one of four values with the following interpretations:

flag = 0   The Read pointer is adjusted from beginning of the file;
flag = 1   The Read pointer is adjusted from its current position;
flag = 2   The Write pointer is adjusted from the end of the file;
flag = 3   The Write pointer is adjusted from its current position.

The file is accessed, and depending on the value of *flag*, the Read or Write pointer is positioned and then adjusted by the value of *offset*. Setting *flag* to 0 or 2 enables the adjustment to be made with reference to the beginning or end of the file, which is frequently easier than keeping track of the position of the pointer.

7. *ntell* : = TELL (*Joe,Read/Write*)
    The current position of the Read or Write pointer of the file *Joe* is assigned to the variable *ntell*.

6.8 Conclusion

The basic characteristics of file systems and important criteria for their design have been outlined. File systems have been discussed as a sequence of levels of software starting from the hardware:

1. the I/O system, which masks the hardware peculiarities and provides message passing and input–output functions in terms of block transfers;

2. The basic file system, which allocates regions on volumes and manages the volumes;

3. the logical file system, which enables symbolic naming and user-oriented operations;

4. the access methods, which implement formatted files and, through the use of several mechanisms, enable the user to identify and access separate records;

5. the data base management system, which provides several logical data structures based on the same physical copy of a file.

Finally, some of the techniques have been illustrated by means of a simple example of a file system.

File systems have been incorporated in many operating systems, starting with the early tape-oriented systems, and over the years have inherited a massive, colorful, and generally imprecise jargon. To shed some light on this body of conflicting terms and describe some elementary ideas, a concept is needed. For instance, processes as a basic computational unit serve the purpose of describing the operations in an operating system. In file systems the basic concepts should be in terms of data structuring, since the main function of file systems deals with data management. Unfortunately, there is no general agreement yet on elementary concepts of data structuring. What is needed is a concept referring to data structuring which is dual to the concept of processes referring to computation. Data management is lagging behind computational activity in terms of understanding its basic functions and operations. As a result, this chapter may seem specialized and *ad hoc* in comparison with previous chapters. Nevertheless, file systems are important, even if they are not as conceptually elegant as other, more developed areas of computer science.

Problems

6.1 Are file systems a poor substitute for virtual memory? Do they provide some additional facilities? Does the virtual memory make the implementation of a file system easier? Justify your answers.

6.2 How big do you think directories are? Are they always core resident? Investigate different techniques for storing directories. What techniques are used to access an entry within a directory? Provide some examples from existing systems.

6.3 For each shared file it is advisable for the system to keep information about all the users which have the file currently open. Discuss the relative merits of keeping just a count of the number of users having the file open at a given time versus having a list of the users identified through either their unique names or back pointers.

6.4 Consider the SUE system as described in Chapter 10. Can you identify the influence of the IBM/360 hardware reflected in the design of the I/O system? What changes in the I/O hardware organization would permit a simpler I/O system?

6.5 Outline an implementation of file descriptors. What hardware features are desirable for the manipulation of these descriptors? Compare your descriptors with the segment descriptors present in some Burroughs machines.

6.6 The process which manages volumes inside an operating system needs to communicate with the operator who physically mounts and removes disk volumes. Design a protocol for conversations between the operator and the process which manages volumes.

6.7   Sharing of data contained in files can be performed through copying. Discuss the relative merits of copying data versus a single shared file. How would copying simplify the design of the file system?

6.8   In a virtual memory system, each process can be identified with the virtual address space it uses. In this case the process can be saved even when it is inactive by keeping its virtual address space intact. In such an environment is the sponsor concept as described in Section 6.4 applicable? Justify your answer.

6.9   Why is a separate "open" command important in a file system? (An "open" command could be implicit in a "read" or "write" command.)

6.10   Survey the different access methods provided by IBM for the /360 or /370 series. Point out any redundancy in terms of facilities provided by the access methods. If you had to choose a single access method on which to base different applications, which one would you choose? Justify your answer.

6.11   A user can manipulate records in files explicitly by using pointers or implicitly by using qualifications and keys. For instance, he can point to a record and then by issuing commands, such as NEXT or LAST, he can pick out relevant records. Alternatively, he can qualify in one statement all the records he needs, for example, records whose salary field is $15,000. The system can then use pointers transparent to the user to obtain the records. Discuss the relative merits of the two approaches.

6.12   Consider a file system where a record field can have the value "null," meaning undefined. Describe a facility in a programming language to handle null as a possible value of a variable or expression in a computation. Remember, run-time checks are more expensive than compile-time checks.

6.13   In a data base management system the data manipulation commands can be issued from a host language, such as COBOL in the IBM IMS system, or they can be integrated in a language, such as the IBM GIS system. Discuss the relative merits of the two approaches.

6.14   Prepare a comparative survey of different file systems available with machines of some leading manufacturers.

6.15   Prepare a survey of data base management systems and their facilities.

6.16 Do a case study of an existing data base management system, such as IBM IMS/GIS/AAS, TDMS, TOTAL, MRI2000.

6.17 Prepare a survey of data communications facilities with associated costs.

6.18 Do a case study of the U.S. Department of Defense ARPA supported network of computers.

7

PROTECTION

7.1 Introduction

A system should be able to prevent users (or processes) from maliciously or erroneously harming other users (or processes). The assumption that users are friendly and infallible is unrealistic. A user can do harm by destroying his own or another user's programs and data, or by degrading the service that all users get. (The ultimate degradation is to "crash" the system.)

In the context above, a user is a person with some computation to do. Inside the system the user may be manifested as a single process, a group of processes, or a block of storage. In this chapter the word "user" will be used rather loosely to indicate those entities within the system which are using the system's facilities to perform some person's computation.

Protection is the general term describing mechanisms which protect items of a system from their environment. A good protection mechanism should not permit a user to interfere with other users. In addition, it should provide some tools to help the user in safeguarding his own programs and data against himself.

Protection mechanisms vary from system to system. In fact, they are sometimes different for different parts of a single system. For instance, in some systems there is one protection mechanism for the file system, another for main memory, etc.

In computer systems all information resides on some storage device. Hence, the information can be protected by dividing the address space of these devices into regions and allowing information to flow between regions in a controlled way. Each region of addressable space must be protected from unauthorized attempts by the rest of its environment to obtain or alter information. As a typical example, consider protection in a file system. Each file should be protected from users who issue unauthorized read and/or write operations.

The regulation of information flow among regions presents two basic problems. First, "walls" must be built around the regions of addressable space with specific "gates" for communication purposes. The only way to access a region is through a gate; the walls are impenetrable. Second, communication across regions must be "policed." That is, there must be a control mechanism at the gate to allow only authorized users to access the region. The walls which surround the regions of addressable space must be related to the addressing mechanism (for example, paging or segmentation). For efficiency reasons, address references within a region should not require extensive checking. Address references to items outside the region must pass through gatelike mechanisms.

For instance, assume that a user has a set of addresses which he is permitted to access. Each address generated by his program is interpreted and checked. A segmented address space, where each segment has a base and limit address, makes checking a straightforward operation. Each address reference is checked to be within the bounds of the base address and base address plus the limit. The address mechanism puts a wall around all addresses which are outside the base–limit bounds.

Segments can also be explicitly protected. Each time a segment is addressed through the segment table, its protection status is checked against the process which generated the reference. In the same way, when a process tries to access a file, its request goes through the file system which checks the privileges of the process against the protection status of the file. There must be no way to access files except through the file system (that is, the gate). A file can be thought of either as a region of addressable space, or merely as a unit within the system requiring protection.

Items in the system which require protection are referred to as *objects* [Lampson, 1971]. Another way of providing walls is to keep the linking path to an object secret. That is, the object is not protected, but its location is known only by certain privileged processes. Other processes can use an internal name to address the object, but the linking path will be revealed only to privileged processes. Such a mechanism does not usually provide adequate protection, since the wall can be penetrated. A user might erroneously or maliciously still be able to reach and destroy the object. However, in a virtual memory environment the large size of the address space makes this interference rather improbable.

A third technique of providing walls is encoding. The information is in an unprotected location, but it is encoded. To decode the information, a process must know the code key, which is provided only to privileged processes. The code is the gate to the information.

Each region of addressable space must be protected by a *protection monitor* which serves as a gate. The monitor allows only certain privileged processes through the gate to access the region. The same monitors which provide synchronization (see Section 2.6.2) can be augmented to provide protection. Each time an access is generated from outside the region (that is, somebody tries to cross the gate), it must go through the appropriate protection monitor. The monitor can be in hardware or software. For instance, the physical protection keys in IBM/360 machines together with the key in the Program Status Word of the executing process form a hardware protection monitor protecting regions of $2K$ bytes in memory. On the other hand, the file system is a software monitor which, among other things, safeguards information on secondary storage. Traditionally, machines were not provided with elaborate protection hardware; a flexible protection mechanism could only be implemented in software. However, machines of the future will probably provide more and more of the basic protection functions in hardware or microprogramming.

A protection monitor is logically located somewhere in the linking path to the object, in order to control the access attempts. The monitor can be local to the object. That is, each object requiring protection has its own protection monitor. Since the access rules are usually the same for some large class of objects, local organization duplicates a great deal of effort. For instance, it is obviously inefficient for each file to have its own mechanism to check protection. Alternatively, there can be a central protection monitor which checks all access attempts in the system. However, since each access has to go through a single central monitor, this scheme often generates a serious bottleneck in the system. This problem can be somewhat relieved, although not completely solved, by implementing the monitor in hardware.

One attractive solution is to do the monitoring in groups. Each protection monitor serves as a gate for a large class of similar objects. A typical example is again the file system, which enforces rules concerning the access privileges to the class of objects called files.

In addition to checking the identity of the process which is attempting access, the protection monitor can also examine data which the monitor allows to be passed. This provides an extra measure of protection for the protected region, since the monitor can check for corrupt data which might harm the region. Clearly, though, this checking is done at the expense of increased overhead in the monitor.

One of the most difficult protection problems is the communication between two mutually suspicious processes. Each process tries to restrict the accesses generated from the other and closely examines the data which it receives. It is important that the two processes come to a mutual understanding of their communication requirements. They may choose to establish a third independent process to serve as protection monitor. This monitor resembles a contract between the processes. The processes agree on a supervisor and thereafter cannot change anything without appealing to "higher authority."

The treatment of the attempted violations of the protection mechanism poses an interesting philosophical question. In most systems unauthorized access is simply refused. The protection monitor can record attempted violations, perhaps reporting frequent violators. It may very well be that processes which attempt violations should be charged with fines, to help defray the "policing" overhead.

7.2 Domains and Capabilities

The notion of regions of addressable space is too general to be useful in describing the protection status of the system. Concepts are needed to understand the design of protection mechanisms. In a protected environment there are passive elements and active elements. Elements which require protection are called objects. An active element which attempts to access objects is referred to as a *subject* [Graham and Denning, 1972]. A typical subject in the system is a process. As an active unit, a process generates requests for operations on protected objects. Files are typical objects. The roles of subject and object sometimes change with time. For instance, two processes may well be guarding against each other, in which case both are subject and object alternately.

Since different subjects are sometimes permitted equivalent privileges with respect to different objects, it is helpful to isolate classes of privileges as separate entities. A *domain* is defined to be a set of access privileges [Lampson, 1969, 1971]. A domain provides the protection context out of which a subject can operate. Instead of associating protection privileges with subjects or processes, privileges are now associated with domains. In this environment each process always operates in the context of some domain. Other processes may share equivalent protection privileges by operating out of the same domain. A process changes its protection status by changing the domain out of which it operates. By separating the protection status into domains, access privileges can be manipulated independently of the subjects operating within the system, thus providing a very flexible environment for sharing protection mechanisms.

In some systems it is expedient to associate a unique domain with each subject. In this organization the processes, as subjects, can have their protection privileges encoded in their process descriptors. Considerable flexibility is lost in such an environment. If a procedure within a process requires a protection status different from the rest of the process, then the procedure must be moved into a separate process. This separate process exists only because two domains cannot be distinguished within a single process.

Objects, subjects, and domains are identified by unique identifiers. This arrangement is necessary to enable the protection monitor to check the validity of an access privilege. A long bit pattern (for example, 64 bits) can be used to provide unique identifiers throughout the system for many years without repetition. For efficiency reasons it is also convenient to have unique identifiers which are unique only within the particular context in which they are used. For instance, process identifiers must be unique with respect to other processes, but they need not be unique compared with file identifiers.

A particular access privilege of a subject over an object is called a *capability* [Dennis and Van Horn, 1966]. Capabilities can be manipulated like any other entity. For instance, read-only access to some particular file is a capability. Read/write access to the same file is a different capability. Confusion occasionally arises because the word "capability" is also used for the particular data structure which encodes an access privilege. The abstract notion of capability will be differentiated from its incarnation in software whenever the use is ambiguous.

The canceling of protection privileges is a controversial issue. Sometimes it is convenient for a subject to assume that its protection privileges are irrevocable. In this case, if a protection privilege becomes invalid, the subject might erroneously attempt an unauthorized access. An alternative viewpoint is to allow the process which issues a protection privilege to recall it at will. For example, a resource manager which issues capabilities is permitted to invalidate all or parts of the capabilities associated with the resource it controls. The subject losing the capability can demand the right to be protected by making the capability inviolate

Lampson, 1971] or by registering a "complaint" with a "higher au-
hority" in the system.

As an example of the use of capabilities, suppose a process is given
he privilege of accessing an object at most n times. Such a restriction
:ould be important for accounting purposes. There are many distinct
vays of granting the restricted access privilege.

1. The process obtains a capability in the form of a "pass." The pro-
ection monitor, acting as a bookkeeper, maintains a counter, initialized
o zero. Each time the process uses the capability, the counter is incre-
nented by one. When the counter reaches n, the protection monitor
:tops honoring the capability.

2. The process obtains n capabilities, which are treated as a book
)f "tickets." Each time an access is made, the protection monitor cancels
ι "ticket," thus invalidating that capability.

3. A count field is introduced in the data structure which implements
he capability and is initialized to n. Each time the capability is used,
he count field is decremented by one. The protection monitor stops
ιonoring the capability when the capability's count field reaches zero.
Γhis type of capability resembles a "ticket" which is punched after each
ιse.

4. The capability's data structure is used as a pointer to indirectly
·eference another capability in which the number n is stored. Each
ime an access is made, the capability is used to indirectly reference
he "common" capability and decrement it by one. When the common
:apability becomes zero, all indirect capabilities become void. This
:cheme allows many subjects to share a common pool of resources repre-
:ented by the common capability; the environment resembles a shared
'checking account" where each indirect capability is a checkbook.

Different uses of capabilities have been outlined conceptually. Imple-
nentations based on these concepts are deferred until Section 7.4. In
he following section the protection status of the system will be
lescribed.

7.3 Describing the Protection Status

The protection status of a system can be described by using a simple
nodel. At any given time there is a set $X = \{x(1), \ldots, x(n)\}$ of
)f domains and a set $Y = \{y(1), \ldots, y(m)\}$ of objects. The *pro-
ection status* is described by a mapping $F: X \times Y \to A$, where $A =$
{$A(1), \ldots, A(s)$} is a set of access attributes, such as read only,
·ead/write, or execute only. Domains are considered independently

of subjects to avoid dwelling on the peculiarities of the subject operations. It is assumed that there is a mechanism to associate a given subject
with a domain at any point of time.

The protection status is by no means static. Domains and objects
are continually created, deleted, and changed according to well-defined
rules. In addition, subjects change domains out of which they operate.
The model provides only a snapshot of the system at any given time.

If the mapping $F(x, y)$ depends only on the identity of x and y,
then the protection status can also be described as a matrix with rows
associated with domain names and columns associated with object names
within the system [Graham and Denning, 1972]. For each domain and
object, the matrix defines the privileges of the domain on the object.
The privileges can be expressed with access attributes, such as read
or modify. Since a domain typically has privileges on very few of the
system's objects, the matrix is usually quite sparse. The matrix model
is not as flexible as the functional model, since the former allows only
the names of the object and domain to influence the access privileges.
The matrix model can be generalized, though, by allowing procedures
(that is, functions of other variables) as the matrix entries.

For example, consider a domain which has access privileges only on
files containing fewer than 1000 records. In the functional model the
protection field of each file can contain both the size and name of the
file, allowing the mapping F to check for the size of the file before
granting access. In the matrix model a special attribute, denoting "access
on small files," should be introduced, which is then used to further
qualify the matrix entry. If instead a procedure is associated with an
entry in the matrix, then access attempts can be verified via the procedure. The procedure is essentially associated with a capability (for example, "access on small files") and it can effectively implement many access
constraints.

The matrix protection scheme must not allow matrix entries to be
changed without control, for then there would be no protection. If domain privileges need to be changed in a flexible manner, then they
have to be protected. This protection can be effected by handling domains as objects. The matrix is augmented to include columns which
correspond to the domains. The domains can now be accessed and
changed.

With this organization the protection monitor need not be completely
responsible for the evolution of domain privileges. For example, consider
the following scheme for controlling the changing of domain privileges
[Lampson, 1971]. An access matrix A is constructed with domains as
rows and domains plus objects as columns. In addition, special privileges,

called *owner* and *control,* and a *copy flag* for each access privilege are provided. The control attribute of a domain $x(i)$ over another domain $x(k)$ implies that $x(i)$ has complete control over $x(k)$. The owner attribute of $x(i)$ over y implies that $x(i)$ owns the object y. The copy flag allows an access privilege to be copied into another domain.

The following rules for changing the matrix entries control the protection status of the system.

1. A domain $x(i)$ can remove access attributes from $A(x(j), y)$ if it has control attribute over $x(j)$.

2. A domain $x(i)$ can copy an access attribute A1 into $A(x(j), y)$ if A1 is in the matrix entry $A(x(i), y)$ and has the copy flag set.

3. A domain $x(i)$ can pass access attributes to $A(x(j), y)$ with or without the copy flag set if it has owner access to y.

The preceding rules do not give the opportunity for recalling access privileges. To give a domain the ability for a recall, the following rule can be introduced.

4. A domain $x(i)$ can remove access attributes from $A(x(j),y)$ if $x(i)$ has owner access to y, provided $x(j)$ does not have protected access to y. Domain $x(j)$ is safeguarded against recall by refusing to accept any access privileges which are not "protected."

The foregoing scheme does not provide a mechanism for relating subjects to domains or for moving a subject from one domain to another. Neither does it deal with the creation of new domains or the deletion of superfluous objects or domains from the protection status description. These mechanisms, however, must be included in any practical implementation.

7.4 Protection Implementation

A protection implementation scheme is a collection of programs and data structures which implement a protection mechanism. There is a wide choice of implementation schemes which can be incorporated in an operating system. As in most implementation problems, there are usually trade-offs in computing overhead, space, and flexibility.

When a matrix is used to represent the protection status, the simplest implementation is to provide a description using triplets [domain, object, access attributes] in a table T. This global table is searched whenever the value of $A(x, y)$ is required. However, this implementation is usually impractical for the following reasons [Lampson, 1971].

1. The table is quite large, making it unrealistic to store it all in main memory. Relevant portions should be stored in main memory and protected adequately.

2. It is difficult to take advantage of special groupings of objects or domains. For example, a public file must have a table entry for each domain.

3. It is often necessary to obtain all objects that a domain either has access to or owns. The table T has to be structured so that such requests can be serviced efficiently.

A second implementation groups all the objects to which a domain has access in a list and attaches it to the domain. This list, called a *capability list*, has entries $[y, A(x, y)]$ which are capabilities corresponding to access privileges of domain x on object y. It would be nice if the hardware provided read-only high-speed arrays which could be used to store the capability lists. The same effect can be obtained, though, by keeping all capability lists in a single storage area which is protected by a separate storage key. Only a highly privileged protection monitor is permitted to access this area.

A third implementation groups all the domains having access to a particular object in a list and attaches it to the object. The entries in the list, called an *access control list*, are of the form $[x, A(x, y)]$; they give the access attributes for every domain which has access privileges to the object y. For each object the subject which created that object provides a procedure and an access control list. The procedure is responsible for checking domains which attempt to access the object.

A fourth implementation uses unique bit patterns in a lock–key mechanism. In every domain there is a list of objects together with a bit pattern for each object; the bit pattern (that is, the key) serves as an identification for the access privileges to the object. Associated with the object there is a list of unique bit patterns (that is, locks) together with associated access privileges for each bit pattern. A subject accessing an object presents the bit pattern (that is, key) to the protection monitor which is safeguarding that object. The monitor matches the bit pattern against the lock associated with the object and grants or refuses the access, depending on the access mode requested.

Provided that keys are not forgeable, the lock–key mechanism is effective and flexible. The bit patterns, which represent capabilities, can be passed around without any reference to their meaning. Also, if the owner of an object wants to recall or change certain access privileges, he merely changes the list of bit patterns (that is, locks) associated with the object.

In addition to knowing the name of the object and its access privileges to the object, a subject must also know where the object is located. This linking information is usually independent of how the object is protected. Linking paths can be provided by the system to everybody upon request freely and without checking. Alternatively, the domains can keep information about linking paths to objects which they may care to access. Sometimes, however, it is convenient to include the linking information within the structure of the protection implementation. For example, if capability lists are used, the linking paths to the objects can be stored in the same area that contains the capabilities. Depending on the organization of the rest of the system, the ease with which linking information can be built in may or may not be an issue in choosing a protection scheme.

The last three implementations offer speed advantages by having a more localized search for access validation. Capability lists and lock–key mechanisms provide a nice vehicle for encoding linking information. However, lock–key mechanisms take a little more space to implement, since the bit patterns must be long enough to prevent duplication.

Recall the model introduced in Section 7.3. The privileges of each domain x can be expressed by a function $F(x,y) = fx(y)$ mapping objects y to access privileges A where $A = \{A(1), \ldots, A(s)\}$ can be read, write, execute, etc. The implementation schemes introduced so far are very primitive in that the functions fx are of the same form for every x. The mappings, although different for different domains and objects, are all implemented essentially by using a table lookup and the matching of bit patterns.

More elaborate implementation schemes can be provided by lifting the restricted form of fx. The structure of domains or objects can be used to provide more efficient implementation schemes. For instance, suppose the domains are strictly ordered with respect to protection privileges; for any two domains $D1$ and $D2$, either $D1$ has all of $D2$'s access privileges or conversely. A number can be assigned to every domain according to the domain ordering. The domain with the fewest privileges is given a 1, the domain with the next fewest the number 2, and so on. Assigned to every object is a number equaling the lowest-numbered domain that is allowed to access the object. Under this scheme an access is granted if the domain number is greater than or equal to the number of the requested object. A similar scheme can be devised to distinguish different access privileges to the same object.

Another useful technique is to group objects with the protection monitors which control them. Each capability (that is, data structure) is separated into three parts, the first referring to a monitor, the second to an object, and the third to an access privilege. Although the capability tends to be large, there are advantages for fast identification of the object and access attribute to which the capability refers.

Although many different protection implementation schemes are theoretically possible, most of them incur a considerable overhead in practice. Sometimes, the best approach is to choose a simple algorithm which is adequate. Complex schemes are conceptually elegant, but they frequently have many undesirable side effects.

7.5 Capability Passing and Format

Any protection mechanism, no matter how sophisticated, can be easily bypassed if the system is loosely structured with many unconventional interfaces. All the malicious user has to do is to access the information by using an unadvertised access path which is not supposed to exist, but which the system allows freely. Returning to the wall and gate analogy, it is like having many holes in the walls, but imploring customers to use the gates. Most commercially available systems suffer from this syndrome. It usually takes extensive changes, not only in the implementation, but also in the basic design, before the existing protection gaps are closed (if they are closable). Therefore, for a system to be safe, the system must be designed so that there are no access paths among entities except those controlled by the protection mechanism.

The example presented in this section is a modified lock–key mechanism which implements protection [Sevcik *et al.*, 1972]. In this scheme processes are uniquely identified with domains. Thus, there is no need for a separate concept of domain. Associated with each process is a list of access privileges (that is, a capability list). Each entry in the list is a small data structure which encodes some access privileges with respect to an object. This data structure is essentially an encoding of the abstract notion of a capability. In this section the words capability and capability list refer to both the abstraction of an access privilege and its particular incarnation.

One of the basic decisions to be made with respect to the protection mechanism is the size and format of capabilities. They should be long enough to contain all the necessary information, but should not consume any more storage than necessary. Variable length is not practical, because of the problem of manipulating variable-length blocks. Within the fixed-length constraint, the format should be flexible enough to accommodate the protection requirements for all parts of the system.

One approach is to allow the format to vary, depending on the protection monitor to which the capability refers [Sevcik *et al.*, 1972]. The capability has five fields, two of fixed length and three of varying length. The overall size of the capability is fixed (64 bits), but the fields within the capability may vary. First, there is a "type" field (8 bits) specifying the capability type. Since each capability type is controlled by a single protection monitor (that is, a protection monitor is a process), the type field uniquely identifies the process which issued the capability. Second, there is a "format" field (8 bits), which specifies how the rest of the capability is used and whether the capability can be passed or copied; it also gives some indication of what happens to the capability if the process owning the capability is destroyed. The remaining 48 bits are separated into fields of three types. A *Boolean* field uses its bits to signify access privileges. Bits can be turned off (thus decreasing privileges) in the Boolean field in a controlled manner. A *numeric* field holds a number usually signifying the amount of a resource allocated to the process through the capability. Processes can only decrease the privileges provided by a capability. Thus, the numeric field can be decreased or split into parts, creating new capabilities. Only the protection monitor which controls the capability can increase a numeric or Boolean field. A *free* field is used at the discretion of the protection monitor to hold any type of information it wishes. The free field can be modified only by the protection monitor which is specified in the capability type, since only it knows how to interpret the field.

Capabilities reside in capability lists, which must be highly protected by using hardware storage keys. Clearly, if processes themselves have access to the capability lists, then the whole protection scheme falls apart. For protection, the lists can be stored in a central monitor, which then assumes control of the capabilities. The kernel described in Section 2.3 can assume this function, or a separate monitor can be constructed. All capabilities are created, manipulated, and passed by using special commands to the central monitor.

A capability can only be created by the protection monitor corresponding to its type. The protection monitor requests that the capability be mounted on a certain capability list; the central monitor can easily check that the protection monitor has this privilege. A process is allowed to inspect capabilities on its own capability list by receiving a core image of the capabilities. This image of a capability cannot help the process in forging access privileges, since the only privileges a process has are by virtue of the capabilities stored on its list in the central monitor. The latter is hardware protected, making tampering very difficult.

It is important that the passing of capabilities among processes be highly controlled. Clearly, if the physical capabilities can be passed among processes, then forgery is possible. This problem is overcome by passing the index of the capability in the capability list instead of the physical data structure. To pass a capability, a process tells the central monitor to move one of its capabilities (for example, the ith one) onto another process's list. The passing can be further controlled if a bit in the format field specifies whether or not the capability can be passed. The central monitor can check this bit before moving the capability.

For example, assume a process wants to execute a privileged operation provided by the file system. The process makes a request and provides the index of the capability, proving it is allowed to do the operation. The file system asks the central monitor for an image of this process's capability. If the capability is acceptable, the file system completes the operation.

Capabilities can also be used for purposes other than protection. Consider a basic file system which provides elementary operations of subsetting files and enforcing protection walls between the different subsets. Assume further that all files consist of an integer multiple of $2K$ word blocks. The basic file system uses capabilities of the type "basic file" having one *Boolean* and three *free* fields. The first free field, called VOLUME, refers to an internal identifier of the volume. The remaining two free fields, START and RANGE, specify the beginning address and the length of the file. The Boolean field indicates which operations on the file are allowable, for example, read, write, execute.

The basic file system uses capabilities essentially as file descriptors. For example, take the SUBSET command: SUBSET (CAPAB INDEX, CAPAB SLOT, START, RANGE). If START and RANGE are within the bounds specified by the file identified by the capability pointed by CAPAB INDEX, then the basic file system creates a new capability (that is, file descriptor) for the subset of the file specified by START and RANGE. The new capability is deposited in the capability slot called CAPAB SLOT.

In the basic file system the capability not only is used to retain linking information for the file through the START, RANGE, and VOLUME, but also serves as a unique identifier. Thus, only one data structure is needed to implement capabilities for protection purposes and file descriptors for file identification purposes.

As a second example, consider the read/write operations which are requested of a device manager constituting a part of the I/O system. The device manager wants to account for the operations. It issues capabilities of the type DEVICE MANAGER, which have a large numeric field specifying the number of I/O operations permitted. The capabilities are distributed to subsystems which need to do I/O. A subsystem is charged when it obtains the capabilities, which it can then distribute freely to its related processes according to flexible policy decisions.

The device capability is eventually acquired by a user process which wants to do I/O. After the OPEN operation, the user process can access the file directly through the device manager, since the device manager knows that the user process has permission to execute the read/write by the open command. As long as the numeric field has a positive value, the process is known to be able to "pay" for the I/O. The device capability is used to count the number of I/O operations. In this case a capability is used for measurement and accounting as well as for protection by encoding information in the numeric field.

Good protection mechanisms are difficult to design. As in the case of other problems in complex systems, a logically complete solution is not necessarily an adequate one. The solution must also be cost effective. The amount of overhead associated with the protection mechanism can be substantial for some applications, especially if all the checking is performed interpretively. If the protection mechanism is very cumbersome, it will be bypassed and, consequently, will be ineffective. Therefore, apart from convenience and security considerations, the designer of a protection mechanism must carefully measure the cost of the design.

7.6 Security

There has been much discussion recently of the control of access to privileged information stored in large-scale data banks. The issues can be separated into three major categories [Gotlieb and Borodin, 1973]. *Information privacy* involves issues of law and ethics controlling the access of information by individuals. Privacy is an attribute of people. They have to decide collectively and individually exactly what their rights to privacy are. *Information confidentiality* involves rules of access to data. Confidentiality applies to data in the real world which, out of privacy considerations, should be protected. *Information security* involves the means and mechanisms to ensure that confidentiality decisions are enforceable. As such, these mechanisms implement confidentiality requirements on the representation of data in the machines.

For instance, strong general feeling can prevail in a country about the privacy of an individual's past emotional and physical problems (that is, his medical history). This general feeling may be written into some form of law, or it may be interpreted as a policy governing the decisions of courts. The issue will be translated into specific laws or government decisions concerning the confidentiality of medical data. These laws or decisions in turn will influence the design of medical information systems to enforce security provisions in the accessing of medical records.

As individuals, everyone shares the concern of citizens for privacy, but the main concern for computer professionals involves questions of information security. The public must be warned about the difficulties involved in the control of access privileges. In addition, techniques must be developed for implementing confidentiality decisions in systems and data banks in a cost-effective manner.

Protection, as discussed in this chapter, deals with the control of information access within the operating system without considering the nature of information. Such mechanisms are *internal*. Internal protection mechanisms use labels, locks, keys, etc. to ensure that an object containing information can only be accessed by privileged subjects in the system. Information security includes some *external* aspects of the system and differs from internal protection primarily in two ways. First, the whole information system is considered, rather than only that part of the system which operates on the computer. The active elements are people. For example, user identification is assumed correct for internal protection purposes, but its verification is of prime importance in security enforcement. Second, the nature and content of data play an important role in determining the access privileges. The security mechanism can base its decisions on the contents of a file, perform data checking during transmission, or insist on certifying the properties of a program operating on a file. Clearly, a secure system must be internally protected, but that alone is not adequate. In this section approaches are discussed which deal with security problems in addition to internal protection.

The following example gives an indication of potential security requirements imposed by selective confidentiality of data [Conway *et al.*, 1972]. Consider an employee personnel file for a large company. The file includes data items called name, salary history, current salary, performance evaluation, department, medical history, and social security number. The following list exemplifies some of the confidentiality decisions concerning access to the file by an individual.

1. A user has complete access to the file.
2. A user has no access to the file.
3. A user may see any portion of the file, but change none of its contents.

4. A user may see exactly one record and may change only some fields of the record.

5. A user may see only the name field and medical history field and alter only the medical history field.

6. A user may alter only "financial" portions of each record, but only at specific times of the day from specific terminals.

7. A user may see and modify only "financial" records with the current salary field below a certain amount (for example, his own salary).

8. A user may see "financial" information in an aggregate way, but not in individual records.

9. A user may see the performance evaluation field, but only for a certain department.

The protection mechanisms which were discussed in the previous sections can very easily handle the first four requirements just listed. They can conceivably handle the rest of the requirements too, but rather inefficiently. In addition, there are the following questions which cannot be handled by an internal mechanism:

How can the identification of the individual be ensured?

What measures can be taken against wiretapping?

What control can be exercised over the disks or tapes when they are off-line?

What happens when the system is not working properly due to malfunction of hardware or software?

A good security environment should attempt to provide solutions to all these problems. It is almost impossible to design an "unbreakable" system (which may be unnecessary in a commercial environment). It is important to make it very difficult and very expensive to bypass the security scheme. The problem of security must be viewed with the complete system in mind. A breach in security is likely to happen in the weakest link of the protection chain, which is not necessarily associated with the most complex or technically advanced operation. A system is only as secure as its weakest point.

One of the most direct methods of breaking a security system is through the trust of a privileged user. This problem is well known, and counter-methods are similar to those provided in manual data systems. Personnel are investigated, high penalties for breach of security are established, and accidental disclosure is minimized by labeling sensitive information. A common method in banks is the authorization in pairs. Since it takes two persons to perform a sensitive operation, both persons have to agree for a malpractice to occur. As an extension, functions of individuals should be separated. For instance, an operator who is also a systems programmer can violate security more easily than one who is not. Finally, the mere presence of a security guard is not necessarily helpful. To be effective, a guard must have a good understanding of the security system and his duties within it, and he must carry them out.

As a general rule, both privileged access and information about the operation of the system should be disclosed to as few persons as possible. The "need to know" serves as the primary criterion.

To protect against unauthorized operation, users are traditionally identified with passwords, but this procedure is not always adequate. More elaborate mechanisms are possible which provide added protection. For example, the user can be provided with a unique number (that is, a one-time password) every time he logs out. He uses this number as a password the next time he logs in. If another person impersonates him in the meantime by producing the password, the user will at least be able to detect that his environment was violated, since his password will be invalid. Another scheme uses arithmetic transformations. When the user identifies himself at log-in, the system provides a pseudo-random number x. The user performs a simple transformation $T(x)$ and sends the result back. The system has the transformation stored in a highly secure area and is able to check the identity of the user. Note that x and $T(x)$ provide very little information for identification of T, and therefore the scheme is not susceptible to wiretapping on the transmission line.

One-time passwords do not protect against infiltrators who attach a terminal to a legitimate user's line. Instead, messages can be identified with unique numbers generated by hardware in the terminal and possibly in the central processor. The source of a message can now be checked. The problem of user identification is also related to the security of the physical location of the terminals and transmission lines.

Any password protection scheme can be violated, assuming that the infiltrator has enough resources and patience. Thus, monitoring enables the system to respond to attempted violations and to enforce penalties. Periodic reports on file activities can serve for performance evaluation and tuning of the system, in addition to providing an indication of misuse or tampering. In the absence of any threat monitoring, a process can generate much overhead in the system by attempting numerous unauthorized accesses. Each access is refused, but it nevertheless requires some attention.

Audit logs of the operations make it possible to detect security violations off-line. Audit logs are hard to interpret, but they provide an audit trail and evidence of breaches of security. As such, they serve as a deterrent to malpractices.

Data in hard copy, removable disks, and tapes must be adequately protected off-line. Security guards, vaults, and other manual systems provide some measure of security. Also, care should be taken for data which is considered useless by the owners, but which can provide a breach of security, for example, old tapes, waste paper, or core images. It is customary to leave main memory and tapes "dirty" after their use. They should be cleared by overwriting random numbers to erase the information. Even when some backup facilities are necessary for integrity purposes, care should be taken to avoid undue proliferation of copies.

In discussing internal protection, little attention has been paid to the data contained in an object. A good security system sometimes has to revert to data transformation and/or investigation of data or program properties to ensure careful monitoring of access.

Reversible encodings of sensitive data can be used to conceal the information. They can protect against transmission wiretapping, unauthorized access to data files, etc. They are especially useful if a highly secure system needs to be attached as a subsystem of an existing system which has marginal security. Substitution of character strings, transposition of characters, and addition of key characters are three common types of transformation which can be combined to increase the complexity associated with breaking the code [Hoffman, 1969].

It is sometimes desirable to control the access of data not only on the file level, according to the user or process privileges, but at the record level, according to the data accessed. This approach avoids proliferation of separate capabilities, especially in a shared information environment. For instance, in the previously described example of a personnel file, a user cannot be restricted from seeing salary items above $15,000 without taking into account the value of the data in the field salary. A separate capability can be associated with records having salary below $15,000. Another capability will be needed if another salary level is desired. Alternatively, data-dependent access decisions can be made interpretively by invoking a procedure in the protection monitor associated with a particular access as represented by a capability. A procedure related to a capability provides a very general form of protection. However, the interpretive nature of the operation implies a certain amount of overhead and consequently should be used only when needed.

The security mechanism may also involve the verification of certain program properties. Such mechanisms fall within the general area of program verification. Consider, for instance, the case where a program should be prevented from retaining statistical information about the data on which it operates. There is no way for a security mechanism to enforce such a condition unless the program is shown to demonstrate the proper behavior by an analysis of its structure. Sometimes it also is a good idea for the compiler to test the generated access attempts at compile time. In such a case, the compiler should be trusted (that is, proven correct) not to erroneously provide the wrong access. In addition, the security mechanism for most systems is implemented with software. It is important that the procedures providing the security be both protected and verified.

Security has become very important recently. People are growing more and more aware of the amount of information provided and being made readily accessible by vast computer-based information systems. Breaches of security were certainly possible before, but were highly impractical in manual systems. Computer-based systems provide easy access to the data. They should therefore disallow unauthorized access rather than rely solely on the impracticality or complexity of obtaining the information.

7.7 Conclusion

Internal protection has been isolated and discussed extensively in this chapter. Different mechanisms have been proposed. An adequate protection mechanism should be one of the prime goals of the designer. Issues of security, which have been briefly outlined, are extremely important, although not very technical in nature.

Computer scientists come under criticism for concealing their activities behind a cloud of mysticism. The security mechanism of a system is an especially sensitive matter. The system designers, programmers, and operators can take advantage of breaches of security. Judging from the number of cases which have gone to court, it is clear that they sometimes do. Therefore, management is extremely suspicious of obscure mechanisms which are claimed to work. A security mechanism should not only work properly, but should be easily understood by nontechnical people, for example, bank managers.

Problems

7.1 Suppose your memory were divided dynamically in two parts, protected and unprotected. One protection bit in every word gives the status of the word as either protected or unprotected. Also, a process can execute in either privileged or unprivileged mode. In privileged mode all memory words are accessible, and the protection bit of each word can be altered. In unprivileged mode only unprotected memory can be accessed and the protection bit cannot be altered. For a system which has an arbitrary number of processes, devise a software method by which every process will have its own storage region protected.

7.2 Suppose we assign a number x to every process X and a number y to every object Y in the system. We then implement protection as follows: "process X has access to object Y iff $x > y$." What structure does this implementation impose on the access privileges of the processes? Relate it to the MULTICS rings of protection [Schroeder and Saltzer, 1971]. Devise another method which imposes a tree structure. Analyze the dynamic characteristics of such schemes.

7.3 Suppose you had no protection hardware in your main memory, as is the case in a small minicomputer. Outline a series of steps which would lead to a reasonably protected system. Is there any way to protect your secondary storage information?

7.4 Suppose you had a one-language installation. What features could you incorporate in the compiler to ensure that users are protected from each other?

7.5 What hardware features are needed for efficient capability manipulation? Sketch a design for a capability-based machine. Can the facilities provided be used for purposes other than protection?

7.6 There are some objects in a system which are more or less public; that is, they can be read by almost everybody, but written over by only a few processes. Devise a method to protect these objects adequately without undue overhead.

7.7 Consider a system where the subjects for protection purposes are procedures. Devise a method for associating a domain to a procedure. If one procedure wishes to call another procedure, the calling procedure must pass its domain to the called procedure, so that the latter can access the necessary objects. How can you pass a domain as an argument for the activation of the procedure?

7.8 Find an example where the ability to recall or cancel a capability is important. Find another example where capability recall can generate serious problems.

7.9 Prepare a list of possible access privileges (for example, read-only, read/write) which are applicable to protect different objects in a system. Suppose these privileges were encoded in a Boolean field of a capability. What is the desired length of the Boolean field? Justify your answer.

7.10 Consider a procedure calculating income tax. The procedure should be invoked only by users who have taxable income less than $15,000. Taxable income is itself an intermediate result of the tax-calculating procedure. In addition, the procedure should not retain any information about the tax situation of a given individual. Outline a mechanism to implement such an environment.

7.11 Consider the basic protection implementation scheme which stores entries of the form ⟨subject, object, access privileges⟩. Outline a method for accessing entries of particular objects or subjects very quickly. What hardware features would be helpful for your implementation?

7.12 Analyze the storage requirements needed for each of the four basic implementations outlined in Section 7.4.

7.13 Devise three good methods for user identification. For each one find a situation for which the method will not work. If a particular subject in the system can assume a false name, then the protection system might break down. For instance, if a process can impersonate a SUE facility (see Chapter 10), then it can tamper with the capabilities associated with the facility. Outline a series of steps which will ensure proper identity verification at least among system processes.

7.14 Prove that for any set of domains and objects, the number of entries in a capability list, access control list, or a table is the same.

7.15 Prepare a survey of hardware memory-protection facilities. Evaluate the merits of base–limit registers, protections keys, Honeywell–MULTICS protection rings, BCC-M1 capabilities, etc.

7.16 Prepare an essay on the different protection mechanisms available in different parts of a large operating system, such as Burroughs MCP, IBM OS/360, or CDC Scope.

7.17 Prepare an essay on the effects of computers on the privacy of individuals in society.

8

DESIGN

8.1 Introduction

Operating systems are rather large and complicated software systems. As such, they cannot be produced with the same informal organizational environment used for small programs. A project should be established with the specific goal of producing the operating system within given constraints in terms of time and resources. As a first step of any serious effort, a proposal should be written. This is true irrespective of the financial sources of the project. The proposal serves at least as much for internal documentation purposes as for a presentation of the project's objectives to the outside world.

The proposal should include the project's objectives in terms of the generality, efficiency, and reliability of the system. The literature should be surveyed for relevant information. Experience from other projects should be exploited whenever feasible. When goals conflict, their relative priorities should be considered. A method of testing the product should be outlined with respect to the stated objectives and acceptance criteria. System specifications, such as the functions of major facilities and the overall internal organization, should be given. The proposal should include time and cost estimates for the completion of the project. Personnel requirements should be clearly stated, taking a realistic view of both the state of the art within the organization and the availability of outside assistance. A schedule should be prepared with frequent checkpoints to assess progress, and a team organization should be outlined. Benefits obtained from the completion of the project should be stressed in the proposal, even if the decision to initiate the project has already been reached for nontechnical reasons, such as marketing strategy. For personal reasons, people like to participate in something that they feel to be important and exciting.

All key project members should participate in writing the proposal. It is important that they take a personal interest in the project from the beginning. The proposal should be widely circulated both among the project members and within the organization. Interested or important persons should be asked to comment on the contents. In the case of outside financing, the proposal serves the very real purpose of obtaining money.

After the proposal is written and accepted, then the project officially starts. The project members should then choose the general design approach that they wish to follow. Tools for the design and production, such as documentation aids, debugging aids, and programming language, should be imported or built. Once these preliminaries have been completed, the real design work can begin.

In this chapter some alternative design approaches are outlined. None of them are absolutely complete and foolproof. The reader should use his judgment in adopting the design methodology which best suits his product, his environment, and last but not least, his personality.

8.2   Design Methodology

Designing is a creative process. There are no exact rules that have to be followed in designing an operating system. One must either learn from his own experience or from the experience of others and then decide which techniques contribute to a good system and which problems should be avoided. However, there are some general guidelines and overall approaches which can be followed.

A design methodology for software is emerging rapidly. To some extent, software design principles are similar to design principles in many other fields. Merely by translating terms, design methodologies for other disciplines are applicable to software design (for example, town planning [Alexander, 1964]). Still, there are principles which are particularly applicable to computer system design. In this section some of the methods which have been used in the design and implementation of operating systems will be examined.

Almost by definition, a design process implies making a series of decisions about the form and substance of the designed product. A design method should assist the designer in ordering his decisions. Knowing that each of his decisions was made in the proper context and at the best time increases the designer's confidence in the correctness of those decisions. In addition, a design method should enable the designer to concentrate on particular aspects or parts of the designed product in isolation. This is especially critical in operating systems, where the complexity of the system precludes the possibility of any one person's grasping all the details at one time. Nevertheless, the designer has to understand thoroughly the gross characteristics of the system as it emerges during the design.

The most powerful tool enabling the designer to divide and conquer the complexity of a system is the concept of abstraction. An *abstraction* is a description of a system, or part of a system, that does not specify all the details completely. An abstraction gives the designer a macroscopic view of the system. As such, it gives a perspective of global relations and properties of major elements of the system which is very difficult to achieve when all the details are present.

Every description, unless it is a physical prototype of the object being described, must be an abstraction. For example, a description of a computer system will probably not specify anything more detailed than basic hardware and software characteristics. The structure of the electronics is hidden from the description. From this point of view it is clear that no description of a physical object is complete unless it is the object itself.

Abstractions are nothing new; they have been used in mathematics for a long time. One of the first abstractions students learn is the separation of properties of numbers, such as arithmetic, from the quantities of physical items which they represent. For example, the numeral 5 is an abstraction of a basket of five apples.

There is no such thing as *the* abstraction of a particular system. Every system has many possible abstractions. Each abstraction gives the viewer a different perspective on what the system looks like or what it does. However, abstractions of a system can be closely related. For instance, one abstraction, $a(2)$, can be a *refinement* of another abstraction, $a(1)$. If $a(2)$ refines $a(1)$, then $a(2)$ describes everything that $a(1)$ describes and the level of detail of $a(2)$ is always at least as great as that of $a(1)$. That is, $a(2)$ is a uniformly more detailed description than $a(1)$.

Let $a(1), \ldots, a(n)$ be a series of abstractions such that for each

i, $a(i + 1)$ is a refinement of the previous abstraction $a(i)$. Each abstraction $a(i)$ is a complete, although not necessarily detailed, description of the entire system. As i increases, the amount of detail in the description increases. When abstractions are nested in this way, it is meaningful to speak of the *level of abstraction,* that is, the amount of detail in the description. A high level of abstraction contains very little detail (that is, highly abstract). A low level of abstraction contains a great deal of detail. Level of abstraction is a relative concept. It makes no sense to speak of a high level of abstraction unless the description involved is being compared to some other description which is more detailed. However, computer system descriptions can be broken down into fairly obvious levels of detail. When a person speaks of a high-level system description, he is usually referring to the gross system characteristics without specifying much detail about the system's structure. A low-level system description generally deals with actual code and perhaps with hardware structure. Therefore, it is quite common to speak of a high- or low-level system description without explicitly stating what high and low level are relative to. It is understood that hardware means low and software means high.

Consider a file system as a module of an operating system. One way of describing the properties of the file system is to list the names of all the commands which it will service and the function performed by each command. This is a rather high-level, macroscopic abstraction of the file system. As such, it gives a basic understanding of what the file system does and how the rest of the operating system can use it. Consider now the set of communicating processes which make up the file system. Together these processes constitute another abstraction which describes the gross internal structure of the file system. Each of the file system's processes can be viewed as a separate unit, composed of a set of data structures and a set of procedures. An informal description of all the procedures and data structures present in each process provides a still lower-level abstraction of the file system. Each procedure and data structure can be further specified in a programming language, such as ALGOL. This provides yet another abstraction of the system. This last abstraction is somewhat different in that it can reasonably be assumed to be of a form which is translatable mechanically into machine language. At this point the abstraction begins to lose its abstract character. It is a concrete representation of the file system rather than an abstraction of its properties.

A second major design concept, closely related to abstraction, is the virtual machine. A *virtual machine* is a set of primitive operations which describes the operation of a system or a part of a system. The machine is called "virtual" because it may not necessarily be implemented in hardware. For example, the ALGOL language describes a virtual machine. The ALGOL virtual machine is usually implemented by means of an ALGOL compiler, which maps the ALGOL language into machine language. Machine language also describes a virtual machine. This virtual machine, though, is implemented as a real machine.

As in levels of abstraction, one can think of levels of virtual machines. The lower the level of a virtual machine, the closer one gets to the hardware. The ALGOL virtual machine is at a higher level than the machine-language virtual machine. A virtual machine is typically implemented by a piece of software operating on another virtual machine. The ALGOL compiler, operating on the machine-language hardware, implements the ALGOL language. The file system written in the ALGOL language and operating on the ALGOL virtual machine implements a virtual machine which is characterized by the file system commands. If a user of the system only sees the ALGOL compiler and the file system, then he is executing on a virtual machine which interprets ALGOL instructions and file commands. If he writes a program package for statistical analysis, then the user of his package sees a virtual machine which does statistical analysis. Thus, each layer of software implements a new (higher) level of virtual machine.

Levels of virtual machines and levels of abstraction are related concepts. An abstraction of a system is a description of that system in some language. The amount of detail permitted by the language specifies the level of abstraction of a description written in that language. For example, assume a system is described both in ALGOL and in assembly language. Clearly, the former description is at a higher level than the latter, since the ALGOL description has less detail. Since they are languages, ALGOL and assembly language also describe virtual machines. Any language which is used to describe a system also specifies a virtual machine, namely, the machine which can execute that language. This is just another way of saying that the language is a tool for describing the system at some level of detail. A language which specifies a high-level virtual machine can be used to generate descriptions of systems at a high level of abstraction. The ultimate in high-level virtual machines would be one that could execute natural-language notation. An English description of the system could then be executed on the English-notation virtual machine to produce a working version of the system!

It is meaningless to ask what the basic modules or building blocks of a system are. They depend heavily upon the level of abstraction at which the system is viewed. A high-level description uses different building blocks than a low-level description. Depending on the language used to describe the system, the building blocks can be procedures, processes, function modules, subsystems, etc.

Given the tools of abstraction, refinement, and virtual machines, the designer is better able to focus his attention on particular parts of the system without losing track of an overall structure. In the following sections, different methods for ordering the design decisions using these concepts are outlined.

8.2.1 Structured Design

Structured design usually implies the use of structure to separate different parts of the system. Each part can then be designed separately. One of the most traditional design methods in operating systems is to design each major module of the system separately; this is sometimes called the *modules–interface* approach. By examining existing systems, one finds an operating system to be composed of an I/O system, a scheduler for processor time, a memory manager, a file system, etc. Each module is isolated and specified (usually in English), and its interface with the other modules is outlined. The modules and their interconnections constitute a high-level abstraction of the system. At this point modules are considered separately for further design and implementation. The same procedure may be repeated within a single module of the system, splitting the work on one module further into individual programming assignments. When all of the modules are designed and implemented, they are linked together according to the prespecified interfaces.

Guaranteeing correct interfaces is a serious problem in the modules–interface approach. The modules and their interfaces are usually specified in a very informal and imprecise manner. Consequently, although individual modules are written according to specifications, they often assume the wrong environment of operation. When the modules are linked together, they do not interface properly. The logical structure and internal representation assumed for a data item which is shared among modules may be different for each module which uses the item. Correcting the conflict in a data item's specification can be quite difficult after the modules are coded. Sometimes it is even necessary to write a special program just for the purpose of correcting the interface between two modules. Special systems have even been proposed for automatic interfacing [Weissman and Stacey, 1973].

In principle, if the interfaces are completely specified, then there should not be any problem. Unfortunately, the original overall design and planning is rarely carried to the level of detail of a programming language. As a result, important decisions which should be made at the beginning by the expert designers are pushed back in the modules. In the end, programmers make decisions with global implications based on a very limited and narrow viewpoint of the system. The decisions may be made at an inappropriate time by marginally qualified persons. For example, if a module which will be critical, such as the operator console manager, is incompletely specified, each module may make a different assumption with respect to how to communicate with the operator console. Patching such an error could be very difficult. This is a case where decisions are not properly ordered. A good design method ought to assist the designer in ordering his decisions correctly.

The proper identification and separation of modules is a difficult task. Parts of the system which are closely related should stay in the same module. It has been suggested that a measure of connectivity between two parts of the system is the number of assumptions one part needs to make about the other [Parnas, 1971]. Too much or too little information about the environment in which neighboring modules operate can have bad consequences in the design of a module. For instance, consider a module A operating on a data structure. A neighboring module B should know the exact protocol for communicating with A. However, it should not know the exact details of the local data structure of A. Parnas suggests that informal use of information about the internal specifications of the other modules can be harmful during the design of one module [Parnas, 1971]. For instance, in the previous example, suppose module B uses the information about the local data structure of A. At this point, if A needs to change its organization, module B might be in considerable trouble. Module B's assumption may not become visible until the entire system crashes.

The module–interface approach is one method of structured design. Specifications for the modules and their interfaces give the structural basis for the design of each module and, together, of the complete system. As an analogy, consider the design of a bridge. The designer knows that a bridge consists of different parts, such as a platform, a base, and supports. Therefore, he can isolate the different parts of the bridge and design them separately. In addition, he should specify how these different parts are going to be connected. If there are any problems in the connections of the parts, the bridge will be hard to build, even if the parts meet their individual specifications. Special solutions will have to be found to interface the parts.

Software designers often start with only a very rough and incomplete skeleton of the system, and prematurely focus their attention on the details of the individual modules. As a result, decisions which affect the system globally are made outside of their proper context and without full realization of their consequences. Premature implementation leads to unstable software systems which often require enormous maintenance efforts. Unfortunately, this situation appears with alarming regularity.

In the following sections two design methods will be discussed which are based on structured design and the principle of abstraction. In essence, they are similar to the modules–interface approach. However, they also severely limit the ways that modules can be split and linked together. This organization forces a certain ordering of design decisions. Although there are shortcomings to a strict ordering, any ordering of decisions is usually better than no ordering at all. The added discipline that ordering imposes on the design process prevents postponing decisions until it is too late.

As discussed in Chapter 1, the main goals of an operating system are to provide users with (1) flexible facilities and (2) an efficient method for sharing the system's resources. Therefore, what the user actually sees is a virtual machine whose characteristics resemble the operating system more than the basic hardware. The operating system bridges the gap between the user's virtual machine and the hardware machine. Thinking of the operating system in this way, its designers can proceed in at least two different ways: either from the hardware up toward the user's virtual machine, or from the user's virtual machine down toward the existing hardware. As previously mentioned, a more flexible user-oriented virtual machine is traditionally considered "higher" than a basic machine. The two design approaches are therefore referred to as *bottom up* and *top down*.

8.2.2   Bottom-Up Design Method

In the bottom-up design method the designer starts with the basic hardware. Bare hardware is a rather inconvenient machine to use for problem solving. Therefore, the designer adds a layer of software. The software together with the underlying hardware provides a set of commands defining a new virtual machine. In the next step another needed feature is isolated, a layer of software is added, and a still more convenient virtual machine is obtained. Layers of software are successively added, each layer implementing one or more desirable features, until finally the virtual machine desired by the users is reached. This is the basic bottom-up design method.

A layer of software together with its supporting layers of software and hardware define a virtual machine. In addition to the facilities supplied by the layer of software, the new virtual machine can provide all of the facilities made available by the underlying virtual machines, only some of those facilities, or none of them. For instance, the basic file system described in Chapter 6 uses the I/O system and, of course, the hardware. The commands provided by the I/O system and the hardware define a virtual machine. Clearly, the user of the basic file system is allowed to invoke those commands provided by that virtual machine. It is a design choice whether the user also automatically has access to the virtual machine underlying the basic file system, namely, the I/O system. The choice can be left up to the basic file system. That is, the basic file system provides its own commands plus any commands of its underlying virtual machine which it chooses to provide. Alternatively, the system structure may be defined such that a user of a virtual machine automatically has all the commands of the underlying virtual machines. This problem can best be understood by viewing the general case.

Let $L(1)$, $L(2)$, . . . , $L(n)$ be a series of software layers where $L(0)$ is the hardware, $L(1)$ the first layer of software, etc. Consider the case where a layer $L(i)$ is only allowed to access the facilities of the virtual machine provided by $L(i-1)$. If a facility of $L(i-2)$ is needed by $L(i)$, then $L(i-1)$ must also provide that facility. Consider another case where a layer $L(i)$ is allowed to access all the facilities provided by $L(1)$, $L(2)$, . . . , $L(i-1)$. Thus, the virtual machine provided by $L(i)$ includes all the commands available to $L(i)$ as well as the commands implemented by $L(i)$. In between these two cases, one can allow $L(i)$ to use only some of the commands provided by $L(1)$, $L(2)$, . . . , $L(i-1)$. For instance, in some systems the first layer of software is the only layer which can issue privileged hardware instructions. The other layers can execute nonprivileged instructions, plus commands to the first layer.

Each case has its advantages and deficiencies. If a layer can only access commands one level down, then the designer of each layer need only keep in mind the preceding layer. Thus, the relevant characteristics of the system are automatically isolated. In the case where all inner layers are accessible, the designer of the next level must sift out those commands he needs as basic operations. Although design considerations made the former case attractive, it can be very inefficient. For example, if a facility provided by $L(1)$ is needed by $L(i)$, then each of $L(2)$, $L(3)$, . . . , $L(i-1)$ must also provide that facility. This means that a request by $L(i)$ for the facility must filter down through $i-1$ layers of software until it reaches layer $L(1)$, which is able to handle the request. This efficiency problem may lead to adoption of the second structure.

An intermediate case is to structure the layers of software as a tree. Each layer can access only the layers which correspond to its ancestors on the tree (for example, see Fig. 2–1). In fact, the tree of pieces of software introduces a tree of virtual machines. Each virtual machine has all the commands provided by its ancestors. In Chapter 10 this organization will be discussed further with reference to the SUE System.

In the bottom-up method of design the designer can concentrate his attention on one level at a time, designing only the extensions from the current top-level virtual machine to the new top-level virtual machine. At the same time, design decisions are made in an order corresponding to the order of virtual machines. First, the decisions are made about the mechanisms which are closest to the hardware, then about the parts of the system which are further from the hardware. The THE system will be outlined as an example of a system designed in this level fashion [Dijkstra, 1968b].

8.2.3 The THE Multiprogramming System

THE is a multiprogramming system which consists of a community of cooperating sequential processes in a paged memory environment. One sequential process corresponds to each user, and one to each input and output peripheral (for buffering); a "segment controller" process is associated with the drum for the purpose of moving pages between main memory and drum; and a "message interpreter" process is associated with the operator's keyboard. The system is structured in six levels of virtual machines.

At level 0, the processor is allocated to processes which are not blocked. Interrupts from the real-time clock are serviced at this level for purposes of time-slicing processes. Above this level, each process has its own virtual processor. That is, processes appear to run independently as if each one had its own processing unit.

The segment controller is at level 1 of the system and handles page swapping between core and drum. Above this level there is a conceptual one-level store. That is, the distinction between drum and core pages has disappeared.

The message interpreter is at level 2. The console keyboard is shared by all processes. When a process sends a message to the operator, it must identify itself. Similarly, when the operator initiates a message, he must identify the process to which the message must be sent. The responsibility of the message interpreter is to route each message to the appropriate process. Above this level, each process can be considered to have its own private console keyboard. Note that if the message interpreter had been placed at a lower level than the segment controller, it would have been necessary to reserve permanent core storage for it, since its underlying virtual machine would not support paging.

Level 3 consists of the processes for buffering input and output streams for peripherals. Above this level, processes communicate with logical devices. The I/O processes must be at a higher level than the message interpreter, because they must be able to communicate with the operator (for example, to signal equipment malfunction).

User processes are at level 4, and the operator is at level 5.

The major advantages of the bottom-up design method result from the structuring that is imposed on the system. Clean interfaces can exist between the different levels and unexpected loops are eliminated, since a process can request service only from a process at a lower level. The bottom-up ordering can also be applied in the implementation of the system. Levels are implemented according to their order going up from the hardware. Each level of implementation defines a new virtual machine which can be constructed and then tested. Testing procedures using this method can be more exhaustive, since one can test each level separately and completely. When a level is thoroughly tested, portions of the next level can be added and testing continued. The hierarchical structuring enables the designer to be more assured of the correctness of the system.

As might be suspected, a major difficulty in using this design method is the choice of levels and the hierarchical ordering. In the THE system it appears that a level is characterized by the allocation of a limited resource to processes at higher levels. The process father–son structure, if it exists, might be related to the level design structure of the system (see also Section 2.3). In the SUE system the father–son process tree is directly related to the hierarchical structure used during the design.

8.2.4 Top-Down Design Method

An alternative way to design a system is to start with the desired features of the user's virtual machine and to work down in successive refinements toward the hardware [Parnas and Darringer, 1967]. The designer initially specifies the virtual machine of the users. The implementation of this virtual machine is not completely specified. Undefined parts are designed further as components of the system. The activity continues until the system is so refined that its basic functions are provided by the hardware or modules directly executable by the hardware, such as ALGOL programs.

Consider again the analogy of the bridge design. A bridge can be designed by considering just its functional specifications. It has to span a certain distance, it has to support a certain amount of vehicular traffic, etc. Then specifications of individual parts can be derived, such as the platform's length, width, and strength and the tower's height and supporting weight. Each part can then be designed according to specifications, for instance, the platform, structure, and surface. The design of the bridge does not necessarily follow the same steps as the construction of the bridge. In actual life the steps for building the bridge are enforced by physical laws. While designing, one may draw a platform without supports. In real life, platforms cannot be suspended in air without proper supports. The physical laws which constrain the bridge's construction do not prevent the testing of intermediate steps of the design, for instance by building models of the bridge and testing an overall gross design of its features.

Top-down design results in a nested set of components. At each point of the design the designer has an abstraction of the functional specifications of a component, and he has to refine that abstraction further into smaller, more detailed parts. For instance, if a person were designing a computer system from the top down, he would probably start with a set of cooperating processes providing the facilities needed in the system. At a lower level of abstraction the procedures and data structures of the system will be specified. Each procedure and data structure can be further refined by designing its parts. The design essentially follows a nested series of abstractions, as discussed in Section 8.2.

Using this approach, the decision whether a system component should be hardware, microprogrammed, or software does not have to be made early in the design. This is an issue which should be based on overall performance and frequency of use rather than on any real difference in the nature of operation of the components.

Simulation can be used from the beginning in order to test the development of the design [Zurcher and Randell, 1969]. This approach encourages the designer to think about *what* functions a component is to perform rather than *how* the component is to implement them. System components can be modeled in greater detail as the design progresses. The initial representation of a component is an algorithm which produces suitable output for a given input with a time delay to simulate the activity of the component. As the design progresses, the algorithm is replaced by a sequenced set of calls on the next set of designed components. At each stage in the development, the design can be evaluated to see that it still conforms to its objectives [Graham *et al.*, 1971; Parnas and Darringer, 1967]. Each abstraction of the system corresponds to a simulation program which is constructed from a hierarchy of procedures. The program specifies how those variables which affect the state of the system at this level of abstraction are manipulated. The program, say P, corresponding to a given abstraction is controlled by the program of the abstraction above, say Q. Q makes more global decisions based on its own variables, which are actually abstractions of the variables of P. Changes in variables of Q correspond to changes in variables of P. Similarly, some of the procedures of P make requests to the programs of lower abstractions to do the work.

When the system has finally been designed, it can be implemented by replacing the basic algorithms at the lowest level of abstraction and the facilities provided by the simulation program with the mechanisms from which the system is to be built. If this is done properly, the system will provide the exact facilities specified in the highest level of abstraction.

The final interface, in which the simulation program becomes the system, may prove to be a major problem. Each refinement of the system was made with a strong emphasis on elegance, simplicity, and understandability. Low-level abstractions will have to interface with actual hardware, which is often unwieldy. As a result, the final interface with the hardware might not be very smooth.

For instance, consider the protection of main memory. At a high level of abstraction the designer may separate and protect memory in variable-sized blocks corresponding to segments. If the system is implemented on IBM/360 hardware, then in a lower level of abstraction protection can only be implemented with $2K$ blocks. This is a structural detail of the real machine that the designer cannot afford to ignore in the initial high-level abstractions. Any inefficiencies in the final hardware interface can greatly influence the overall performance of the system.

When the top-down method of design is used, the levels tend to localize the effects of changes to the system. If a change is to be made in the design, variables at the appropriate level need to be examined, while variables at the lowest level do not have to be considered. If one object used in a certain level of abstraction requires changes, then only part of the design supporting that particular object needs to be changed. The rest of the design can stay the same. For instance, if a module is constructed from three processes, A, B, and C, then a change in the specifications for B only affects further refinements of B. Refinements of A and C remain unchanged.

A program simulating the higher levels of abstraction can be run to verify the sound design and performance of the system. In this testing environment many procedures that are invoked return immediately without doing anything. The reason is that the procedures do not yet have the code to actually perform the computation. Testing at this level can still verify the logical correctness of some of the mechanisms of the system. Care should be taken that when the procedures are filled with actual code, the code conforms directly to the assumed specifications.

Alternatively, the system can be designed top down but implemented bottom up. The overall structural design is obtained top down, but the modules are actually integrated bottom up. This way all the advantages of bottom-up implementation are present, without sacrificing the global view obtained from top-down design.

There is much discussion between proponents of the bottom-up and top-down design methods. Many believe that top-down design corresponds better to the design philosophy of making the grosser and more important decisions early and the more detailed implementation decisions later. However, top-down design requires a good understanding of the system early in the design process. Bottom-up design may require less understanding, since each layer of software is added to an already completely specified virtual machine. As a result, some people preach top-down but practice bottom-up design, especially in the case of operating systems. The point of this discussion is not to conclude in favor of either approach. The thrust of this section, and indeed of the entire chapter, is that design need not be completely *ad hoc*. The fact that design approaches are being compared on the basis of technical merit is encouraging. It suggests that the design of software may be closer to the realm of science than art.

8.2.5   Concluding Remarks on Structured Design

There are other ways of structuring design decisions. The design does not have to be directly related to the hierarchy of virtual machines which bridge the gap between the existing hardware and the user virtual machine. One good example is "make the easy decisions first." That is, all the decisions which do not greatly affect the performance of the system should be dispensed with quickly. Of course, it is not always easy to identify a decision which carries little importance. A gross performance error may be introduced by making an important decision in a casual way. The opposite approach is to concentrate on a part of the system where there is very little confidence. By attacking a difficult module initially, understanding can be gained which will be valuable in the course of a formal bottom-up or top-down method.

Sometimes a certain layer of software of the system carries so much importance that it is completely designed first. One such layer is the virtual machine that provides all the basic resource allocation functions, usually referred to as the *nucleus* of the operating system [Brinch Hansen, 1970]. The main purposes of the nucleus are to implement processes and their communication mechanisms and to provide some basic functions for sharing the hardware. For example, the SUE System (see Chapter 10) has a small part, called the kernel, which provides primitives to manipulate processes, main memory, and protection capabilities. The SUE nucleus implements a virtual machine providing I/O, a basic file system, and resource management. The kernel and nucleus provide a fixed intermediate virtual machine which guides and constrains the rest of the operating system design.

Elegant design methodologies are occasionally bypassed for the sake of practicality. Sometimes a lower level has to use an operation provided by a higher-level virtual machine, thus apparently contradicting the hierarchy of the system. For instance, in a system designed according to levels of virtual machines, it is rather unrealistic to store all the hardware error-handling routines in main memory, since they take up too much space. If the routines are stored on a peripheral device, then when an error occurs, the appropriate routine must be brought into main memory. The file system is useful for performing the action. However, the error is usually detected by the I/O system, which is a lower-level virtual machine than the file system. Hence, the I/O system has to request service from a virtual machine above it, namely, the file system.

That structured design is sometimes difficult to apply does not mean that it is inappropriate. Structured design is a tool for disciplining the design process. At specific times, though, a designer may decide to diverge slightly from the techniques of structure, for his own good reasons and at his own risk.

8.3   A Design Approach

Based on the previous methods and some general principles of design, an outline will be given of the design of the software constituting an operating system. The basic assumption is that a description of the functions of the system is given, together with the hardware or at least the hardware's complete specifications. The design proceeds in five steps. There is nothing conceptually important which distinguishes the different steps. They are separated to provide additional discipline in the design process. Although the steps are performed in order, some backtracking is often necessary. During the design, decisions are made with some degree of uncertainty. They cannot always be right. Hence, the designer may have to repeat one of the steps several times.

1. *Skeletal Design* A gross skeletal design of the system should be outlined as a first approximation of the different modules and their interfaces. The gap between the system's functional specification and the hardware's facilities is bridged with a structured set of modules. The design proceeds in a top-down fashion, as outlined in Section 8.2.4. Some virtual machines may be predefined, such as the system nucleus. The intermediate abstractions of the system are tested for validity either by using simulation or at least by reading over their descriptions very carefully.

2. *Module specification and interfaces* Exact functions and interfaces are specified for the modules described in the previous step. Each module is initially described at a high level of abstraction. The description is refined in a top-down fashion to further specify each module. Eventually, all modules and interfaces are described, using detailed abstractions. This description allows close examination of the behavior of the system's components. Some of the logical problems of the system, such as deadlock possibilities, can be detected at this level.

3. *Design of general mechanisms* Enough is now known about the general flavor of the system to specify in detail the basic mechanisms for: (a) process implementation; (b) process communication; (c) protection; (d) memory allocation.

Some backtracking to previous steps might be necessary. A particular mechanism can be improved by making some restrictions on the interaction among the different modules. For instance, imposing a hierarchy on processes in the system may simplify the process communication mechanism.

4. *Gross design of modules* Each module in the system can now be designed separately. The module can be divided into a number of processes and/or procedures whose interaction should be clearly specified. The flow of control and the parameters passed within the module should be clearly stated for each initiation of the module.

By now there is a detailed enough picture of the system to allow us to consider its overall performance. Some simple calculations should be made regarding the time required for certain frequent operations which will greatly affect the efficiency of the system. Repetition of the previous steps may be necessary, especially if the performance of the system does not meet the original specifications.

5. *Detailed design of each module* Each module is designed in detail, programmed, and tested independently. It is difficult to separate the

detailed design from the programming itself. In Chapter 9 a top-down programming method is described which is a natural extension of top-down design.

The integration of modules in the system can proceed in a bottom-up fashion to allow careful testing. Careless design may generate problems during the testing phase. Although teams frequently work in parallel, they have to integrate the modules in a certain order. If one of the modules is not ready, the need might arise for a simulated environment to facilitate integration and testing of other individual modules.

Needless to say, this final phase is critical. All the problems which were not attacked properly in the previous steps will show up now. The outlined design steps may have to be repeated many times, occasionally forcing the designer to return to the original specifications. These problems should be expected. In practice, design steps rarely proceed in a completely preordered fashion either top–down or bottom–up. However, uncontrolled repetition of steps, where the previous design is not directly involved, should be avoided. Continual modifications to meet new requirements can lead to such uncontrolled repetition. For instance, the marketing people may keep shifting the specification of the system. The result can be utter confusion for designers and programmers, causing significant delays in the project.

One of the great dangers in designing is overdesign. There is a temptation to include an extra feature if it does not appear to affect final implementation. A wiser approach is to exclude additional features until they are required. Useless generality has a considerable effect on both the performance and the implementation complexity of a product. It is better that the system be designed to be extensible. Then, generalizations and added features can be incorporated later on.

Marketing considerations may impose strict, unrealistic deadlines which are impossible to meet. As a result, many *ad hoc* decisions in the design are made. The final product might not be able to survive all the inconsistencies of "reckless" design. Although it is possible to patch a demonstration prototype of the system, it may be necesary to start designing all over again afterward. There is no substitute for careful design, especially in the initial phases. No amount of patching up can improve a badly designed system.

To speed up the design process, large operating systems have traditionally been implemented by using a large number of persons. Large numbers of improperly trained people are assigned to work on the project. Communications among people and among the modules they are trying to design becomes a problem. Most of the real talent is wasted in managing the project. These remarks lead us naturally to the problems of project management.

8.4 Project Management

To say that software is usually not produced within the originally specified cost and time constraints is probably an understatement. Experience has shown that considerable delays and cost overruns are so often present that they are almost accepted as a fact of life in software production. One can always multiply time estimates by a large safety factor to account for bad management and uncertain events affecting the project. However, this approach can hardly be considered good engineering.

The reasons for the difficulties in managing software projects can be divided according to two schools of thought.

1. *Poor Management* Due to the gap between managerial and computer science education, there are very few persons with adequate technical and managerial skills. As a result, software projects are managed either by good technical people with limited managerial talent or experience, or by experienced managers who do not really understand the designed system and communicate poorly with the software engineers.

2. *Random Activity* It is very hard to plan adequately during the production of software. Product specifications are liable to be shifted. Personnel changes are frequent and painful. Planning tools and data are lacking. To manage software projects, one has to use special techniques, which take into account the nature of the project. For instance, it must be accepted from the beginning that the final product will be quite different than the one originally proposed.

Software design projects sometimes operate in an environment which would give nightmares to any manager. For instance, when a bridge engineer successfully designs a bridge, he is expected to go on and design another bridge. When a software engineer is successful in designing a software system, he usually moves to a different, more complicated system, or to a managerial position, or to an academic environment. Consequently, most project members are new to the project activity, and they get an education while doing useful work.

The overall goal of project management should be to produce the desired product within the stated design goals, specifications, and available resources. The initial problem is to find a common dialect of natural language for communication purposes. Unfortunately, the terms in the area of software do not always convey the same meaning to everybody. It may be helpful to adopt an easily readable (!) manual of an existing system as a preliminary term dictionary. Project members may use the manual as a basis for the language spoken and written during the lifetime of the project.

Proper project documentation is important. It is a good idea to have a workbook for the project. Each project member should carry a copy, which should be updated regularly. Major decisions, working papers, technical papers, minutes of meetings—everything that is judged important to the project—should go into the workbook. (One team member can be responsible for the updating.) Material can be condensed periodically. Old versions can go in a special section at the back. The workbook should give not only the current status of the project, but a complete history as well. The workbook can thus form the basis of adequate documentation. It will also aid in performing a postmortem of the project after its completion or its abrupt stop.

Checkpoints of the project should be carefully followed and accompanied by checkpoint reports. Checkpoint reports should not be regarded as a burden for the project; they should provide some real benefits and feedback. Every checkpoint report should always go as far back as the original objectives, specifications, and benefits of the proposed project. If the need arises for a modified proposal, then it should be written before design work continues.

If the team is *small* (five to seven persons, so they can get around a table for lunch), two or three meetings per week of all the members is desirable. One meeting should be more technical and one very informal. Frequent informal conversations should be encouraged. Parnas suggests that too much communication between the members might negatively affect modularity [Parnas, 1971], since people would tend to use informal information to bypass standard interfaces. Overcoming this problem is a matter of management and discipline.

If the project team is not small, informal communication is almost hopeless. Some questions should be asked about the project, for example, why is it so large? Could it be smaller? The usual communication mechanisms should be used (such as memoranda), but it should be realized that much of the talent in the project may well be expended on communications.

Some existing systems have been designed by a "large" team of persons. A "large" software project is usually defined as one with more than 25 members, or with at least two levels of management. The problems of managing large projects have been outlined in the two NATO reports on Software Engineering [Naur and Randell, 1969; Buxton and Randell, 1970]. There has been a tendency to discount the necessity for large software projects. Instead of hiring enormous numbers of inexperienced people, a few highly trained persons are given good tools with which to produce the project. It seems that productivity and joint intellectual output increase as more people get involved in a project, but that productivity eventually reaches a plateau. The point of diminishing returns varies according to the managerial talent in the project. One of the reasons for less productivity in large projects is that with more than five to seven members, a formal managerial structure is needed. A large software project requires managers who are "skilled, flexible, tolerant, informed, extremely tactful, and unfortunately rare" [Naur and Randell, 1969]. Such people may exist, but to think that they are readily available for managing software projects is an illusion.

According to "Conway's law," a system's structure resembles that of the organization which produces it [Conway, 1968]. The interfaces between different functional modules of a system will be as good or bad as the interfaces between the groups which work on the modules. If the team is small, there is adequate communication and project members get involved in the design of more than one functional module. This situation has some immediate advantages. There can be at least one chief designer (preferably two) who understands the complete design. This person cannot be the project manager, since no manager can both manage the project and keep all the design details under control. The chief designer of the system should be freed from other menial time-consuming tasks, so he can devote most of his time to being a sounding board for ideas of other designers. In small projects, members take part in more than one module's design, and they begin to view the system globally. They do not try to optimize locally, with the obvious disastrous effect. In addition, there is less need for formal lines of management. Democracy can work in small enough numbers.

To keep the project small, the proper environment should be generated to increase the productivity of each designer and programmer. One organization approach which enables the designer to spend his valuable time in design has received much attention. This is the "chief programmer method" [Baker, 1972; Mills, 1971]. The main idea is to bring experienced and talented persons back from management to actual design and programming. The chief programmer, together with his backup programmer, designs and writes most of the programs. They are assisted by a program librarian, who does all the routine work of submitting runs, updating manuals, etc. In addition, the team employs a few programmers to develop the small individual programs according to the specifications and interfaces of the chief programmer. Finally, a manager and systems analyst complement the team.

The chief programmer method establishes a small well-organized team centered around a very talented programmer, who does most of the program design. The programs themselves should be designed in a structured top-down manner. Each person in the team has a well-defined function. The librarian handles all the information about runs and updates; thus, programs are no longer the property of each individual programmer.

The chief programmer method, combined with structured programming techniques, has been used in practice with remarkable success, as in the New York Times information system project [Baker, 1972]. The productivity of the team was far above average. Programs worked right quickly, eliminating the very costly testing phase. The time spent in organization, planning, and careful design paid off in the final stages of system validation.

8.5 Concluding Remarks

Some organizational problems arising in a software project have been discussed. An operating system is a product of careful design and good organization. A number of approaches and design methods have been outlined. They do not constitute a tight design methodology. On the contrary, it is hard to imagine a precise design methodology. Design is a creative process which cannot be absolutely controlled and constrained. It cannot be algorithmic, but neither should it be uncontrolled. It seems that unconstrained design is as difficult as design which is overconstrained. Somewhere in the middle lie the good techniques. Structure helps to achieve that middle ground. The designer still has much flexibility, but he is also guided by the overall structure of the system.

One of the most precious resources in the development of an operating system, or of any other software system, is the designer's time. Software design tools can be very valuable in maximizing the designer's efficacy. In some design projects, however, software tools are either unavailable or poorly used. Therefore, the designer has to rely more on his own competence. Unfortunately, competence and design talent are scarce resources. In many institutions, research work is concentrated on generating design tools which will take some of the unnecessary burden out of design. Project PEARL [Snowdon, 1972], Project LOGOS [Rose, 1972], and Project ISDOS [Teichrow and Sayani, 1971], among others, are trying to create environments for design which provide the designer with tools for the description, verification, and analysis of the designed system.

Problems

8.1 Define a measure of connectivity between two modules in a software system. Can you use this measure to evaluate the complexity of an entire system?

8.2 Outline a series of virtual machines which describe the operating system of your installation. How are the virtual machines related? How would you describe the virtual machine associated with a given language processor, such as the FORTRAN compiler?

8.3 Hardware designers have their own design methodology. Investigate their techniques. Are they structured? Are they similar to software design?

8.4 Automatic interface systems have been proposed in the literature [Weissman and Stacey, 1973]. Outline the use of a monitor, as described in Chapter 2, to provide standard interfaces between modules in a system. Give examples.

8.5 In most engineering disciplines there are handbooks with many observations from past experience which are very helpful to the designer. What material do you consider applicable for a handbook of software engineering?

8.6 Consider a system structured as a hierarchy of virtual machines. Give some examples of facilities provided in low-level virtual machines which you would like to mask from some of the higher-level virtual machines. How would you achieve it? You can use as a framework the different levels of a file system.

8.7 Can you find an alternative way to order the levels of the THE system as described in Section 8.2.3? Justify your answer.

8.8 PERT analysis of projects has become a primary management tool in many fields. This design tool, however, has not been used extensively in software projects. Why?

8.9 Discuss the relation between hierarchies of processes as outlined in Section 2.3 and hierarchies of virtual machines. What is the role of the interprocess communication? Consider the SUE System described in Chapter 10. How are processes and their communication related to the system's virtual machines and their structure?

8.10 Investigate the properties of some simulation languages, such as GPSS, Simula 67, and Simscript. Choose one language which is appropriate for evaluating a system during design. Justify your choice.

8.11 Perform an experiment comparing two process communication mechanisms, for example, mailboxes and facilities, in connection with the SUE System. What conclusions can you draw from your experiment regarding the use of simulation during the design phase?

CHAPTER
9

IMPLEMENTATION

9.1 Introduction

There is no clear distinction between the design and implementation phases of software system development. If the system is developed in a structured manner, say from the top down, then the design turns smoothly and gradually into a concrete implementation. The only difference is perhaps that a programming language is used to describe the implementation of the system, instead of a more abstract or informal notation. However, if an appropriate programming language is chosen, it can also be used during the design phase to describe parts of the system. The subjects of design and implementation are discussed in separate chapters only to emphasize different aspects and properties of the final product.

What are the desired properties of a software system, or of any program for that matter? Minimally, it has to be reliable, efficient, and understandable. An operating system has to be reliable; unreliable software is almost worthless, no matter how many services it pretends to provide. For some applications, the cost of failure is much higher than the cost of the computer system. For instance, unreliable software may have hidden errors which can violate the system's and the users' data without warning. A failure may affect data that is very expensive to duplicate. Software must be designed and implemented with care if it is to be reliable. Reliability does not just happen. As Randell has observed, reliability is not an add-on feature. An inherently unstable and unreliable system is very hard to improve. For each change to correct an error, another error is frequently introduced inadvertently.

An operating system has to be efficient. Since it occupies the machine a large portion of the time and consumes much of the machine's resources, the operating system's efficiency can have a considerable effect on the overall performance of the computer system. However, different parts of the system do not contribute equally to overall efficiency. In fact, it has been observed that only a very small part of the operating system accounts for most of the usage of processor time. Therefore, efficiency requirements carry more importance in some parts of the system than in others.

Convenience factors often reduce the importance of efficiency. Extra machine capacity and speed due to technological innovation is frequently used to make machines more convenient, rather than to increase the amount of real work they can accomplish. Reliability considerations also occasionally take precedence over efficiency. Still, there are many applications, such as real-time or process control systems, where the speed of response is critical. The relative importance given to reliability, efficiency, and convenience should depend on the type of service which the system must provide.

Understandability of an operating system is extremely important. Programs are written not only for machines to execute, but also for other people to read. Operating systems continuously evolve; new extensions are introduced constantly. In addition, the maintenance effort requires extensive and detailed documentation. If the programs display "nice" properties which increase their readability, the documenting of the system will be simplified. For example, the programs should be nicely paragraphed, have appropriate comments, and make use of mnemonic variable names.

An operating system that is reliable, efficient, and understandable is not easily produced. A conscious and sometimes painful effort is necessary to achieve these characteristics. Since the programmer is responsible for the implementation, programming tools have to enforce some discipline. Clearly, the main tool used by programmers is the programming language. The language influences the programming style and, hence, the properties of the programs. Therefore, choosing a programming language is one of the first decisions that an implementation group should make.

9.2   Choice of Implementation Language

Traditionally, operating systems have been written in assembly language. This practice was assumed to lead to more efficient programs than those written in high-level languages. To a large extent, available programming languages were more oriented toward scientific and business applications (for example, FORTRAN and COBOL). Their properties were not particularly attractive for systems programming. Recently, some operating systems have been written in higher-level languages (for example, MULTICS in PL/I [Corbato, 1969]), and the system designers have found many advantages over assembly language. These findings have led to discussions on the comparative advantages of using high-level languages for system implementation [Sammet, 1971].

High-level languages have a structure which can help the programmer write better programs. Algorithms can be programmed more easily in the high-level language, since the programmer need not worry about the details of generating clever assembler code. This also speeds up implementation, since in principle a programmer can write the same number of debugged assembly language or high-level language statements per day. However, the main advantages do not come during the writing phase of programs, but rather in understanding, testing, and debugging them. Programs in high-level languages also tend to be self-documenting, so that programmers can read each other's listings. This is particularly important when programs have to be maintained.

The main argument against high-level languages is that execution may be slow. However, an analysis of the frequency of execution of parts of the system usually shows that only a few modules account for most of the operating system's executing time. Thus, the extra effort for coding most of the modules in assembly language is wasted. The frequently used modules can be rewritten to be more efficient once they have been identified. In the MULTICS System tremendous speed improvements were made by recoding small parts of the system in assembly language, such as the page fault mechanism [Saltzer and Gintell, 1970]. For reasons of maintenance and documentation, some of this assembly code was later rewritten in a high-level language (PL/I) with the same advantages in terms of speed. Thus, the improvement seemed to be due to concentrating extra effort on critical code rather than to the use of assembly language. Assembly-language programs tend to have global inefficiencies which far outweigh the local efficiencies.

Given that one should use a high-level language for implementation, the question is, which one? There exist many interesting languages designed primarily for systems programming, such as BCPL, PL/360, LIS, BLISS, LSD, and SUE. Moreover, the population of system languages keeps increasing every year. Some general-purpose high-level languages are also good candidates, such as PL/I and PASCAL. Although it is difficult to make an objective choice for one particular language, basic guidelines for the choice can be outlined [Atwood *et al.*, 1972].

The system language must facilitate a clean programming style. It must be convenient to write compact programs, whose control structure is easily visible and amenable to demonstrations of correctness. Data structures must be flexible, powerful, and intuitive. The GO TO statement has come under much criticism, because of its general and uncontrolled nature [Dijkstra, 1968c]. It can be used in a program for many completely different situations, some of which greatly reduce the readability of the program.

The system language must be readable. Programs written in some powerful languages are totally incomprehensible except to the programmer who wrote them. Inscrutable programming should not be encouraged by the language. Rather, the language should encourage clarity of expression in its constructs, naming rules, comment facilities, and paragraphing conventions.

The system language must actively assist in the detection and isolation of syntactic and logical errors. Language constructs should not be prone to misunderstanding and errors. In addition, facilities should be available for both compile-time and run-time checking, based on useful redundancy built into the language.

The system language must be compilable into efficient code. The language cannot allow powerful constructs which inherently produce bad code; neither can it be so restrictive that the programmer has difficulty expressing a construct which is "natural" in the machine. While the programmer should not normally need to worry about machine idiosyncrasies, the system language must give him precise control over both the emission of instructions and the allocation of storage and registers when he wishes it.

The language has a great influence on the programs which are written in it. Programmers do not usually make the same errors in different programming languages. Certain constructs introduce more frequent errors. Such frequent errors are characteristic errors of the language rather than of the programmer. The reasons for characteristic errors may be related to complexities of the constructs, poor definition, unnatural behavior, etc. The foregoing guidelines can help to isolate those aspects of a language which inhibit good systems programming.

For instance, consider the CASE statement in ALGOL W discussed by Ichbiah and Rissen [1971]. The CASE statement has a form like that in Fig. 9–1, where the actions A, B, C are taken according to the value of I = 1,2,3. Frequent errors arise from the CASE statement due to omission of cases or rearrangement of the cases.

Now consider the modified version of the CASE construction in Fig. 9–2, where a SPACE of labels, called COLOR, is defined to be (RED, ORANGE, GREEN). The variable LIGHT is declared to be of type COLOR, meaning that it can only take on the values RED, ORANGE, or GREEN. The cases are chosen according to their labels and not numbers. They can therefore be rearranged, or one of them can be omitted, without difficulty. In the modified version of the CASE statement the numbers associated with the cases do not have to be known to the programmer. The compiler assigns numbers which are invisible to the programmer. Thus, the modified CASE statement eliminates problems associated with ordering of cases.

In addition to language constructs, the choice of language must also consider the compilers which are available for it. The compiler is in a position to do much checking, especially if the language has the proper characteristics. At least the compiler should catch most of the clerical errors, such as missing punctuation.

Consider, for instance, the FORTRAN program in Fig. 9–3 [Elspas *et al.*, 1971]. The program is syntactically correct but does not make any sense. The value of Z is changed without using the previous value at all. This type of discrepancy can be discovered at compile time.

Obviously, the compiler cannot ensure absolute reliability, since some

```
          CASE I OF
            BEGIN
              A;
              B;
              C
            END
```

FIG. 9–1   ALGOL W CASE statement.

```
SPACE COLOR : (RED, ORANGE, GREEN) ;
TYPE COLOR LIGHT;
      ⋮
CASE LIGHT/COLOR OF
    GREEN :    A;
    RED :      B;
    ORANGE :   C;
END
```

FIG. 9–2   Revised CASE statement.

Z = simple arithmetic expression
*A*1
*A*2
:
AN
Z = a different arithmetic expression

FIG. 9–3 Example program. (A1, . . . , AN make no reference to Z, do not have branching instructions, and are not the target of GO TO's.)

semantic information is not available until run time. Still, useful redundancy in the syntax of language can give clues to help the compiler locate suspicious-looking code. Certain constraints imposed on the language give the compiler more information which is useful for error detection. However, language constraints and redundancy are sometimes incompatible with a philosophy of very flexible and powerful language constructs.

Unfortunately, very little is known about program behavior, especially with respect to common errors. Programmers themselves cannot always judge what is wrong with a language. Experimental data is needed concerning the type and frequency of errors made using different programming languages. This type of information would be invaluable in choosing language properties which lead to good programs. Most of the language evaluation done to date has concentrated on subjective arguments concerning style and clarity. Language designers have very few facts concerning language usage on which to base their arguments during language design.

The programming language is the most heavily used tool during implementation. Its properties can greatly influence the properties of the final product. However, like any other tool, it has to be used properly. This brings us naturally to the topic of programming style.

9.3 Program Engineering

There are many ways to judge the quality of a program. Performance of a program can be measured in terms of reliability, program clarity, output clarity, storage utilization, running time, ease of maintenance, and ease of change. During the implementation phase, measures of the programming effort, such as programming time, may be optimized, in addition to measures of program quality. Some of these objectives are compatible, such as program readability and ease of maintenance. Other objectives are in conflict, such as small number of statements and development time. The choice of objectives significantly affects the quality of the final product.

Experiments have shown wide differences in achievement among different programming teams working on the same program under different goals [Weinberg, 1971]. For instance, it is reported that two programming teams P (prompt) and E (efficient) were given the same assignment with different objectives. Team P was to produce a working program as quickly as possible, while team E was to produce a highly efficient program (that is, one requiring low processor time). Group P estimated 39 runs and finished with 29 runs. Group E estimated 22 runs and finished after 69 runs. Both teams had equally good programmers. The experiment shows that the objectives given to a programming team can tremendously influence its performance and its time estimates. The foregoing observations appear to hold irrespective of programmers' experience and performance. Therefore, programming objectives should be taken very seriously. Unfortunately, in most cases the objectives are not clearly stated, and when conflicts occur, the relative weights are not specified. Consequently, the programming team makes arbitrary decisions on objectives which result in delays and costly reruns. In another experiment, programming teams showed differences of as much as five times in terms of amount of core and number of statements for the same programming assignment given different goals [Weinberg, 1971]. The remarkable thing is that all teams ranked very high on their individual objectives. They achieved what was asked from them. This was not a case of distinction between "good" programmers and "bad" programmers, but rather one of choosing the desired goals.

The performance of programmers themselves varies, depending on their education, experience, and talent. It is widely rumored that a "good" programmer can have 30 times the productivity of a "bad" programmer. However, it is very hard to outline what a good programmer should do. Considering the amount of programming that is done, surprisingly little is known about what good programming practice should entail. The object of program engineering is to enable reasonably competent people to enhance their capabilities by using the right tools and procedures.

Many experiments are currently under way to generate tools and principles for successful program engineering. One of the main contributions in this field is the idea of structured programming [Dijkstra, 1968c; Dahl *et al.*, 1972; Mills, 1972]. Structured programming is a well-organized way of developing a program from the top down. It should not be confused with GO-TO-less programming. One can write unstructured programs in a language without the GO TO statement. On the other hand, a well-organized programmer can write a well-structured program in assembly language, for example, by properly using macros.

For the purpose of this book the following definitions will be adopted.

1. *GO-TO-less programming* is programming without using GO TO statements, for example, in a language that does not have the GO TO as a control statement.

2. *Structured programming* is a highly organized way of developing a program from the top down. A description of the program is successively refined until the level of abstraction of the description is that of the programming language.

3. A *structured program* is a program which is clear and understandable as a result of the use of proper control statements, paragraphing rules, and variable names.

Structured programs are usually produced through structured programming in a language with proper characteristics. However, good language characteristics, such as the absence of GO TO statements, do not guarantee good programs. For example, consider the following FORTRAN excerpt [Kernighan and Plaugher, 1973].

$$\text{DO } 10 \ I = 1, N$$
$$\text{DO } 10 \ J = 1, N$$
$$10 \quad V(I, J) = (I/J) * (J/I)$$

The program does not have any GO TO statements. On the other hand it is unclear, cryptic, and even inefficient. The program's function is to generate an identity matrix by clearing all the matrix entries to zero, except the diagonal, which is set to one. The program relies on the truncation properties of FORTRAN integer division to achieve this result. The same result can be obtained with a less clever, but much better, program.

$$\text{DO } 20 \ I = 1, N$$
$$\text{DO } 10 \ J = 1, N$$
$$10 \qquad V(I, J) = 0.0$$
$$20 \quad V(I, I) = 1.0$$

A structured program is written by first describing the entire function of the program at a high level of abstraction. Procedures and data structures are then redefined in more and more detail. When the level of detail of the program's description corresponds to the programming language, then the program is finished. The following example illustrates the approach [Mills, 1971]. The specification of the program's function is *Add member to library*. It is expanded with the single letters serving as identifiers for functions. The phrases in italics may be expanded into substantial descriptions using a programming language.

Specifications (Level 0)

f = *Add member to library*
    f expands to: g THEN *h*
                (that is, first execute *g*,
                     then execute *h*)

Subspecifications (Level 1)

g = *Update library index*
h = *Add member text to library text*
    g expands to: IF *p* THEN *i* ELSE *j*
                (that is, if *p* is true, then execute *i*,
                   otherwise execute *j*)

Subspecifications (Level 2)

p = *Member name is in index*
i = *Update text pointer*
j = *Add name and text pointer to index*

Restatement of two levels of expansion

f =   (IF *Member name is in index*
         THEN *Update text pointer*
         ELSE *Add name and text pointer to index*)
     THEN *Add member text to library text*

The abstractions of functions, shown above in parentheses, are of considerable value in understanding a low-level description of the program. At each level the specifications of the function letters can be a single programming language statement, a procedure, a group of procedures, or an English-language description of what the function does. As the level of abstraction becomes more detailed, the function descriptions look more like the programming language. Furthermore, since the whole program is defined at each level of abstraction, the program can be hand tested, or even simulated, many times during its development.

A structured program is a rather vague concept, usually associated with the product of structured programming. To a certain extent, though, the structure of a structured program is a psychological issue. Structure is in the eye of the beholder; it is not always detectable. Structured programming produces the program in a highly organized way. The structure of the resulting program may or may not be readily apparent to the casual reader, unless it is retained via a macro facility. Devices such as mnemonic variable names, strict paragraphing rules which emphasize the control structure, and comments to explain obscure code all help to bring the program's structure to the surface, where it can be observed.

Currently, there is much emphasis on the readability and understandability of programs [Weinberg, 1971]. Reading of programs is a very interesting exercise. Weinberg observes the paradoxical phenomenon that programmers learn how to write in programming languages before they learn how to read programs in the language [Weinberg, 1971]. How can a programmer be expected to write great programs (or poetry), if he cannot read programs (or English)? Structured programs generally are easier to read than unstructured ones. As pointed out by McIlroy, a program that reads well will probably run well. This is not a statement of cause and effect; rather, it is an observation that programs which cannot be easily understood often have hidden errors which the programmer could not see. Such errors occur far less frequently when the effects of the program can be easily understood.

Structured programming techniques can be applied equally well in the design of data structures [Dahl et al., 1972]. Data structures are very important in operating systems. In fact, when designing and implementing an operating system, one should concurrently design the data structures and the programs. Sometimes, in cases where many processes or procedures share the same data structures, it is better to start designing the data structures before the programs. One test of the adequate structuring of data in a program is the absence of unrestricted pointers. Unrestricted pointers are analogous to the GO TO statement, in that the net effect of the use of the pointer is difficult to predict by reading the program. It is better to define explicitly the data structure and use associated operations to retrieve the data, such as "pop" and "push" for a stack.

Designers of some systems programming languages are aware of the importance of data structures. They have developed many tools for structuring data, such as the programmer-defined data types in PASCAL [Wirth, 1971]. The tools enable the programmer to define high-level operations for the manipulation of his data structures. For instance, in some languages the programmer is free to declare data structures which can be further implemented using procedures for their basic operations.

Although structured programming may slow down the speed of initially writing the program, it greatly reduces the time required for the testing and validation phases [Baker, 1972]. Programmers tend to be more productive, and the programs they write are almost uniformly better. Structured programming enables the programmer to obtain a global view of the problem and a deep understanding of the relations between the different modules. The resulting program is easier to understand and to describe; its correctness can even be more easily validated. The description of the structure which is superimposed on the program during the program design process provides good documentation of the program's behavior. This greatly reduces the documentation and maintenance effort. Recent results have established that the method is practical [Baker, 1972]. There is strong evidence that structured programming may be the first step toward an effective programming methodology.

Good quality programs do not come easily. There are many ways of writing bad programs and very few ways of writing good ones. Writing good programs is far more intellectually taxing than writing bad programs. Knowing this, programmers should realize that they are engaged in an important activity which must be taken seriously to be done well.

9.4   Program Verification

Program verification consists of several phases:

1. *Predictive analysis* refers to the careful scrutiny and analysis of the program's behavior before it is executed in a machine.

2. *Testing* refers to the activity of searching for errors by initiating the program with sample inputs.

3. *Debugging* refers to the activity of searching for the causes of errors found during testing and modifying the program to correct them.

4. *Validation* refers to the final check of the program, usually by the person who wrote it.

5. *Certification* refers to the checking performed by the organization in which the program was written, before it is released for use in a production environment.

All five phases are important. The main tools for program verification, however, are associated with testing and with proving the program's correctness.

Exhaustive testing may verify the correctness of a program, but it is hardly practical in general. As pointed out by Dijkstra, testing can show the presence of errors but never their absence. To be even moderately effective, testing must be performed in a highly organized way.

One practical approach is to concentrate on covering all paths of control in the program. The inherent assumption is that if a piece of code is ever exercised and an error is present, then the final result (or intermediate results, if they are printed) will be affected. Clearly, there are cases in which the assumption is invalid. Usually, though, covering all control paths is a good start in catching errors. It does not prove the program correct, but it eliminates many obvious errors. Another simple and frequently effective procedure is to test exceptional conditions, for example, extreme values in the domain of the variables. Experience has shown that extreme conditions (for example, when a queue is empty) are often neglected when a program is written.

An approach which further reduces the effort required is to test each module separately. The following argument motivates the approach. Suppose it takes one unit of work to test a control path. Consider a procedure which has n paths to cover. Suppose it is called from m places in another procedure; that is, there are m paths containing calls. If the procedures are tested independently, n units of work will be needed to test the paths in the first procedure and m units to test the second, for a total of $n + m$ units of work. On the other hand, if both are considered together, there are $n * m$ paths through the combined program, requiring $n * m$ units of work. Clearly, testing independently involves much less work.

Testing modules independently has the disadvantage that problems in the interface may not show up until the modules are combined. For instance, in the previous example the called procedure may have side effects which affect the calling procedure. Global testing of the combined program will disclose this kind of problem. However, it may be difficult to find test cases for the complete program which cover all possible paths and, in particular, the ones which have undesirable side effects. If the system is structured as a series of virtual machines, then the modules of each level can be verified independently of higher levels. These modules can then be used in verifying the next level without being tested further. If the interfaces are strictly predefined and are uniform throughout the system, it may be possible to ensure that no interface problems with respect to a module can appear at a level higher than that module.

9.4.1 Program Correctness

A program representing an algorithm can be proved mathematically to be correct. The work on this topic follows essentially two approaches. The first approach is to give a conventional manual mathematical proof that the program is doing what it is intended to do. The second approach states the properties of the program in a formal manner, using a mathematical model, and expresses the correctness of the program with a formula in predicate calculus which can then be verified automatically by a mechanical theorem prover [King, 1969]. The latter method is very interesting conceptually. Unfortunately, the state of the art in theorem provers is not yet adequate to be used in proving the correctness of systems.

The manual proof approach dates back to Von Neumann, but it has acquired practical significance only recently [Floyd, 1971; Hoare, 1971; London, 1970]. In principle, it is quite simple. At various points in the program, say $p(1), \ldots, p(n)$, the programmer provides *assertions* of invariant conditions among the variables at those points. There is at least one assertion about the input variables of the program, one assertion in every possible control path, and one assertion about the output variables, which specifies what the program is supposed to produce. The *verification process* takes the following steps.

Assume that $p(i)$ is an assertion and $p(j)$ is the following assertion in some control path of the program. Prove that the code between $p(i)$ and $p(j)$ is such that if $p(i)$ is true, and the statements between $p(i)$ and $p(j)$ are executed, then $p(j)$ is true. If this verification process is performed for all adjacent pairs of assertions, for all paths of control, then the program is correct by induction, if it ever halts. The verification process shows only partial correctness (that is, up to halting) and it should be supplemented by another halting proof. The interested reader can find examples of this technique in the literature [Elspas *et al.*, 1972; London, 1970].

Some comments on the application of the verification process seem pertinent. First, if the program cannot be proved correct, it may be that the program is correct but that the wrong assertions were used. Therefore, the creative part of the proof is to develop the assertions, which can be very hard for fair-sized programs. The proofs of programs also tend to be very long and tedious. The problem of verifying correctness of such proofs is apparent. The effort in proving a program correct is of such magnitude that it often precludes the application of the method in any large scale. Finally, a proof of this type does not guard against clerical errors, such as keypunching. Neither does it safeguard a particular program from errors in the hardware, which the proof usually assumes to be correct. Most important, though, is that viewing a whole software system as one program for verification purposes is unrealistic, considering the present state of the art.

The method of assertions is a very general and flexible method which can be used heuristically without necessarily claiming a proof. For instance, in some languages (for example, SUE [Clark and Horning, 1971]), the programmer can specify assertions, which produce error-checking code when the compiler is in the "debug" mode. In this way the assertions are verified for some inputs. The same assertions are inserted as comments when the compiler is in the "regular" mode. A similar approach has been suggested for interactive programming. In such an environment a programmer makes assertions which the system tries to verify or prove erroneous. Feedback from the system helps the programmer understand his program's properties [Snowdon, 1972].

Proving correctness of programs has been discussed so far as an activity which is independent of the design and implementation of a program. This is far from true. First, it should be obvious that proving somebody else's program correct may be much harder than proving one's own. In addition, the structure and design of the programs greatly influence the complexity and sometimes even the possibility of a correctness proof. Therefore, correctness proofs should not be considered separate; rather, they should be an integral part of the design and implementation effort. The correctness proof might even drive the design of the programs in certain directions. A combination of structured programming techniques and program proof techniques during design and coding seems to be the best method of achieving a very reliable program [Hoare, 1969]. In this and the next section correctness proofs are discussed separately from design, but the reader should always bear in mind that they are a proper part of design and implementation. They are only separated to be emphasized properly.

Manual program proofs complement testing and influence both a clean programming style and careful design of programs. The latter by itself is a worthwhile goal. In the next section the general method will be discussed more specifically as it applies to operating systems.

9.4.2 System Correctness

Operating systems may be too large to prove correct, but a precise statement of the properties, assumptions, and theorems involved greatly influences their reliability. As a side benefit, a tremendous understanding of the operation of the programs is obtained while trying to prove their correctness. By the time all necessary properties, assertions, and theorems are formally stated, the system is sufficiently analyzed informally to ensure its correctness for all practical purposes.

In addition, the proof of the system's correctness needs very rigorous specifications of assumptions about inputs and other factors affecting the program's environment. This aspect minimizes the danger of incorrect operation of the system module due to inappropriate activation. The style and structure of the programs are also favorably affected when the implementer knows that the program is eventually to be proven correct. Thus, even though the current state of the art probably precludes our proving large systems completely correct, attempting and planning to use correctness methods is a beneficial practice in itself.

The correctness property of a simple sequential program is expressed as a function from inputs to outputs, or as a straightforward relation among the variables of the program. Such a property can be proved more or less directly from the semantics of the programming language, using the verification process as sketched in Section 9.4.1. System correctness presents several additional problems [Ballard and Tsichritzis, 1973].

Before any attempt is made at proving correctness, the correctness properties must be clearly stated. It is often very difficult to give exact specifications of facilities which each module of the system provides. To specify what the whole operating system does as a unit is even more difficult. There may be some obvious restrictions, for example, no deadlock. However, many properties, such as real-time constraints, are not easy to formalize. Even when the required properties are understood, they are often not conveniently expressable by using a function between inputs and outputs. Consider, for example, a process operating on a large shared data structure. One important property is that the process leaves the data structure consistent after its operation, for example, it leaves a linked list properly threaded. The consistency can be expressed by using the semantics of the pointers, but it is rather clumsy to describe it by using a function between inputs and outputs.

There is a natural or logical parallelism inherent in the operation of most systems. Techniques are therefore needed to deal with the parallelism. Sometimes arbitrary timing conditions have to be investigated which generate many separate cases to prove.

Some of the processes in a system conceptually go on forever. In fact, one of the desired properties of an operating system is that it never stops. The nice cause and effect relationship and simple control of call and return statements in a sequential procedure implementing a function do not always exist in an operating system. Rather, there are continuously evolving processes which can be described by using histories of their internal states. Such processes receive a stream of inputs and send a stream of outputs. The order of inputs and outputs may be permuted by an arbitrarily complex scheduling mechanism in each process.

Some processes are close to the hardware. There is nothing conceptually difficult about the operation of the hardware, but it is usually messy to describe. One of the reasons is that hardware can malfunction in many exotic ways. These possibilities are disregarded in practice, but they have to be stated in a correctness proof. A precise description of the hardware properties is needed as part of the basis of the proof.

Most of the foregoing difficulties in proving the correctness of systems can be taken into account if the state framework described in Section 2.2 is adopted [Horning and Randell, 1973]. The system can be represented at any instant of time by its state. The semantics of a program can be described in terms of the program's effect on the state of the system, which is specified by the values of certain state variables. The progress of the system is represented by its state history. The state framework enables one to describe each process at any level of abstraction. A property can therefore be described as a relation between states. For example, in the verification of a sequential program, the states correspond to the points where assertions have been specified. The correctness proof is inductive with respect to the sequence of such states followed during execution.

The problem with the state framework is that it is too detailed. Special attention must be paid to specific states or groups of states for the proof to go through. In sequential program correctness it is a difficult art to choose assertions. In the system framework it is very hard to choose appropriate sequences of interesting states.

Consider a system and its state history. A correctness property can usually be specified as a relation of states or groups of states at a very high level of abstraction. At a low level, the properties of the programs (that is, the scripts that the processes follow) are represented as relations of states, closely related to the code and progression of control of the process. The correctness proof should bridge the gap between the different levels. It usually follows four steps [Ballard and Tsichritzis, 1973]:

1. Properties of each process's environment are clearly and formally stated. They usually refer to the correctness of the machine on which the process executes, and assumptions about the initiation of the process.

2. Properties of sequences of low-level states corresponding to activations of the process are proved using the program and semantics of the programming language. The structure of the program, and properties of the programming language, have a considerable effect on the difficulty of this step.

3. Appropriate higher-level states and/or groups of states are chosen. Properties of all possible sequences of these states are proved by induc-

tion, using properties derived from step 2. The induction itself is not always straightforward.

4. The correctness properties are formalized in terms of relations among higher-level states. These relations are derived from the theorems of step 3. The structure of the system is important here. If it is well structured, the properties involved can be quite concisely stated.

Verification of program and system properties is receiving much attention [Mills, 1973]. The current emphasis on software reliability makes close scrutiny of the programming effort important. The goal is to develop techniques for program construction and verification which will result in ultrareliable systems. The current feeling is that a combination of structured programming and program correctness methods can be adequate. It has been suggested by Mills that the right techniques exist, but that people do not have the confidence to use them properly. Consider an analogy due to Mills. Five-year-old children can play a perfect game of tic-tac-toe, but they do not know that their game is perfect. Consequently, they do not concentrate, and they occasionally lose a game. Seven-year-old children know that their strategy is perfect. Therefore, they do not lose a game, unless they are not interested. Perhaps it is time to stop programming the way a five year old plays tic-tac-toe, and to adopt the seven year old's strategy. Great programs can be written by those who want to take the time and concentration to do so.

9.5 Performance Evaluation

As computer systems increase in complexity, so does the difficulty in evaluating them. In early systems, most of the development effort went into design and implementation. Performance evaluation was merely an afterthought. However, with the proliferation of different hardware and software products, many of which claim to do the same thing, the attention of both manufacturers and users has focused on finding reasonable methods for assessing system performance even during the design phase.

In evaluating computer systems it is difficult to distinguish between hardware and software characteristics. The first attempts at judging system performance centered around hardware speed; software played only a minor role. In modern multiprogrammed systems, though, it is not particularly useful to know the traits of the "bare" machine, that is, the machine less its software. System attributes like throughput and turnaround time are as much a function of the operating system and the workload as of the hardware itself. Thus, it is appropriate that the operating system designer deal seriously with the problems of measuring system performance.

To evaluate computer systems effectively, goals must be clearly defined. In an environment where the potentially unlimited number of parameters is exceeded only by the amount of data which can be collected, it is easy to become inundated by a mass of detail. Consequently, it is necessary to limit the investigation to relevant attributes, so that the cost of evaluation can be kept within reasonable bounds. These relevant attributes can be isolated only if the objectives of evaluation are understood.

Specifically, there are three basic reasons for performance measurement: selection evaluation, performance projection, and performance monitoring [Lucas, 1971]. *Selection evaluation* is applicable where several existing systems are compared. The usual motivation is to pick the combination of hardware and software which best suits the user's needs. From these needs, a set of selection criteria is chosen; then, the systems are compared, based on these criteria. Note that at least one prototype of each system must exist to make a meaningful comparison. *Performance projection* is generally made on systems which are not yet implemented. Designers can use prediction methods to try out ideas before committing themselves in hardware. *Performance monitoring* is concerned with characteristics of a system which is already in operation. Improvements in the local configuration can be made, based on data which pinpoints system inefficiencies.

Given a goal for evaluation, what attributes are consistent with meeting the objective? The choice of relevant characteristics is often as difficult as the actual measurement of these characteristics. In fact, the difficulty in collecting certain data accurately may influence the choice of attributes to be investigated. Also, some characteristics will be more useful than others in making an evaluation decision. The deciding factor may well be how much money is available for the evaluation process. In Section 9.5.2 the most commonly used measures of computer system performance are discussed. Section 9.5.3 presents the various techniques which can be used to determine real values for such measures.

9.5.1   Goals of Evaluation

The three goals of evaluation previously mentioned correspond roughly to the design, purchase, and use of a machine. In addition to describing each objective in detail, it will be shown how these types of evaluation can have an important impact on systems yet to be developed.

At every stage during the building of a system, the ability to predict performance can aid the designer in testing new ideas before actually implementing them. Such predictions can be made with the aid of analytic or simulation models, usually the latter. Several alternative designs can be compared by measuring each one's effect on the entire system using the model. In addition, the characteristics of the final system can be determined before going into production. Undesirable system traits can be corrected during design, when such changes are easiest to make. Knowing the specifications of the final system can also give the marketing people a head start on selling the system to users.

Despite these obvious advantages in projecting the performance of systems while they are being designed, logistic problems have often reduced the effect of such predictions in the past. Since most of the available financial resources are directed to the design, the performance prediction often lags behind the design by months. Useful analyses, when they appear, are usually too late to help. If prediction is to be useful in designing computer systems, it must receive a high enough priority to keep pace with the rest of the project.

A second, though less utilized, aspect of projection is in the modification of existing systems. Also, projection can be used to determine the effects of anticipated changes in system workload. The system manager can use such data to plan for future modifications to the system configuration.

Selection evaluation involves the analysis of several existing systems for the purpose of choosing the configuration which best suits the user's needs. Speed, reliability, and cost all enter into such a selection. Systems can be ranked, based on each attribute which the user finds important. Alternatively, a combination of attributes, called a *figure of merit,* can be calculated. This number is a weighted sum of attributes which can be used for a single ranking of systems. The system with the highest figure of merit is considered to be the best of the systems tested.

Selection evaluation can be combined with performance projection in extending an existing system. Using projection, the effect of adding a unit, such as a peripheral or a software package, can be determined. Then units produced by different manufacturers can be compared, and the best among them can be chosen (that is, selection evaluation).

Monitoring is both a tool of system design and a technique for performance evaluation. Following changes in user and system characteristics can help keep a system "tuned" to operate efficiently. Good monitoring facilities, therefore, should be a goal of any installation. They can also be thought of as a technique to aid in selection and projection. Data regarding the operation of a system is useful both for ranking it and for predicting changes under varying loads and configurations. Specific monitoring methods will be discussed in Section 9.5.2.

In addition to helping in the design, selection, and monitoring of systems, performance evaluation may influence the design of future systems. By discovering characteristics of system workloads and user demands, performance evaluation helps designers tailor new systems to meet known needs. Unreliable and inefficient designs can be isolated and modified. Perhaps the most important long-range use of evaluation is in fixing standards for system performance. A program certification bureau, not unlike Underwriters Laboratories, could help in producing a minimum level of performance for computer software. However, more research is required into what constitutes "good" performance before such standards can be established.

9.5.2 Performance Measures

There are three main measures of performance: throughput, turn-around (or response) time, and availability [Calingaert, 1967]. The workload capability is measured by *throughput,* that is, the amount of work which can be done per unit time (on the average). *Turnaround time* is the average time a job takes to go through a batch system; *response time* refers to the time required by an interactive system to respond to a user command. *Availability* is a measure of how much of each day the system can do useful work. Both maintenance time and unexpected down time are included in this measure. Sometimes mean time between failures can be used in lieu of availability. The preceding measures are user oriented, in that they quantify what the system is capable of doing for its users. These measures do not necessarily pinpoint why the system is giving the service that it gives.

Another class of measures, called *efficiency measures,* gives clues to how the system is operating internally. Internal characteristics, such as overhead, resource utilization, and machine speed, are not inherently important to the user community (except perhaps for their effect on pricing). In fact, optimizing some of these measures may be detrimental to the user. For example, increasing resource utilization may increase turnaround time for some users. However, such performance attributes are of considerable help to the designer and manager in locating the causes of inefficient system operation.

Although the types of performance measures which are useful for evaluation are well known, it is not always clear exactly how these measurements can be made. This is particularly true of efficiency measures where internal characteristics of the system may be hidden from view. The types of techniques that are available to determine these characteristics are the subject of the next section.

9.5.3 Methods of Quantifying Performance

Techniques for performance evaluation vary widely, depending on the attribute being measured and the resources available to do the analysis. Evaluation methods can be categorized into three areas: analytic, empirical, and simulation methods. The analytic approach abstracts the system into a mathematical model. The model is then analyzed, and the results are applied to the original system. Empirical methods involve the collection of data on a real system. This data can then either be cited directly (for example, instruction speeds) or used as input to another analysis (for example, a trace-driven simulation). A simulation model is an abstraction of a real system where much of the unnecessary detail has been eliminated. Collecting data about the model is assumed to be easier than collecting similar data from the original system. This data is then used to describe attributes of the system being modeled.

None of the foregoing techniques are ideal for all evaluation problems. For each method, however, there are situations in which it excels. In the following discussion the major strengths, weaknesses, and important applications of each technique are presented.

9.5.3.1 ANALYTIC METHODS

There are several types of mathematical models which are applied to computer system evaluation. One of the most popular approaches is queueing theory. This technique has been applied to scheduling problems involving both CPUs and peripheral devices. In these models a function which describes the distribution over time of arrivals of tasks is hypothesized. A scheduling discipline for the processor is chosen. Then, given properties of the processor itself, such as time required per task, characteristics of the system are derived. For example, in a queue of processes to be executed on a CPU, it may be helpful to know expected waiting time for each task, the total time to service each task (that is, turnaround), and the average number of jobs serviced per unit time (that is, throughput). Queuing theoretic models have been particularly successful in the analysis of CPU, drum, and disk scheduling. Coffman [1969] and Fuller and Baskett [1972] have analyzed drum units for expected queue lengths and waiting times under different scheduling disciplines and drum organizations. Disk scheduling policies have been examined for average waiting time [Turnbull, 1972] and for expected seek time [Teorey and Pinkerton, 1972]. For an introduction to queuing theoretic methods, the reader is referred to the books by Morse [1958] and Coffman and Denning [1973].

Techniques of combinatoric analysis and mathematical programming have also been applied to system evaluation. Combinatoric arguments have been used to prove the optimality of several scheduling disciplines [Sevcik, 1971]. Linear and dynamic programming methods have also been applied to system analysis. This approach is generally more applicable during the design than the evaluation stage. However, all of these methods have serious disadvantages.

The key problem with analytical techniques is their inability to model complex interactions of several subsystems. For a single subsystem, such as a peripheral device, certain simplifying assumptions make analysis possible; but these asumptions are often invalid when the system is viewed from a more global viewpoint. The proliferation of variables and probability distributions usually destroys the simplicity of the abstraction which permitted analytic solutions.

In addition, some parts of the system are difficult to represent mathematically. Large pieces of software are unwieldy to analyze theoretically. Even those system components which can be modeled produce techniques which are often overly sensitive to parameter changes. That is, a small modification in component structure may destroy the applicability of the technique. Also, many simplifying assumptions are of dubious validity. For example, multiprogramming can produce effects which are a function of processor scheduling policy. Although these effects are usually considered to be random, it is not always clear that empirical evidence supports this hypothesis. However, most of these limitations apply more to global situations. For evaluation of the performance of small subsystems, analytic techniques can produce reasonable results which can be applied to real machines. In addition, they are very useful in deciding what to measure and how to evaluate empirical data.

9.5.3.2 EMPIRICAL TECHNIQUES

Probably the most common techniques for evaluating performance involve the collection of data from a system in operation. These empirical techniques fall into two classes. One set of methods applies system specifications, such as CPU cycle time and instruction times, to sample loads. In particular, analyses of instructions, instruction mixes, and kernel programs use this method. The second group of methods collects data from running programs. Artificial or real programs can be run on different machines to obtain comparative data.

One of the early methods of system evaluation uses the instruction cycle time and the add instruction time as basic measures. Although these times do give a vague indication of overall machine speed, they are clearly inadequate as an accurate measure. Far too many machine features are ignored when only cycle and add time are considered. No one instruction is representative of machine speed. In addition, input–output, which is the limiting factor in many systems, is difficult to consider when using this technique.

The objections to the cycle and add time approach can be overcome somewhat by using a weighted average of instruction speeds. This average, called an *instruction mix,* can favor instructions in proportion to how often they get executed in an average program. Different mixes can be devised for different applications. A scientific mix weights arithmetic instructions heavily, while a business mix heavily weights instructions related to data handling instead. The calculated average instruction speed is used as a measure of machine power.

A *kernel* program (note: no relation to SUE-type kernel) is a program which calculates a standard function that is supposed to be representative of a machine's average load. The program is timed by applying the known instruction speeds to each machine-language statement; the sum over all instructions, weighted by the execution frequency of each instruction, is the estimated execution time. The main advantage of kernel programs over instruction mixes is that special programming features of the system can be utilized. Multiple address or stack instructions can be used to their greatest advantage in reducing kernel program execution time. Many features which have low frequencies of use in an instruction mix may have a significant effect when used in a kernel program. Most applications of this technique use a weighted average of several kernel programs to include a wide range of computing problems.

In addition to measuring hardware speed, kernel programs have limited use in evaluating critical hardware bottlenecks and in evaluating software. By observing which instructions contribute most to total execution time, the designer can see where improvement in instruction speed will be most effective. Also, the examination of code generated from the kernel program by different compilers provides a rough measure of performance of the compiler.

A *benchmark* program is a coded algorithm which computes a useful, common function that is typical of system load. Benchmarks differ from kernels because they are real programs. They compute genuine business and scientific applications. Kernel programs, on the other hand, may be only parts of functions which are assumed to represent an average computation.

To get a reasonable distribution of applications, a large number of benchmarks are generally run. Benchmarks are the first technique encountered here which include I/O and system software considerations. Since benchmarks are actually executed, the effects of I/O delays and operating system overhead enter into the timings.

The addition of system software to the evaluation creates new problems. It is difficult to compare fast and optimizing compilers. Similarly, slow operating systems sometimes provide more facilities than faster ones; thus, timing is not always a fair basis of comparison. Also, unlike hardware, software generally changes over the life of a machine. System support by the manufacturer includes improving old programs and providing new functions. Occasionally, an unreliable software system may have its bugs repaired in a matter of months, making it comparable to a formerly superior system. A company's reputation for improving its software can influence the evaluation. Therefore, the flexibility of making software changes introduces a parameter which is quite difficult to measure.

A *synthetic* program is a (usually machine-independent) procedure which tests a variety of system properties (for example, I/O, instruction speed, operating system) in a uniform way. Synthetic programs differ from kernels in that the former are completely coded to run. They differ from benchmarks since they do not represent real applications and may not exist before the evaluation.

Synthetic programs are designed to behave much like real ones. They compute, do I/O, and perhaps call some system functions. Their advantage over benchmarks is that the programs can be kept simple, easy to write, and portable.

The most frequently used tools for performance evaluation are undoubtedly hardware and software monitors. A *monitor* is a program or hard-wired "black box" which collects performance data during normal system operation. Monitors can collect a wide variety of data, including address traces, reference counts, channel utilization, storage utilization, and job statistics. Monitoring is the one empirical technique which makes the internal system operation visible.

Hardware monitors are generally built as appendages to the original system, although modern computer systems include some monitoring facilities. Virtually any kind of information traffic can be measured by such devices. However, hardware monitors are fairly indiscriminate about the data they collect (for example, a complete address trace occupies reels of tape in a matter of minutes). Therefore, they must be used selectively, so that only a sampling of the events are collected. Device utilization and access counts are most easily obtained by hardware monitoring methods.

Properties of user programs and system routines are best monitored in the software. Job statistics such as resource usage and system routine calling frequencies can easily be watched by means of a small program patch. However, extra software monitoring also consumes CPU time and memory space, thus degrading system performance. Hardware monitors, though usually more expensive, do not affect the host system. Since some monitoring will be done during the entire life of the system (for example, job execution time), the trade-off between the cost of hardware monitors and the degradation due to software monitors must be considered.

It has been shown that careful software monitoring techniques can limit the effect on system performance to under 1% of total CPU time. Unfortunately, many systems are not easy to monitor, since they were not designed with monitoring considerations in mind. For instance, the ability to insert small procedures in any communication path can be a useful tool for monitoring.

9.5.4 Simulation Methods

Simulation provides an economically feasible way of testing a system and evaluating the effect on it of design changes. The main elements of the system are modeled in a computer program; the execution of the program simulates the operation of the system itself. There are essentially two types of simulations: trace driven and model driven. The trace-driven type uses data which was monitored from the system being studied. This data provides a sample of system behavior for input to the simulator. In a model-driven simulation, components behave according to a probability function. For example, in the simulation of a drum channel, access time may be modeled by a uniform probability distribution (that is, model driven) or by an actual trace of observed access delays (that is, trace driven). The choice of method depends on whether trace data is available and on how accurately system behavior can be modeled by a probability function.

The assumption behind the simulation method is that it is easier to program and monitor a simulated system than the system itself. While this is true on the average, neither method is particularly cheap. The expense in the simulation depends on how much detail of the system is retained in the model. More detail means a more accurate model which probably runs slower. A speedup in run time can be obtained by simplifying the model at the expense of accuracy. The point at which the additional detail no longer justifies the increased cost is often difficult to determine. Since the simulation model must be statistically validated before its results can be trusted, choosing the amount of detail is more than just a question of economics.

The cost of simulation is prohibitive for most evaluations of existing systems. However, it is useful for projecting the performance of a system during the design stage. Design suggestions can be tested on the simulation model to determine their effectiveness. One problem of logistics is to give the simulation people sufficient resources to keep pace with the rest of the design project. Many unsuccessful simulation attempts have failed because of a large time lag between the design of a component and its inclusion in the simulation model. When properly used, simulation is a powerful evaluation tool. Still, it is unlikely that it will become inexpensive enough or accurate enough to replace analytic or empirical methods in the near future.

With the exception of the few analytic techniques which are of practical value, performance evaluation methods are presently more art than science. Most techniques are *ad hoc*. The techniques which can be validated are usually too expensive. Simulation is clearly effective, but its cost is beyond the reach of most computer operations.

9.6 Conclusion

In Chapters 8 and 9 the design and implementation of good quality software have been discussed. In actual practice, if any one or all of the outlined techniques are followed, the final product will still fall short of the perfect software system. To ensure final "real world" reliability and efficiency, weakness must be admitted as a fact and errors anticipated. Each module of the system and the users themselves should operate defensively. Appropriate operational procedures are important. For instance, the integrity of information should be preserved by using frequent incremental and/or complete dumps. Key information of the system (for example, directories) should not only be safeguarded, but duplicated. Finally, good restart facilities can minimize the effect of failures.

A software product is never completely frozen. It has a life cycle involving modifications. Therefore, a practical aspect is the maintenance of the produced software. Functional changes and known errors force new releases of the system. A very interesting study by Belady and Lehman [1971] investigates the rate of increase of maintenance effort, using a model. It is shown that with certain conditions the maintenance effort can increase exponentially with time. The results were also verified with measurements of maintenance efforts for an existing system. This finding suggests that some software systems may eventually be candidates for retirement. It is easier to rewrite them than to maintain them. This has interesting philosophical implications. Software is designed and implemented; it then lives (hopefully) and eventually it may die.

Problems

9.1 Discuss the relative merits of PL/I as a system implementation language. What desirable features are missing? What superfluous features could be dispensed with? Argue your case.

9.2 Discuss the merits and drawbacks of using a fast diagnostic student compiler, such as WATFIV or PL/C, as a means of teaching good programming practices.

9.3 Read some programs either written by your colleagues or documented in the literature and prepare a critique of each one. Read one of your old programs and write a critique. Can you point out a program in the literature which you consider an example of excellent programming?

9.4 Prepare a list of steps required for putting a system onto a new machine (that is, system generation). Prepare a list of steps required for starting the system (that is, initial processor loading).

9.5 One programming practice is to write your program fast and then use good debugging techniques and careful testing to find the errors. Discuss the merits of this technique as compared with those of structured programming. Outline an experiment to compare programming techniques.

9.6 Prove the correctness of the producer–consumer relationship programmed in Fig. 2–7. You must rigorously define the operations on semaphores and the properties of their implementation. At this point, how much assurance would you be willing to give that the program will not malfunction?

9.7 Discuss the effect of program structure on correctness proofs. Is there any relation between the structure of the program and the structure of the proof? Justify your answers by elaborating on a particular example of a program and its proof, for example, London [1970] or Hoare [1971].

9.8 Outline a certification plan for products of a software house. That is, prepare a series of steps which verify such desired properties of a program as reliability, performance, documentation, etc.

9.9 What is the worst hardware failure in a system? How can you surmount the loss of system integrity in such a situation?

9.10 Find examples of constructs in PL/I which in your opinion give rise to frequent errors. Would you eliminate the constructs? Would you replace them with other constructs?

9.11 Hardware redundancy is sometimes used to increase reliability. Is the concept of redundancy relevant in terms of increasing software reliability? Give an example.

9.12 Identify three programs in the literature which are either incorrect, ill structured, or inefficient. Propose alternative programs to remedy the situation.

9.13 Define a set of control statements which can be used to eliminate the need for GO TO statements. Prove that they are sufficient. Can you prove that each one of them is necessary?

9.14 Why are so many people against the GO TO statement, whereas few people propose elimination of the JUMP instruction from hardware?

9.15 Assume you are in a position to acquire a new software package. Outline a list of realistic performance criteria which you would expect the package to satisfy. Compare your list with a standard software contract.

9.16 Suppose you had an installation with brand X main frame, brand Y peripherals, operating system developed by X, data base system developed by Z, and application programs developed by you. Outline a procedure to pinpoint an error and notify the appropriate maintenance team.

9.17 Prepare a comparative study of different system implementation languages.

9.18 Prepare a list of tools for performance evaluation. Give examples of their use.

9.19 Prepare a case study of equipment selection. For instance, discuss the advantages of an IBM versus a CDC installation for your university.

EXAMPLES OF SYSTEMS

10.1 Introduction

The study of operating systems is not a theoretical field where ideas are studied for their own sake. A person studies operating systems in order to learn how to design, build, and use them. In addition to studying isolated issues, it is important to see how all the elements fit together in a complete system. Process communication primitives, protection mechanisms, memory management organization, and I/O systems are not designed in a vacuum. These elements interact, and must be designed and used with that interaction in mind. In this chapter two operating systems are described to help the reader visualize how the major components described earlier in the book interact in a complete system.

The two systems described are the Venus Operating System, developed at the MITRE Corporation [Liskov, 1972; Huberman, 1970], and the SUE nucleus, designed at the University of Toronto [Sevcik *et al.*, 1972]. These systems were chosen for both their widely differing characteristics and their clean structure. The systems are very different with respect to size, hardware structure, synchronization methods, protection, and scope. However, both systems were designed using a structured approach. Levels of abstraction and virtual machines are clearly visible in the overall system structure, which makes them particularly easy to describe in a concise, lucid manner.

The SUE nucleus is designed to run on the IBM/360 family of machines. One of the main objectives of the SUE project was to apply state-of-the-art techniques for building structured systems for a common machine. At this writing, the system is completely designed and partially implemented.

The Venus system is a complete interactive system for a small microprogrammable machine, the Interdata 3. This machine is hardly similar to the large, fast, and expensive IBM/360s. In fact, it is quite the opposite. Unlike Project SUE, the Venus group could define their own hardware characteristics via the microprogram. The ability to define their own hardware structure had a highly beneficial effect on the design of the operating system. This is in contrast to SUE, where the idiosyncrasies of the /360 hardware components made elegant structuring of the operating system a difficult task.

Both Venus and SUE use processes as the basic computational unit. After an initial try at using mailboxes, the SUE group ultimately settled on a highly structured communication mechanism called "facilities," [Sevcik, et al., 1972]. Synchronization in Venus is accomplished by means of semaphores. The two systems provide good examples of the use of high- and low-level primitives for synchronization.

Venus and SUE differ in several other ways. Users in Venus essentially share the entire machine and memory space, making protection difficult. On the other hand, processes in SUE are highly protected via a capability mechanism. SUE provides a capability-based disk file system; Venus provides an unprotected tape file system. In fact, beyond the basic design approach of building a structured system, SUE and Venus have very little else in common. The main characteristics of the two systems are summarized in Table 10–1.

The remainder of this chapter is devoted to the system descriptions. SUE is described in Section 10.2 and Venus in Section 10.3. In the final section, a number of other systems are briefly mentioned with references for the interested reader.

10.2 The SUE System

10.2.1 Introduction

SUE is the name of an operating system nucleus designed at the University of Toronto for the IBM/360 family of machines. SUE is not

TABLE 10–1
Comparison of SUE and Venus

Feature	SUE	Venus
Hardware	Fast, large, expensive	Slow, small, inexpensive
Hardware structure	Fixed instruction set	Microprogrammable
Memory structure	Static relocation via base register	Segmented and paged
Scope of system	Nucleus of a multiprogramming system	Complete interactive system
Process synchronization	Facilities	Semaphores
I/O hardware	Hardware channels, control units, and devices	Microprogrammed channel, hardware channels for tape and disk
Protection	Capability-based protection	No protection mechanisms
Accounting	Capabilities	Microprogram maintains basic process statistics
Functions provided	Disk file system Teletype I/O system Resource manager Multiple subsystem connections	Tape file system Teletype I/O system Shared segments through common dictionaries Assembler, editor, and debugger

a complete system in the sense of OS/360. Rather, it is the *nucleus*
of an operating system (see Section 1.2). A simple disk file system;
a structure for resource allocation, protection, and accounting; a typewriter I/O system; and the ability to create and destroy asynchronous
processes are furnished as the basic tools for building several protected,
independent subsystems to run under SUE (for example, a text editor,
a batch system, or an interactive system). The description of the SUE
nucleus is in two parts. In Section 10.2.2 the structure of process communication and resource allocation in SUE is outlined. In later sections
the actual facilities that SUE provides for its users are described.

10.2.2   The Structure of SUE

10.2.2.1   PROCESSES AND COMMUNICATION

The SUE nucleus is composed of a group of asynchronous processes,
each executing on its own virtual processor. Every process, after the
first one, is created by another process. Consequently, each process has

a creator, called its *father,* and it can have some number of processes which it has created, called *sons.* The ordering of processes defines a directed graph called the *creation tree* (Fig. 10–1). An arc is directed from node A to node B if and only if process A is process B's father. The creation tree serves as the basic structure for the system. In particular, it specifies all possible communication paths among processes.

The process communication mechanism in SUE is a modified form of Hoare's monitor, called facilities. A *facility* is a process which accepts service requests from descendants via facility calls. Facilities are implemented using the three primitive operations *Facility Call, Accept Facility Call,* and *Complete Facility Call.* The Facility Call operation is a request from the calling process for service provided by one of its ancestors (that is, a father, grandfather, great grandfather, etc. on the creation tree). The calling process specifies the nature of the service request by passing several parameters to the facility. When a process invokes this primitive, its execution is temporarily suspended. It resumes operation only after its service request has been completed.

Each facility services requests of one or more different types, the type being specified as a calling parameter. Service requests are honored by means of the Accept Facility Call primitive, which has the effect

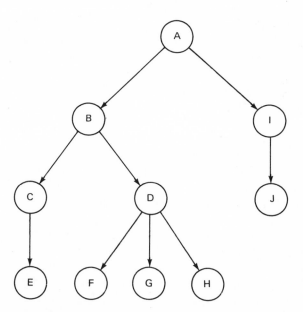

FIG. 10–1 SUE-type creation tree. (An arc is directed from node A to node B if process A is process B's father.)

of notifying the facility that issued the Accept of the next pending request of a particular type (that is, the oldest unaccepted Facility Call of that type). If no such request exists, the facility is blocked until such a request appears. By altering a parameter, the facility can make the Accept "conditional," in which case it will not be blocked if there are no pending requests. After accepting a Facility Call, the facility performs some action in response to the service request. The facility then permits the calling process to continue execution by invoking the Complete Facility Call primitive.

In SUE the facility mechanism is used to implement levels of virtual machines. Each process on the creation tree can provide facilities to all of its descendants. For example, if process B in Fig. 10–1 were providing the "file system facility," then all of B's descendants (that is, C, D, E, F, G, and H) could use the file system by invoking a Facility Call which would be served by B. One can think of processes C, D, . . . , H as running on a virtual machine which includes a file system. When a process invokes a facility call, it is unaware of which facility is servicing the call. It merely knows that its virtual machine supports that facility. Thus, each process is using a virtual machine which is completely defined by the facilities which its ancestors provide. Figure 10–2 shows the actual creation tree for the SUE nucleus. The functions of specific facilities are defined in later sections.

The facilities discussed above are called *CPU processes*. In addition to CPU processes, there are two types of pseudo-processes in SUE, called *calendar clock processes* and *buffer processes*. Neither buffer processes nor calendar clock processes consume processor time. Every CPU process has the right to spawn children of any of the three types, although it has to relinquish some of its resources, such as memory and processor speed, to each son it creates. When created, the process has the following function, depending on its type.

1. *Calendar Clock Process*   This process is essentially an alarm clock which does a facility call on its father when a specified time interval has elapsed. When created, the process is waiting to receive its first time interval from its father.

2. *Buffer Process*   A CPU process can buffer its facility calls by creating a buffer process son. The buffer process does a facility call on its father, followed by a facility call on a specified ancestor. The buffer process (not the father) has to wait for the service request to be completed. When the facility call is completed, the buffer process again calls its father, thereby notifying the father that the buffered facility call has been completed.

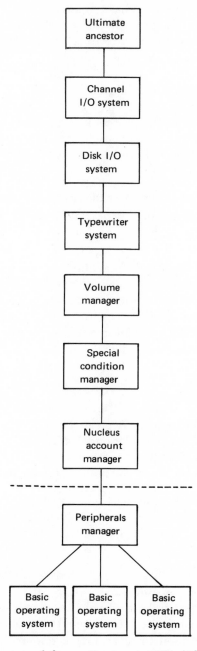

FIG. 10–2 The structure of the creation tree in SUE. (The dashed line indicates the boundary of the SUE nucleus.)

Buffer processes are quite similar to message slots in a mailbox system. When a CPU process wants to invoke a facility, it can create a buffer son (that is, send a message), which makes the call. After the specified facility call is completed, the buffer process again calls its father (that is, replies to the message). In the interim, while the buffer process is waiting to be serviced by the ancestor which it called, the buffer's father (which awaits a reply) can continue to do other work.

3. *CPU Processes*   A CPU process is a garden-variety sequential process. A CPU process can declare itself a facility process in the system, in which case it will be allowed to service facility calls according to its location on the facility tree.

10.2.2.2   RESOURCES, CAPABILITIES, AND PROTECTION

Resource claims within the SUE system are managed by means of capabilities (see Section 7.2). A capability is a 64-bit record which specifies the availability of some resource to a process. Corresponding to each process there is a list of capabilities which determines the process's allotment of resources which are provided by ancestors.

Every capability has an associated manager, generally either the facility which originally created the capability or the Kernel (see next section). A capability can be modified either explicitly, by the capability's manager, or implicitly, by a facility in the Complete Facility Call primitive.

Each capability has a field specifying its manager and a set of flags which govern the ability to:

1. pass the capability to a newly created son;
2. pass the capability in completing a facility call;
3. adjust the capability after it is created;
4. destroy the capability without notifying the manager.

There are three different formats for capabilities: Boolean, numeric, and uninterpreted. Depending on the format, the remaining bits of the capability (after the manager specification and flags) are interpreted as follows.

1. *Boolean*   the capability is interpreted as a mask to allow limited access to a resource. For example, in a file capability, one process may have read–write access while another has read-only access.

2. *Numeric*   the capability is interpreted as an integer. Numeric capabilities are generally used for consumable resources, such as CPU time or number of I/O operations remaining.

3. *Uninterpreted*   the information has meaning only to the process which created the capability.

Capabilities are useful for both the protection and the management of resources. Since nearly all resources in the system are represented as capabilities, there exists a uniform method of creating, manipulating, and destroying them using the capability operations: *Create Capability*, *Inspect Capability*, and *Modify Capability*. Capabilities are also secure. In transmitting resource information from one process to another (using a capability as a parameter in a facility call), only the slot number of the capability on the capability list is actually passed. The capability lists are protected from the processes so that no process can "forge" a capability. A process informs another process of its access rights by passing a capability slot number; the second process can now inspect the slot's contents. Only the Kernel can modify the capability lists, making it impossible for any other process to lie about its resource allotment.

Capabilities also provide a mechanism for accounting for resource usage. A process receives its initial resource allotment from its father when it is created via its capability list. The process, which is held responsible for its allocation, may either consume the resources itself or pass them on to its sons. If each process keeps records of the capabilities it has allocated, a complete accounting of all resources is always available by examining each process's capability list.

10.2.2.3   THE KERNEL

Processes, facility primitives, and capabilities are not intrinsic to the IBM/360 hardware, but are implemented by the first level of software, called the *Kernel*. The Kernel is not a process in the sense of the facilities shown in Fig. 10–2. Rather, it is a program which modifies the basic IBM/360 machine structure to include primitive operations to manage processes, interrupts, memory, capabilities, facilities, peripheral devices, and real-time clocks. The virtual machine supplied by the Kernel, which includes the unprivileged IBM/360 instruction set and the Kernel primitives, is the machine which the processes actually see. One can think of the Kernel as modifying the hardware to create a virtual machine which is more convenient for programming the SUE nucleus. The reader should compare this virtual machine to the virtual machine provided by the Venus microprogram.

The Kernel executes in privileged mode with interrupts disabled in memory key zero (that is, it has access to all of memory). In fact, it is the only piece of software in the system with any of these characteristics. The Kernel essentially has unrestricted use of the entire machine. Consequently, no process can shield itself from the Kernel. The Kernel also is secure from the rest of the system, since no process is allowed to run in the memory key of the Kernel's memory. Hence, no process can either maliciously or unintentionally modify the Kernel.

The Kernel provides seven functions to the rest of the nucleus.

1. *Processes*   The Kernel provides primitives to create, destroy, start execution of, and stop execution of processes. Each process is allocated a process descriptor and capability list within the Kernel. Process descriptors can then be inspected or modified by the process itself or by its father. When created, a process is in a stopped state; it can be started at any time by its father. Once started, the process executes on its own virtual processor. Interrupts are invisible to it, as they are all serviced by the Kernel. The process continues to run (time sliced with all other active processes) until it is stopped or trapped.

2. *Traps*   When an exceptional condition arises, the process which is associated with the condition is "trapped." A trap causes the affected process to be stopped, and the Kernel sends a message to its father informing it of the problem. For example, a process can be waiting for an interrupt from a peripheral device. When the interrupt occurs, the process is trapped by the Kernel. Its father then takes measures to notify the process (usually by modifying its descriptor) and restarts it. Most traps are expected; special procedures in each facility are provided for servicing them.

3. *Facilities*   The Kernel implements facilities and the three facility primitives as described in Section 10.2.2.1.

4. *Capabilities*   Attached to each process descriptor is a complete list of the capabilities which the process possesses. The Create Capability primitive allows a process to mint a new capability, which is then added to its capability list. The Inspect Capability and Modify Capability primitives permit existing capabilities to be manipulated. Capabilities are formatted as described in the previous section.

5. *Memory Management*   The Kernel provides three primitive operations for managing memory. *Set Process Key* sets the memory protection key in which the process runs. Naturally, the process must have a capability to run in this key. *Set Storage Key* resets the storage key of a 2K-byte block which is either owned by or available to the process. *Create System Area* allocates a block of storage for process descriptors. Since the Kernel needs descriptor space for every process in the system, a process must provide the Kernel with memory for the descriptor of each process it creates. Memory blocks (which are accounted for in

capabilities) can be transferred among processes by means of the capability primitives.

6. *Clocks*   A *Calendar Clock*, which contains the date and time of day, and a *Run Clock*, which for each process contains the amount of processor time used, are maintained by the Kernel. These clocks can be initialized or inspected by certain privileged processes.

7. *I/O Management*   All I/O operations on peripheral devices are controlled within the Kernel. The two primitives *Request I/O Operation* and *Request I/O Status* allow channels to be initiated and channel statuses to be inspected. The details of these operations, which are highly IBM/360 hardware dependent, are beyond the scope of this description.

10.2.3   The Functions Provided by SUE

In Section 10.2.2 the first level of software in SUE, namely the Kernel, was described. Using the Kernel's virtual machine, a system of seven asynchronous processes (Fig. 10–2) provides the basic set of nucleus facilities. The outline of these processes presented in this section constitutes a concise specification of the services offered by the SUE nucleus.

10.2.3.1   THE ULTIMATE ANCESTOR

This facility lies at the root of the SUE creation tree. In addition to servicing traps for the Channel I/O System (since it is that process's father), the Ultimate Ancestor implements the system's main operator terminal, called the *Archconsole*. All processes can "talk" to the operator's console by using a facility call, since each is a descendant of the Ultimate Ancestor.

10.2.3.2   THE CHANNEL I/O SYSTEM

The Channel I/O System, the second major component in the creation tree, is responsible for creating virtual I/O device control units. That is, delays due to busy control units, channel errors, or unexpected interrupts are transparent to the users of this facility. The primitive provided by this process, called *Execute Channel Program,* initiates the given channel program via the Kernel's Request I/O Operation.

Since channel programs generally take a long time to complete, a process will invoke the Execute Channel Program facility through a buffer son if it has anything useful to do in the interim.

10.2.3.3   THE DISK I/O SYSTEM

The Disk I/O System provides a simple file system and an interface for foreign (that is, non-SUE-formatted) disks. All disk requests, whether they are for standard SUE files or for specially formatted foreign volumes, must be cleared through this process. When a process wishes to access a file (that is, read or write) it must present three capabilities. The first capability proves ownership of the memory key of the core area to be written into or read from. The second capability identifies the process as a legitimate user of the file. The third capability, a count of the number of disk operations allotted to the process, is decremented by one for each I/O operation performed.

All SUE files are composed of contiguous 2K-byte blocks. Read and write operations on disk always work on a multiple of these uniform-length records. A process which owns a file may mint a new capability for a contiguous group of records within its file area. This file operation, called "subsetting," allows a process to share part of its file with a descendant. The disk system, however, need not maintain a record of who owns which part of each disk. If a process shows a valid file capability for a certain block of records, then it is permitted to access those records. Thus, it is the responsibility of the process which subsetted its file to know who has access rights to it.

Processes which want to format their own disks must identify themselves to the disk system. The disk system then mints a capability which permits such a process to write on its disk in a non-SUE format.

Finally, the Disk I/O System provides a facility to start and stop logical drives. These commands, which are used primarily by the Volume Manager, activate and deactivate disk drives.

10.2.3.4   TYPEWRITER SYSTEM

The *Typewriter System* provides an interface for processes to communicate with the outside world through typewriter terminals. A user, when signing on a terminal, specifies the name of the process with which he wants to communicate. A process which wants to communicate with a terminal does a facility call on the Typewriter System, defining the name by which it expects to be addressed. Then the first typewriter which signs on using that name is assigned to that process, thereby completing the facility call. Once given a terminal to talk to, the process generally creates two buffer sons. One passes messages to and from the terminal; the other alerts the process when an Attention signal is received. The I/O is actually initiated by the Typewriter System itself.

10.2.3.5   VOLUME MANAGER

The mounting and dismounting of disk volumes is overseen by the Volume Manager. A process may ask for a disk pack to be mounted by invoking a facility call on the Volume Manager. The process must present capabilities to prove ownership of the requested volume and of the logical drive on which it will be mounted. Each volume is represented by a unique six-character name, which the Volume Manager maps into a 1-byte number. This number serves as an internal identification on the volume label. The Volume Manager, after checking the calling process's capabilities, sends a message to the appropriate typewriter terminal (that is, the operator console) requesting the volume to be mounted. After the volume is mounted, a facility call is made to the Disk I/O System requesting the drive to be started. Volumes are dismounted in an analogous fashion.

10.2.3.6 SPECIAL CONDITION MANAGER

The Special Condition Manager is a link between the Ultimate Ancestor and several external devices. On command from the Ultimate Ancestor, the Special Condition Manager establishes contact with the typewriter terminal (via the Typewriter System) which claims to be the Archconsole. In case of some serious system failure, the Ultimate Ancestor may request the Special Condition Manager to record some data on disk before expiring. Also, accounting information is recorded via this path as a matter of course.

Note that this communication path (that is, from Ultimate Ancestor to Special Condition Manager) is a violation of the system structure, since a process is not allowed to invoke the services of any of its descendants. It is, in fact, the only such violation. The reason for it is clear. The Ultimate Ancestor, being at the root of the creation tree, is in a position to know more about the system than any other process. However, in order to make use of its unique position, it has to communicate with the Disk I/O System and the Typewriter System, both of which lie below it on the creation tree. In violating the system structure, the Special Condition Manager creates the needed path from the Ultimate Ancestor to these other processes. This anomaly in the structure requires special care in order to avoid such deadlock situations as when Ultimate Ancestor calls Special Condition Manager, which calls Ultimate Ancestor again (that is, both processes wait forever).

10.2.3.7 NUCLEUS ACCOUNT MANAGER

The Nucleus Account Manager supervises the operation of suboperating systems which run under the SUE nucleus (for example, a batch system, interactive system, or text editor). Its two main functions are to allocate system resources among the active users, and to implement a nucleus console which serves as the operator console for the suboperating system.

To start up his suboperating system, a nucleus console user signs on the typewriter terminal and requests to speak to the Nucleus Account Manager. After establishing communications, the nucleus console user asks that a certain set of resources be allocated to his system (for example, memory, processor speed, disk drives). If these requests do not exceed the maximum allowed for this subsystem and if the resources are currently available, then the subsystem is started up. Otherwise, the Nucleus Account Manager notifies the nucleus console of the problem and asks that the resource request be reduced.

After start-up, the nucleus console user becomes the main operator console for the suboperating system. He may inquire about status, ask to alter resource allocation, communicate with his system, or terminate the system. The resource usage of the suboperating system is stored by the Nucleus Account Manager in disk files and can later be used for billing purposes.

Below the Nucleus Account Manager on the creation tree it would be appropriate to have a facility which manages peripheral devices, such as card readers and line printers. Although a peripherals manager was not included within the SUE nucleus, it is likely to be the first facility residing on the creation tree outside of the nucleus.

10.3   The Venus Operating System

The Venus Operating System is an interactive, multiprogrammed system built at the MITRE Corporation for a small, slow, microprogrammable machine, the Interdata 3. The Venus machine, that is, the Interdata 3 with the Venus microprogram, is paged and segmented. Each segment, which contains either a procedure or data, is accessible by any user in the system (typically, there are three users). Before operating, a user may have one or more card decks read into the system and stored as segments. The user then signs onto a teletype terminal. Commands invoked from the terminal cause files to be read from magnetic tape into segments. Other commands cause the execution of one or more procedure segments. Procedure execution may occur in debugging mode. To test a program, the user can specify a program "breakpoint"; when the breakpoint location is reached, a debugging routine gains control and the user can interactively examine the state of his program. The results of the completed computation are stored in an output segment, which can then be spooled out to the line printer or stored on magnetic tape.

The main design objective of Venus was to show that "good" hardware architecture could significantly simplify software system design. Toward this end, the machine structure was permitted to influence the system structure. In fact, since the machine is microprogrammable, the designers could mold the machine's characteristics to fit their needs. Given a clean hardware base, levels of virtual machines were added to produce a structured system with few errors.

10.3.1 The Hardware

The Interdata 3 is a small microprogrammable machine with a 2000-instruction micromemory. The Venus system supports a configuration consisting of $64K$ bytes of core memory, two magnetic tape drives, a half-megabyte disk (for paging), several teletypes, a line printer, and a card reader. There are hardware channels which can access main memory, one for the tape drives and one for the disk. Channels for the other devices are simulated by the microprogram. In between instruction cycles the microprogram services any device which needs attention (including the tape and disk drives). The software is therefore relieved of real-time constraints normally associated with the servicing of I/O interrupts. The channel interface is discussed further in Section 10.3.4.

Since external device terminations do not raise interrupts, the lower levels of the Venus system are relieved of a complex bookkeeping chore. In systems which have I/O interrupts it is sometimes difficult to decide to whom an I/O completion interrupt belongs. For instance, if a disk interrupt occurs in such a system, a software "interrupt handler" has to figure out which process initiated the disk. If several processes are sharing the disk, this may not be easy. This kind of problem never occurs in Venus. All interrupts are associated with the *running* process for conditions such as arithmetic overflow and illegal instruction execution. Thus, there is never any ambiguity as to which process caused the interrupt.

10.3.2 Processes

The Venus microprogram supports 16 processes. Each process is defined by a core-resident work area and an address space which encompasses every segment in the machine. The work area contains space for the general registers, the program counter, and other process-related information (for example, links for the semaphore queues and a software-defined priority).

Processes communicate by means of semaphores. Associated with each semaphore is a header element consisting of the value of the semaphore and a pointer to the first process on the blocked list for that semaphore. Processes which are blocked on a given semaphore are singly linked through their work areas to the semaphore's header element. When a process executes a P operation on a semaphore, then the microprogram decrements the semaphore by one. If the resulting value is nonnegative, then the process continues; otherwise, its operation is suspended, and it is added to the corresponding semaphore queue. When a V operation on a semaphore releases a process, the process on the semaphore's waiting list with the highest priority is removed. If there are several highest priority processes, then the oldest one of them is removed. A process which is not blocked on any semaphore queue is either *ready to run* or *running*. Ready-to-run processes are linked on the "ready queue" and are scheduled in the same order as the semaphore queues. Thus, the running process always has a priority at least as high as all the processes on the ready queue, because a process released by a V operation can preempt the running process.

Semaphores are used by processes to synchronize with each other, to synchronize with I/O devices, and to communicate messages via queues. The last two applications are discussed in later sections.

10.3.3   Virtual Memory

The Venus machine supports a segmented memory with paging, which is implemented through the microcode. Pages are 256 bytes long, and a segment can contain up to 256 pages. Address references are calculated through one of the eight register pairs; a segment register contains the segment name, and its corresponding general register contains the page number and the displacement within the page. Each segment register also has an "extension"; the extension is a register which maps the page number in the general register into a core address (that is, the page frame in which the page resides). To access a word in storage, a program references only the general register. The microprogram uses the corresponding segment register and extension to determine which segment contains the page. It is the program's responsibility to load the correct segment name into the appropriate segment register.

The segment register extension and page fault mechanism are under the control of the microprogram. When a word is accessed through a general register, the microprogram examines the extension of the associated segment register. If the extension refers to the same page as the general register, then the page is in core and its address is in the extension. If the extension does not refer to the general register page, then the microprogram must search for it. First, the *core page table*, which contains a list of all the pages currently in core, is searched. If the page is in core, then the segment register extension is adjusted to point to the page and the program can continue. If the page is not in core, then the software *page fault handler* is invoked; it locates the desired page on disk, stores it somewhere in core, updates the core page table, and returns to the point of invocation in the microcode. Note that the page fault handler is a subroutine of the microcode and should therefore be considered part of the Venus machine.

Page replacement in Venus is implemented by the least-recently-used rule. Every page which is associated with some segment register extension must be locked in core. In addition, several pages are locked in core for processes and the operating system, such as the core page table, process work areas, and the page fault handler. All other pages are linked on an "aged" list and are candidates for replacement. A page is added to the end of the aged list when it is no longer referenced by any extensions. Thus, pages on the aged list are ordered according to the length of time since they were last accessed. The page fault handler removes the top page from the aged list and uses its core page frame for the new page. It then adjusts the segment register extension and core page table before returning.

Processes and virtual memory are implemented in the microcode. That is, the Interdata 3 does not supply built-in paging hardware or multiprogramming. Therefore, both the memory and process organization represent decisions by the designers in writing the microcode; essentially, the microprogrammable hardware allowed them to build their own machine. Where speed was more important, the functions could be implemented in microcode (for example, calculating physical memory addresses from virtual memory addresses). Where flexibility was desirable, the functions could be pushed up into the software (for example, the page fault handler). In designing their hardware, the designers of Venus were actually choosing specifications for their lowest-level virtual machine.

Compare the Venus microprogrammed machine to the two lowest levels of the THE system. The Venus system implements independent cooperating processes and virtual memory in the firmware, while THE implements the same functions in software. In fact, there is no reason why these functions could not be built into the hardware. Doing so would correspond to implementing the level 1 *virtual* machine of THE as a *real* machine.

10.3.4   Extensions to the Microprogram

There are three software appendages which increase the flexibility of the Venus microprogram: dictionaries, queues, and the poller.

10.3.4.1   DICTIONARIES

Segments are identified by unique 15-bit names, which from a user's viewpoint are not particularly convenient. The Venus software therefore provides a set of dictionaries which map external, user-supplied segment names into internal 15-bit names. Each external name specifies a dictionary and a name within the dictionary. A central dictionary maps the external dictionary names into their internal names. Thus, the two-level external naming mechanism gives users a flexible way of sharing segments without keeping track of internal segment identifiers.

10.3.4.2   QUEUES

Semaphores are used to implement a mechanism for process synchronization. Processes communicate by passing messages through a set of queues. These queues may only be accessed by using a set of system-defined procedures which use semaphores to guarantee mutual exclusion.

10.3.4.3   THE POLLER

The number of processes in Venus is limited by the number of process work areas which can be kept core resident. Assuming a maximum of six user processes, there are only ten processes left for the system, which is not enough. Therefore, a simple procedure called the *poller* is provided, which allows several processes to share a single virtual machine (that is, work area). When an event occurs which affects the poller's virtual machine, all the processes sharing that virtual machine are polled until one of them acknowledges the event. The choice of which processes share the poller's virtual machine is made based on the global efficiency of the system.

10.3.5   I/O System

Venus provides deadlock-free resource management of all I/O devices, plus the CPU, disk, and system segments. One of the best examples of the application of the level approach to resource management in Venus is the I/O system. For this reason, and because it is a major component of the operating system, the I/O system is described in detail.

The Venus I/O system is built as a series of virtual machines (Fig. 10–3). At level 0 is the microprogrammed device channel. The channel accepts commands to transfer an in-core buffer of data to or from a specified device. If the device is a teletype terminal, line printer, or card reader, then the microprogram actually performs the transfer, moving data 1 byte at a time. Data transfers to and from the tape and disk drives are performed by hardware channels. However, the termination of I/O on any device, including the tape and disk drives, is picked up by the microprogrammed channel, which signals the completion of an I/O command by executing a V on a semaphore associated with the invoking process.

On level 1 a *controller* process is created for the tape drives, card reader, printer, and each teletype (the disk has been given to the virtual memory subsystem). The controllers run on the level 0 virtual machine, improving device characteristics for their users. While level 0 users must provide core buffers for memory transfers, the controllers accept buffers from virtual memory segments. That is, the controller takes responsibility for moving the data from a segment buffer into a core buffer. In addition, the length of transfers is fixed at one record, the record size being device dependent (for example, one card or one line). A controller can be activated at any time, whether or not the device is free. It will execute the I/O command as soon as the device becomes available. When the requested transfer has been completed, it signals the invoking process via a semaphore which was specified in the command.

On level 2 a procedure called the *teletype requester* is implemented. The teletype requester provides an interface between user and system processes and the teletype controllers. Higher-level I/O processes can use the teletype requester to communicate with the teletype terminals.

Level 3 consists of *driver* processes for the card reader, line printer, and magnetic tape drives. A driver, which uses the controller commands to do I/O, provides a virtual device which moves one segment at a time. It merges input buffers into a single segment and breaks up output segments into the proper size for the controllers. The card reader driver builds segments from card images as long as the reader hopper is not empty. Synchronization is needed to obtain the completed segment. The printer driver must be activated by a process command to print a segment. It does not notify its user when printing is completed. The tape driver must be activated by a process command to read/write a segment. The invoking process must wait until the read/write has been completed.

Level 4 consists of a *requester* procedure for each driver. The requester simplifies the interface between the driver and the user processes

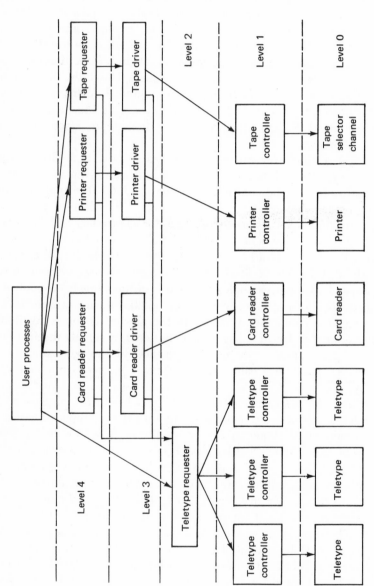

FIG. 10-3 Venus I/O system.

by helping in the construction of segments and synchronization of command sequences (for example, to the tape driver).

The Venus I/O system is a good example of the application of Dijkstra's level of abstraction approach. Each level in the I/O system abstracts out unnecessary details and provides a more convenient virtual machine for user processes. The underlying virtual machine, the Venus machine itself, supplies useful tools, such as semaphore operations and a segmented–paged memory, which are used to implement the I/O system on all levels.

10.4 Other Systems

There are many other systems which have been described in the literature. In this section a few such systems are mentioned to provide direction for the interested reader.

The THE [Dijkstra, 1698b] and RC4000 [Brinch Hansen, 1970] operating systems are highly structured systems built for small (and rather uncommon) machines. Both systems were innovative and have received considerable attention as prototypes for how operating systems should be structured.

The MULTICS system [Organick, 1972] is a large-scale, sophisticated computer utility built for GE Honeywell machines at MIT. The system is based on a complex segmented–paged addressing scheme which provides a dynamic environment for flexible sharing.

Although systems such as those just mentioned are nice for pedagogical reasons, they are not representative of the operating systems which are used most in the real world. Sayers [1971] and Hoare and Perrot [1972] describe a number of practical systems for popular machines. As a first step in understanding such systems, the reader should try to obtain information about the system with which he normally must interface. Knowing the external characteristics of a system often helps in understanding its internal machinations.

Most of these systems were implemented before the impact of structured system design. They are not easy to understand and sometimes are difficult to use. On the job one rarely finds systems as elegant as SUE or Venus. However, practical systems do accomplish much useful work for a great many people.

There are people who feel that systems are either elegant or practical, but cannot be both. We do not subscribe to this philosophy: it is self-defeating. Systems can be designed to be understandable and well structured without adversely affecting their ultimate success in the real world.

Problems

10.1 Prepare a case study of an existing operating system. The following are examples for case studies.

IBM OS/360 (MFT/MVT), DOS/360, 1800 Multiprogramming Executive, OS/VS, VM/370

DEC PDP-10 Time Sharing System, PDP-11 DOS System, PDP-11 RSX-11D, PDP-11 MUMPS, PDP-11 RSTS, PDP-8 Time Sharing System

CDC 6400/6500/6600 Scope 3 Operating System, CDC 3300/3500 Master Operating System

Univac 1108 Exec 8 Operating System

Honeywell 600 system, Honeywell 200 Mod 4 Operating System

MULTICS System

Compatible Time Sharing System (CTSS)

XDS Sigma 2 Real-Time Batch Monitor, Sigma 5/7 Batch Time Sharing Monitor

Burroughs B5500 system, B6500 Master Control Program

Hewlett Packard 3000 Operating System

ILLIAC IV Operating System

Michigan Terminal System

CAL 6000 Time Sharing System

10.2 Hardware components are becoming less expensive and more powerful. Some of the functions of an operating system traditionally performed by software can be taken over by hardware. What functions of an operating system do you think most appropriate to be implemented by hardware? Are there any reasons why the whole operating system should not be in hardware?

10.3 Prepare a survey of the use of computers in banking systems.

10.4 Prepare a case study of an airline reservation system, such as the American Airlines SABRE system, Air Canada Reservec system, BOAC reservation system (BOADICEA), United Airlines reservation system, or IBM PARS.

10.5 Prepare a comparative survey of minicomputer operating systems.

10.6 Terminology in operating systems is very dependent on the local environment and organization. Prepare a glossary of terms found in manuals of at least three manufacturers or major users of computer equipment. Make sure to establish all the aliases of commonly used concepts, for example, processes.

I

DATA STRUCTURES

A *data structure* is a group of one or more data elements which are structurally related to each other. The two fundamental problems in manipulating data structures are *creation* and *maintenance*. The latter activity includes such operations as *inserting* elements into the structure, *deleting* elements from the structure, and *locating* elements within the structure. There exists a large variety of data structures because different applications stress one of the foregoing operations. An attempt is then made to do that operation very efficiently in terms of space or computation requirements.

The use of complex data structures is pervasive in operating systems. In this chapter some basic concepts in the storage and retrieval of structured information are outlined. This is not intended to be an introductory presentation, but rather a review of material which is needed as background for this book. The uninitiated reader is encouraged to consult a good text on data structures, such as that of Knuth [1968].

I.1 Definition of Terms

If an *element* is defined to be the logical unit of information, then a *list* is a sequence of elements $[e(1), e(2), \ldots, e(n)]$ linearly ordered. That is, each pair of elements $e(k)$ and $e(k+1)$ are related in the sense that $e(k)$ precedes $e(k+1)$ and $e(k+1)$ succeeds $e(k)$. Lists can be formed wherever the need for tables of ordered information arises (for example, list of available storage blocks, list of active jobs, list of user files).

By imposing limitations on how elements can be added to and removed from the list, new structures can be defined. For example, a *stack* is defined to be a list in which insertions and deletions are made at one end. A *queue* is a list in which insertions and deletions are made at opposite ends.

I.2   Sequential Allocation of Lists

The items of the list can be stored in sequential locations of memory. Let $\text{MEMORY}(y)$ denote the address in the physical memory of an item named y. Consider a list x where the first element of the list is stored at some base address (that is, $\text{MEMORY}(x(0))$ is the base address). Then if each item has fixed size denoted by L, sequential allocation is characterized by

$$\text{MEMORY}(x(i+1)) = \text{MEMORY}(x(i)) + L, \quad i \geq 1$$

Assume there are four lists (A, B, C, and D) in memory, which are all sequentially allocated in areas of the same name. In Fig. I–1 area B is about to overrun the area used by list C, even though there are plenty of unused locations to the right of C and D. In such a situation there are two common strategies which can be used to solve the problem.

The first method, called *compaction*, attempts to relocate some of the smaller lists to make additional room for the larger ones. Applying compaction, B's available space can be extended as shown in Fig. I–2. By moving C and D into higher addresses, additional space was freed for B.

A second method, called *indirection*, involves the use of links. A *link*

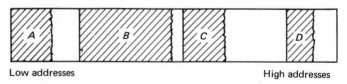

Low addresses   High addresses

FIG. I–1   Memory map I. (The cross-hatched areas represent storage which is in use.)

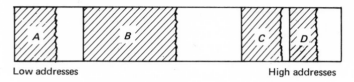

Low addresses   High addresses

FIG. I–2   Memory map II.

s an element of storage which contains an address pointing to another
word of storage. By placing a link at the end of a crowded area to
point to an empty space, a large list can be given additional room to
grow without redistributing memory. In Fig. I–3 area B of Fig. I–1 is
extended by using indirection. When indirection is used to fill memory
gaps, then sequential allocation is only applicable to contiguous areas
within the list. This is in contrast to compaction, which permits the
method of sequential allocation to be maintained in the whole list.

I.3 Linked Lists

In the (singly) linked list representation each element of the list
contains two items: the data associated with the element (called DATA)
and a link pointing to the next element on the list (called POINTER).
In Fig. I–4 a four-element linked list is shown. A special element, called
the *list head,* points to the first element of the list. The last element
has a pointer of "null," denoting the end of the list. Since actual memory
locations are irrelevant to the list's logical structure, links are indicated
by arrows rather than addresses to the appropriate elements.

Lists can also be *doubly linked.* An element *x* is doubly linked when
it has two pointers: one points to the element to the left of *x* and
the other points to the element to the right of *x*. A four-element doubly
linked list is shown in Fig. I–5.

Although a doubly linked list needs 50 percent more storage (for
the extra pointer) than its singly linked counterpart, it simplifies insertions to and deletions from the list. Given only a pointer to an element,
one can easily delete the element from a doubly linked list, since its

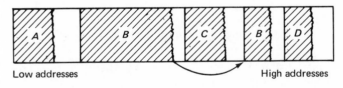

Low addresses   High addresses

FIG. I–3   Memory map III. (Pointer is to the continuation of list *B*).

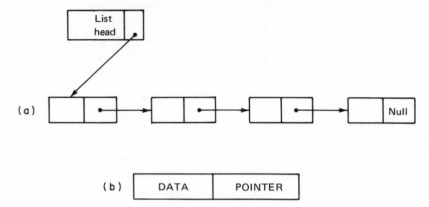

FIG. I–4   (a) Singly linked list where each element is of the form (b).

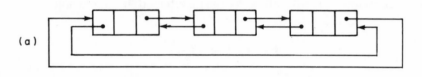

FIG. I–5   (a) Doubly linked list where each element is of the form (b).

left pointer is known. In a singly linked list one must search the list from the beginning to adjust the pointer which used to point to the deleted element.

A *circular list,* in which elements are arranged in a loop, is a list where the last element points to the first. By adding more link fields to the elements, more complex data structures can be obtained. These *multiply linked* lists can be constructed to assume arbitrary graphical structures (for example, cycles, trees, networks).

I.4   Management of Linked Lists

In any linked list management scheme an operation is needed which obtains unused elements from storage. The approach often taken is to maintain a singly linked list of unused elements, called the *free list,* pointed to by a header element. There are basically two strategies which are used for adding elements to the free list.

I.4.1 User-Defined Management

In this scheme it is the users' responsibility to return elements to the free list when they are no longer needed. One way to return an element x to the free list is to set the POINTER of x to point to the first element of the free list and to adjust the free list header element to point to x. Thus, x is the new first free list element. The free list can be initialized by linking up memory before the program begins execution; the free list header points to the first element of memory and the last element points to "null." However, if memory is reasonably large, this procedure can be quite time consuming. Alternatively, one can put a bound on memory that can be used for free elements. The first time through, elements are allocated sequentially until the upper bound is reached. Used elements are returned to an initially empty free list. When the original bounded allocation runs out, the explicit management technique through the free list is resumed. This method also finds application in the next strategy.

I.4.2 System Management

The programmer can be released from his obligation of explicitly returning unused elements to the free list by writing a utility program to deal with deleted elements. Two types of strategies are possible.

The first is *use counts* or *reference counts*. A new field is incorporated into each element x that stores a count of the number of other elements which reference x (that is, how many other links point to x). As elements are added to and removed from the system, the reference count is continually updated. If the reference count reaches zero, then the element is no longer accessible to the program and is available to be reallocated. Therefore, the system can safely return the element to the free list.

There are several problems with this method. First, elements organized in a circular list are never returned to free storage. Even if no list which is accessible to the program points to the circular list, the nonzero reference count within the circular list prevents their being released. This is difficult to overcome, especially when circular lists are embedded in more complex structures. Second, the extra field in each element which records the reference count "wastes" a significant portion of the available memory. One can sometimes circumvent the latter problem by recording the count only in the header element of each list, reducing somewhat the amount of storage needed. However, if most lists are short, waste may still be significant. A third problem occurs when a program aborts because of an error. The program may no longer be able to access an item, but the reference count does not get decremented. Thus, the list will never be deallocated. Sometimes, though, this property is desirable. If the aborted program is restarted, it can often make a good attempt at rebuilding data structures by using the reference counts.

The second approach is called *garbage collection.* In this method the user's program runs along until no more free storage is available, at which time a "garbage collector" program is invoked to pick up all the discarded elements. The garbage collection algorithm makes use of a "mark bit" in each element. The routine starts by setting the mark bits on all elements to zero. Then, starting with the fixed set of storage elements which the user program accesses directly (often the list heads), the garbage collector turns on the mark bits of all elements it can reach from these base elements by following the pointers. All unmarked elements are now known to be inaccessible to the user and can be linked to a free storage list. There are two important problems with this method. The first is that if memory is nearly full, the garbage collector program itself has little working storage for itself and consequently runs slowly. In addition, if most of the elements are still in use, there will be very many bits to mark. Second, the garbage collector, if called in the middle of a list manipulation, may accidently treat part of a real list as garbage, since it is temporarily not linked to the user program. It is often not easy to distinguish between pieces of active lists and real garbage.

Using garbage collection or reference counts, one finds that memory becomes fragmented into small blocks of free storage scattered among the active list elements. Compaction is a method applied after the mark bits (or use counts) have been set, whereby all list elements which are currently active are moved into contiguous locations at the top of memory. The effect of this process is to eliminate the need for a free list, since all free elements can be found in sequential locations at the end of memory. When most of the elements are inactive, considerable time and space can be saved by using this method, since a free list need not be linked together. As in the other techniques, one can construct pathological cases where compaction is intolerably inefficient.

I.5   Stacks

A *LIFO* (last-in–first-out) *list,* usually called a *stack,* is a list in which all insertions and deletions are made at one end of the list. The operations which add and remove elements from the stack are called PUSH and POP, respectively. In a sequential allocation scheme a stack can be implemented with a base address and a pointer to the stack top. PUSH and POP can also be implemented in a singly linked list which has a header element. To PUSH an element x onto the stack, the POINTER of x is assigned the address of the top stack element (which is stored in the stack header). Then the stack header is assigned the address of x. To POP an element off the stack, the contents of the stack header are assigned to some free variable and the header is adjusted to point to the POINTER of the former top element.

Perhaps the most common use of stacks is in language–parsing algorithms and graph traversal. Although stacks are found more often in compilers than in operating systems, they have been included here for completeness.

I.6 Queues

A *FIFO* (first-in–first-out) *list*, or *queue*, is a list in which all insertions are made at one end of the list, and all deletions are made from the other end. The INSERT and DELETE operations on queues, corresponding to PUSH and POP on stacks, require two pointers—one to the top of the list (for insertions) and one to the bottom of the list (for deletions). In queues (as well as in stacks) underflow (that is, deleting from an empty list) and overflow (that is, inserting into a full list) must be handled as error conditions.

FIFO queues find numerous applications in operating systems. When there is no extra information given, users who are waiting for some resource are generally served on a first-come–first-served (FIFO) basis.

I.7 Dequeues

In a *dequeue* (doubly ended queue) insertions and deletions may each be made at either end of the list. As in the FIFO case, two pointers are required, one to each end of the dequeue. The sequentially allocated case presents no new serious problems over LIFO and FIFO other than keeping both an upper and lower bound for memory, since the list grows in two directions. However, the linked list case is significantly more complicated. Unlike stacks and queues, a singly linked list is not sufficient, since one cannot delete an element from both ends without searching for a previous element. The solution is to doubly link the list, with the effect of making the insertion and deletion algorithms both more complex and more time consuming. The dequeue can also be stored as a circular list with two internal pointers to the two ends.

I.8   Tables

A *table* is a data structure in which deletions and insertions may be made at any point. There are several mechanisms which are generally employed to implement tables. In the *hash coding* technique, the content or name of the element in the table is used to calculate the address at which the element is stored. For example, if elements have unique identifiers, then the internal (that is, bit) representation of each identifier can undergo a simple arithmetic transformation which results in an address within the bounds of the table. Ideally, the hash coding function generates different addresses for different elements. When this is not the case, elements which hash to the same address are linked. For example, assume that a hashing function maps the names A and T into a single address K. Only one of the elements can be stored at K, say A. The element T is stored at some other address K', and the element at K is linked to K'. If a third element hashed to address K, then it would be stored at a new address K'', and the element at K' would be linked to K''. When a program tries to access the table by using the hashing function, it must check that the desired element is in fact stored at the location to which the element's name hashes. If it is not stored at that location, then the program must trace through the linked list, beginning at that location, until it finds the element.

A second approach for addressing tables is to store the names in a *directory*, together with the element addresses. To access an element, a table lookup is performed to determine where the element is located. The assumption is that it takes less time to search a sorted directory than to search the table itself. When the directory search is implemented in hardware (usually a parallel search), one has an *associative memory;* the hardware associates element names with memory locations in special hardware registers which can be searched quickly. Hash coding and directories are similar in that they both try to find the element without searching the table directly.

II

COMPUTATIONAL STRUCTURES

II.1 Introduction

Systems in which several processes may execute concurrently can exhibit a number of problems that do not exist in sequential systems. A large portion of the theoretical research in the area of operating systems has been concentrated on the development of models (sometimes called *program schemata*) to analyze the properties of concurrent systems. In fact, there are over 25 distinct models documented in the literature [Bernstein, 1973]. In this appendix three of these models are described as representative examples: Petri nets, computational schemata, and reusable resource graphs.

II.2 Petri Nets

Petri nets were introduced as a tool to describe concurrency among operations in general systems [Holt and Commoner, 1970]. They can be used to answer a number of interesting questions relating to deadlock in a computer system. In addition, Petri nets can be found embedded in subtle forms in many different models for parallel computation. Thus, they are a good starting point for a discussion of schemata.

A *Petri net* is defined to be a labeled directed graph with two node types, called *places* and *transitions*, such that every edge connects a place to a transition or a transition to a place. Places are denoted by circles, transitions by bars, and edges by directed arcs. A *marking* M of a Petri net is a function from place labels into the nonnegative integers. A marking is denoted by assigning a number of *tokens* to each place, corresponding to the marking function. Let N be a Petri net, P be the set of places in N, and $n(P)$ be the number of places in P. The places of N are uniquely labeled from the set of names $\{1, 2, 3, \ldots, n(P)\}$. A marking M can now be thought of as an $n(P)$-element vector, where the ith element of the vector denotes the number of tokens on the ith place. These concepts are illustrated in Fig. II–1.

The marking of a net can be changed by *firing* a transition. A transition t is said to be *firable* if there is at least one token on each place x for each arc directed from x to t. The firing of a transition t (given that t is firable) performs the following transformation: for each edge directed from a place x into transition t, the number of tokens on x is decremented by one; for each edge directed from t to a place y, the number of tokens on y is incremented by one. Referring again to Fig. II–1, transitions a and b are firable, while transitions c and d are not. If transition a fires, the marking $M' = [1, 1, 0]$ is reached. Now, transitions a, b, and c are firable. When c fires, the new marking is $M'' = [2, 0, 0]$.

In a Petri net the only restriction on concurrent execution of transitions

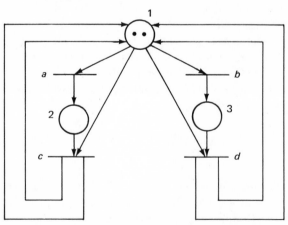

FIG. II–1 A Petri net which can hang up. (The marking M for this Petri net is $M = [2, 0, 0]$; $P = \{1, 2, 3\}$; $n(P) = 3$; $a, b, c,$ and d are transitions.)

is that imposed by the number of tokens on a place. Thus, in the original marking of Fig. II–1 transitions a and b could fire simultaneously. That two transitions are firable at the same instant does not necessarily imply that they can fire concurrently. If the marking in Fig. II–1 were $M = [1, 0, 0]$, both a and b would be firable, but could not fired simultaneously. This is because a and b each require a token to be removed from place 1 (that is, two tokens altogether) in order to fire.

Semantically, places stand for *conditions* and transitions for *events* in a system. The input places of a transition t (that is, those places with edges directed into t) correspond to the conditions which affect the occurrence of the event t. The output places of t correspond to the effect on the system of an occurrence of the event. A token is present on a place if the condition represented by the place holds. The operation of firing implies that if all the conditions upon which one event depends are holding, then the event occurs and its output conditions hold.

Consider a Petri net N with an initial marking $M(0)$. An *execution sequence* of N is a sequence of markings $M(0), M(1), M(2), \ldots$ where $M(i + 1)$ is obtained from $M(i)$ by firing a transition. In general, there are many possible execution sequences for a given Petri net with an initial marking. A marking M is *live* if all possible execution sequences beginning with $M(0)$ are infinite. When a marking is reached where no transitions can fire, the Petri net is said to hang up (that is, deadlock). If a system is modeled by a Petri net with some initial marking which is live, then the system as a whole will never hang up, since it is impossible to reach a marking where no event can occur.

In Fig. II–1, assume an initial marking of $M(0) = [2, 0, 0]$. If a and b each fire, the marking $M(2) = [0, 1, 1]$ is reached. The Petri net is now dead. No transitions can fire. Hence, the marking $M(0)$ is not live. In fact, there are no live markings for this Petri net. No matter how many tokens are put on place 1, one can always fire transitions a and b until all the tokens are on places 2 and 3. As soon as place 1 is empty, the Petri net is "dead."

Two transitions are said to be in *conflict* if they are mutually exclusive (that is, if they cannot both fire at the same time). Although precise conditions under which conflict occurs have not been formalized, it is clear that the notion of conflict is intimately related to the type of hang-up situation encountered in Fig. II–1 (that is, transitions c and d conflict under marking $M(0)$).

A *marked graph* is a Petri net in which exactly one edge is directed to and from each place. Marked graphs are somewhat less general than Petri nets, and are consequently easier to analyze. There are a number of theorems proved about marked graphs which relate to hang-up and finiteness properties. In particular, it has been shown that, for a strongly connected marked graph, there exists a dead transition (that is, one that can never fire) if and only if there exists a directed cycle with no tokens on it. If the transition corresponds to a process, then this theorem has implications for a system modeled by marked graphs. No comparable statement for general Petri nets has been found. In the marked graph of Fig. II–2 transition a is dead, since edges 1 and 2 form a directed cycle containing no tokens.

A marking M on a Petri net N is *safe* if in all markings obtained from M by firing transitions, there is no possibility for any place to have more than one token. There are a number of results which relate liveness to safety in a marked graph.

A Petri net is a *transition diagram* if all transitions have at most one input and one output. Although many nice theorems have been obtained for both marked graphs and transition diagrams, the relationships in operating systems usually demand the complete descriptive power of general Petri nets.

For example, consider a simple mutual exclusion relationship between two processes, A and B (Fig. II–3). Transition $A1$ ($B1$) fires when process A (B) wants to enter its critical section. Transition $A2$ ($B2$) fires when process A (B) leaves its critical section. For $A1$ and $B1$ to be mutually exclusive, they must share an input place (that is, "mutex"). Therefore, since mutex has two outputs, this Petri net is not a marked graph. Also, since $A1$ and $B1$ want to fire only if they are ready (that

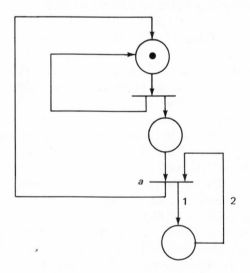

FIG. II–2   Transition a is dead.

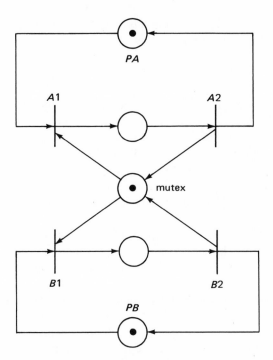

FIG. II–3   Mutual exclusion using Petri nets.

is, *PA* or *PB* contains a token) and mutex is available (that is, mutex contains a token), *A1* and *B1* need two inputs each. Therefore, the Petri net is not a transition diagram. That this model of a simple relationship between two processes is a general Petri net is not particularly encouraging with respect to the applicability of theorems about less general models.

II.3   Computational Schemata

Although Petri nets appear to be sufficient to describe the interaction of events in a system, they are not completely general from a computational point of view. For instance, the "not" operation (that is, a transition fires if and only if a place is empty) cannot be modeled by a Petri net. In this section an example of a computationally complete schema is outlined. A *computational schema* is a representation in graphical form of an asynchronous system, consisting of a set of *operators* (that is, processes) which act on a set of *registers* (that is, memory locations). Each schema is completely defined by two graphs, a *data flow graph* and a *control graph*.

II.3.1   Definitions

The data flow graph specifies the *domain* and *range* registers of each operator. A directed edge from an operator z to a register r indicates that r is in the range of z. A directed edge from r to z indicates that r is in the domain of z. In Fig. II–4 the data flow graph of a computational schema is specified. Operators and registers are represented by circles and squares, respectively.

The control graph specifies the sequence in which the operators execute. Every operator (represented by a circle) is connected to some number of *control counters* (represented by squares), each of which has a nonnegative integer content. The numbers written inside the squares are the *initial values* for the counters. An example of a control graph of a computational schema is given in Fig. II–5.

If all the counters directed into an operator node (that is, *input* counters) have values greater than zero, then the operator is said to be *defined*. At any time while an operator is defined it may execute, changing the registers as specified by the data flow graph and modifying the control graph counters as follows: all input counters to the operator are decreased by one; each output counter is increased by some nonnegative integer. If the increment for the output counter is a constant, it is written on the edge, as in operators a and c of Fig. II–5. To permit sequencing to depend on the data, the change in output counters is

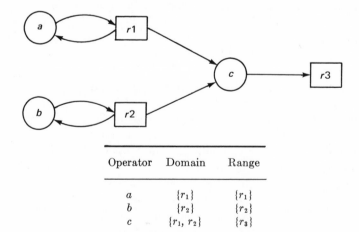

Operator	Domain	Range
a	$\{r_1\}$	$\{r_1\}$
b	$\{r_2\}$	$\{r_2\}$
c	$\{r_1, r_2\}$	$\{r_3\}$

FIG. II–4   Data flow graph.

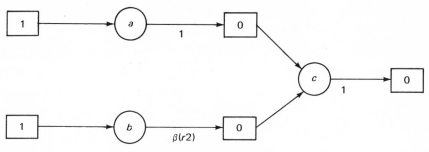

FIG. II–5   Control graph.

allowed to be a function of the values of the registers referenced by the operator, as in operator b of Fig. II–5.

Note the similarity of the control graph to a Petri net. If operators and counters are thought of as transitions and places, the only significant difference between the two representations is the data–dependent counter increment.

Usually, the operators in the data flow graph are represented as arbitrary functions, and control decisions (based on counter values) in the control graph are represented as arbitrary predicates. When this is the case, the schema is said to be *uninterpreted*. An *interpretation* for the schema is an assignment of actual functions and predicates for the function and predicate symbols. The interpretation generally includes a domain of values for the registers. The schema defined by Fig. II–4 and II–5 is uninterpreted. An interpretation for this schema would include

1. a domain of values for $r1$, $r2$, and $r3$;
2. a specification of functions for the operators a, b, and c;
3. an integer–valued function for $\beta(\ )$ in the control graph.

An *execution sequence* of a schema is a (possibly infinite) sequence of operator names $X1, X2, \ldots, Xn, \ldots$ such that each operator Xi is defined (that is, all its input counters ≥ 1) with the values of the counters which result from executing the preceding operators in the sequence. An execution sequence $X1, \ldots, Xn$ is *complete* if no operators are defined after the execution of $X1, \ldots, Xn$. Every execution sequence defines a *history array* which contains, for each register, the sequence of values that the register contains. Table II–1 relates the notions of execution sequence and history array.

II.3.2   Determinacy, Functionality, and Deadlock

Since no particular timing is associated with operators, the order in which operators will start and complete cannot always be predicted.

TABLE II-1

History Array of a Computational
Schema[a]

Register	Values
r_1	x_1 $a(x_1)$
r_2	x_2 $b(x_1)$
r_3	x_3 $c(a(x_1), b(x_2))$

[a] Consider the schema represented by the graphs of figures
II-4 and II-5. The only complete
execution sequences are a,b,c and
b,a,c. This history array corresponds to both of these sequences.

Any valid execution sequence is a possible sequence of events. In general, one would like the schema to "do the same thing" every time
it executes. It is possible, however, that the results of the computation
depend on the execution sequence. When a schema yields identical results for all valid execution sequences under all interpretations, the
schema is said to be *determinate*.

Consider the computational schema in Fig. II-6. Assume the operator
a stores zero in register *r*1. Operator *b* reads *r*1 and stores it in *r*2.
Clearly, the result in *r*2 is different, depending on whether *b* executes
before or after *a*. However, the control graph allows both execution
sequences (that is, a, b and b, a). Consequently, the schema is
nondeterminate.

Two operators are said to *conflict* at a register *r* if one of them changes
r and the other either changes or references *r*. A *race condition* exists
in a schema, and the schema is nondeterminate, if two operators which

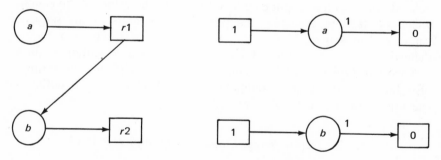

FIG. II-6 A nondeterminate computational schema.

conflict at some register can be defined at the same time. In Fig. II–6 operators a and b conflict at register $r1$. A race condition exists, since they are both initially defined.

A schema is *completely functional* if for every execution sequence every register goes through the same sequence of values that is, all history arrays for the schema are the same. If a race condition exists, a schema will not be completely functional for all interpretations.

Instead of requiring that the schema be completely functional, a subset of registers can be defined to be *output registers*. When all history arrays for the output registers are equivalent for every execution sequence, the schema is said to be *output functional*. In Fig. II–7 if registers $r3$ and $r5$ are the only output registers, then the schema is output functional. It is not completely functional, since $r2$ has two possible histories (that is, $[a(r1), c(r4)]$ or $[c(r4), a(r1)]$).

Another form of nondeterminate execution that may occur is that a schema may "hang up" prematurely if certain sequences of events happen (for example, Fig. II–8). This notion is analogous to "liveness"

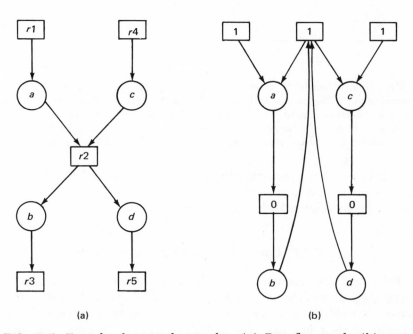

(a)   (b)

FIG. II–7 Example of output functionality. (a) Data flow graph; (b) control graph. (If registers $r3$ and $r5$ are the only output registers, then the schema is output functional. It is not completely functional since $r2$ has two possible histories (that is, $[a(r1), c(r4)]$ or $[c(r4), a(r1)]$).)

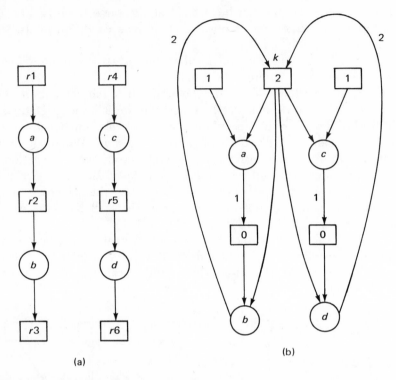

(a)

(b)

FIG. II–8 Example of a schema which hangs up. (a) Data flow graph; (b) control graph. (The counter labeled k represents a resource required by each operator, but not released until b or d completes. The execution sequences a, b, c, d, and c, d, a, b compute the intended results in $r3$ and $r6$, but if a executes first, followed by c, neither b nor d can proceed, and the execution does not finish properly.

in a Petri net. Note the similarity between Fig. II–8 and Fig. II–1. They are essentially the same system modeled in two different schemes, Petri nets and computational schemata.

II.3.3   Conclusions on Program Schemata

Petri nets and computational schemata are but two examples of a large class of models for parallel systems. Unfortunately, these models have not yielded much direct benefit to the operating system designer, in spite of their intuitive appeal. However, there do exist noncomputational models which abstract out the actual functions being calculated and concentrate on specific problems relating to resource sharing. In the next section one such model is investigated.

II.4   A Model for the Deadlock Problem

In both Petri nets and computational schemata, the problem of reaching a deadlock state was encountered. Several noncomputational models have been developed to study deadlocks (for example, Coffman *et al.* [1971], Habermann [1969], Hebalkar [1970], Holt [1972]). As an example of such models, R. C. Holt's reusable resource model is outlined [Holt, 1972].

In the reusable resource model, a system is thought of as a set of *processes* and a set of *resources,* each resource containing a fixed number of units. A process can change the state of the system by either *requesting, acquiring,* or *releasing* a unit of a resource. In graphical form, processes and resources are represented by squares and circles, respectively. Each square contains a number of tokens, corresponding to the number of existing units of that resource. An edge directed from a process to a resource indicates a request for one unit of that resource. An edge directed from a resource to a process represents the assignment of a resource to a process. Since each unit of each resource can be assigned to at most one process at a time, the number of edges from a resource to other processes cannot exceed the total number of units of that resource.

Figure II–9a represents one state in a reusable resource system. Process $P1$ requests two units of $R1$ and one unit of $R2$. $P2$ owns two units of $R1$ and wants one unit of $R2$. Assume $P1$ were now to acquire the one unit of $R2$ which it requests. If the rule is adopted that a process must acquire all of its requested resources before releasing any of them, then granting $P1$'s request produces a deadlock state. $P1$ cannot continue

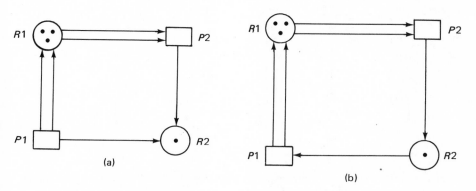

(a)

(b)

FIG. II–9 Example of reusable resource graph. (a) Initial state; (b) state after P_1 has acquired one unit of R_2.

until $P2$ releases a unit of $R1$, and $P2$ cannot continue until $P1$ releases its unit of $R2$.

Using this formalism, one can discover deadlock situations by *reducing* the graph according to the following rule: for every unblocked process, that is, those processes all of whose requests can be met, delete all edges to and from the process. A graph is *completely reducible* if it has no edges after being reduced. It is a theorem that a system in this model is free of deadlock if it is completely reducible. In Fig. II–10 the system of Fig. II–9a is reduced. No reductions are possible to graph II–9b, since both processes are blocked.

In a graph the *progeny* of a node a is the set of all nodes which lie on a path from a. A *knot* is a set of nodes K where the progeny of each node in K is exactly K. In Fig. II–11 {$R1$, $R2$, $P1$, $P2$} constitute a knot. A state is called *expedient* if every process which has a request is blocked. Thus, the system in Fig. II–11 is expedient. Holt proves that in an expedient system, a knot is a sufficient condition for deadlock.

Resources, such as messages, which vary in number during the operation of a system are termed *consumable*. Using both consumable and reusable resources, one can create a reasonable representation of a computer system in this model. A number of algorithms have been proposed which apply this model to the run time detection and prevention of deadlocks [Holt, 1972].

Reusable resource graphs model the states of the system in terms of requests and allocations of resources to processes. However, system states can be modeled in other ways. For example, Holt relates his model to Petri nets, showing how Petri net states can model resource graph states.

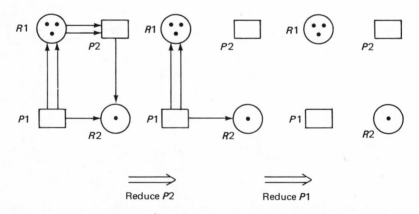

FIG. II–10   Reducing a reusable resource graph.

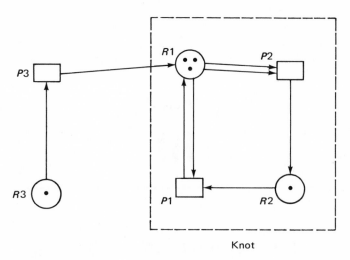

FIG. II–11   Deadlock in a reusable resource graph. (P_1 and P_2 are deadlocked, since they are contained in the knot.)

The preceding discussion of Holt's model is a bit cavalier. The model is actually quite comprehensive, describing a variety of interesting activities among cooperating processes. The discussion here was necessarily brief due to space limitations. Details of the model are given by Holt [1972].

II.5   Conclusion

Throughout this book a conscious effort has been made to avoid undue formalism. Mathematical models and/or results are only important when they give some additional insight into or hint at the solution of a serious problem. Unfortunately, most of the theoretical results obtained under the auspices and with the motivation of problems in operating systems are not readily applicable. This does not mean that they should be discarded. Good theory is by itself gratifying. It helps students visualize and comprehend concepts. Sometimes it even suggests some new ideas.

In this appendix some theoretical models have been presented that give some insight into the problems encountered with parallel operations. As such they can help the designer to understand better the structure and the interrelations of processes in an operating system.

APPENDIX

A TOY OPERATING SYSTEM

III.1 Introduction

In a course on operating systems students learn principles and basic techniques. Examples and exercises help them to understand how these techniques can be applied practically. Unfortunately, lectures are not enough. For a student to appreciate some of the problems, he has to face them himself. When he realizes the importance of a problem, then he will earnestly absorb the pertinent material. True knowledge comes when somebody needs it. The purpose of having a student construct a "toy operating system" is to force the student to face some of the realities of software design.

In constructing the system the students are organized into teams of two or three. Coordinating their efforts in a software design project is an experience in itself. In an undergraduate computer science curriculum students write many programs, but they are usually "toy" programs which can be written without any discipline. A toy operating system is by no means a toy program. It is an intricate program which must be designed, implemented, and tested in an organized manner. A student has no hope of sitting in front of a piece of paper and getting all the ideas in a single stroke of lightning. Nor can he design an operating system, even a toy one, without really understanding much of the material described in various chapters of this book.

The main problem in giving students practical experience in operating systems is cost. They cannot be allowed to tamper with the production operating system of the university. It is too costly in terms of money and can degrade the service provided to other users. Therefore, an environment has to be generated which simulates many of the problems of an operating system. The main requirement in implementing such an environment is the existence of a language which allows coroutines or parallel processing, such as PL/I with multitasking. At the University of Toronto the toy system is programmed in the TOPPS language, which provides parallel processes and basic synchronization primitives [Holt and Kinread, 1972]. The TOPPS language does not use the multitasking capability of the system (that is, IBM OS/360), but rather simulates the multiprocessing in an interpretive manner. This has the effect of considerably reducing the cost of the programs and eliminating the possibility of deadlocking the real system.

The assignment is to write a spooled, multiprogrammed system in the parallel programming language. The entire system can be thought of as a group of cooperating hardware devices and software processes. The hardware devices are simulated by programs which are supplied to the students as part of the project specifications. Since the operating system is written in the same language that is used to simulate the hardware, the interface problems between the "hardware" and software are negligible. Elimination of hardware interface problems is one of the keys in reducing the scale of the assignment. On a real machine, hardware complexities would surely make the project unmanageable for a one-term course.

The assignment used at the University of Toronto is based on a toy operating system project designed by R. C. Holt. Similar projects have been documented in the literature [Shaw and Weiderman, 1971].

In the next section suggestions for designing a simulated machine are presented. Many of these suggestions are based on our experience [Czarnick, et al., 1973]. In Section III.3 the basic issues in writing a small operating system for the simulated machine are discussed.

III.2 Simulated Hardware

The main feature of the simulated hardware machine is that it provides a very clean interface for the toy operating system. It is best to avoid a complex interrupt or program trap structure and fancy machine language. Similarly, the commands which initiate each of the hardware devices should be simple. It is hard enough to write a system for a simple, well-designed machine. Although hardware complexities in the real world make for interesting implementation problems, they also make for a project which is too large for a one-semester course.

The hardware system consists of a reader, printer, CPU, main memory, and a secondary storage device, such as a drum. The heart of the system is the CPU, which executes user programs that are stored in main memory. Although any small, simple machine language which is easy to interpret will do as a user language, a more elegant assembly or high-level language may be attempted. Main memory, which can be represented by an array in the parallel programming language, stores user programs and data. The CPU is initiated by passing it a "process state word," which consists of the values of all of its internal registers, such as instruction counter, general registers, and page table register or base–limit register. The CPU then executes instructions until a program "interrupts." An interrupt may be due to an I/O request or to an attempted illegal action. The operating system must be invoked at this point to take appropriate action. The method of invocation depends on the control structures available in the parallel processing language.

The reader and printer can be started by passing a main memory address and perhaps a length field. The drum needs two addresses and an operation code indicating in which direction the data is to be moved. Again, the method by which these devices notify the toy operating system of I/O completion depends on the language being used.

The operating system for the machine is written in the parallel processing language, not in the user language. One way to visualize it is that the parallel processing language implements one user (that is, simulated-CPU) process, one simulated-printer process, one simulated-reader process, one simulated-drum process, and an arbitrary number of system processes. User programs can only execute on that one CPU process. Every system program is allowed to have its own virtual processor. The system processes must multiprogram the one user process among all the users.

The foregoing machine is only a suggested outline. Virtually any reasonable machine architecture is possible. However, in the context of a course, a complex machine is feasible only if the hardware simulation programs are given to the students as part of the project specifications. Even then, complex machines tend to need complex systems. Pedagogically, it may be better to keep the project simple [Czarnick, et al., 1973].

III.3   The Toy Operating System

The requirements of the toy operating system are to spool input and output and to execute users' jobs in a multiprogramming environment.

Most existing operating systems have at least these basic capabilities, namely, spooling and multiprogramming. The operating system reads incoming jobs from the reader and places them on the drum. As space becomes available, jobs are brought into main memory where they are multiprogrammed. When a job is suspended to wait for an I/O operation, another job may be given the CPU. Printed output from jobs is buffered in main memory and eventually placed back on the drum. Finally, the output is spooled from the drum to the printer. Naturally, many of these activities occur concurrently. That is, jobs are being read in and printed out in parallel with the operation of the drum and CPU.

The operating system must perform many functions. It reads new jobs onto the drum, prints completed jobs from the drum, loads jobs from the drum into main memory, services user program traps, schedules jobs for the CPU, and unloads jobs from main memory when they are completed. There are many possible structures for these independent facilities. Each facility may be a separate process, or several facilities may be grouped together into one process. For example, one type of organization is to associate one process with each of the three peripheral devices to queue requests to these devices. A fourth process can then be responsible for keeping track of user jobs and scheduling the CPU.

III.4   Conclusion

The toy operating system project described in the previous sections gives students an opportunity for practical design experience. Students become familiar with the different resources available in a system and their allocation schemes. However, there are problems of logistics in running such a project [Czarnick, et al., 1973].

The first problem is cost. Each team of students can consume approximately 15 minutes of IBM 370/165 time for the completion of the project. The reader can extrapolate this cost to his own machine. By most standards, this is rather expensive. Costs can be reduced somewhat by reducing the complexity of the system. It may also be advisable to limit the amount of computing time each team may spend. In any case, experimenting with operating systems cannot be very cheap.

The second problem with the project is complexity. Many undergraduate students find it hard to complete the project in a one-semester course. Students should be encouraged to keep their system simple. Alternatively, students may be given a very simple uniprogrammed system as part of the project specifications and be asked to expand it into a spooled, multiprogrammed system for the project. This procedure has the extra advantage of cutting down the costs of running the project.

The third problem is initial effort. It takes some work to start the project. Many computer installations do not support a parallel processing language, which is clearly an essential ingredient. Also, an assignment of this size requires detailed specifications. A complete description of the assignment will typically run from 10 to 20 pages [Czarnick, *et al.*, 1973].

The fourth problem is operational. Supervising such a project takes quite a bit of time. Students should be graded for their overall performance, including quality of the design, documentation, number of runs needed, etc. Also, grading of the projects is time consuming. Teaching assistants for the course should be good program readers.

At the University of Toronto students have been enthusiastic about the project and find it a worthwhile experience. However, ambitious system designs sometimes put a tremendous load on the students, affecting their work in other courses and upsetting the administration with late course grades. Nevertheless, if the project is well specified and details such as the hardware simulation programs are given in advance, then a basic system such as the one described in Section III.3 can be completed by most students with approximately the amount of effort commensurate with a one-semester course.

ANNOTATED REFERENCES

CACM   Communications of the Association for Computing Machinery
JACM   Journal of the Association for Computing Machinery
SJCC   Spring Joint Computer Conference
FJCC   Fall Joint Computer Conference
AFIPS   American Federation of Information Processing Societies

Abate, J., and Dubner, H. [1969]. "Optimizing The Performance of a Drum-Like Storage," *IEEE Trans. Computers* 18, No. 11 (Nov.), 992–997.

A fixed-head storage device with one head per track is analyzed under the shortest-rotational-latency-time-first queuing discipline. The work was motivated by a newly introduced hardware device which scheduled according to that algorithm. The system is described and an analytic estimate of average queue length and waiting time is presented.

Aho, A. V., Denning, P. J., and Ullman, J. D. [1971]. "Principles of Optimal Page Replacement," *JACM* 18, No. 1 (Jan.), 80–93.

It is shown that under certain assumptions, demand paging does at least as well as any other page placement rule. A theoretical model is then developed to examine the cost of certain page replacement algorithms.

Alexander, C. [1964]. *Notes on the Synthesis of Form.* Harvard Univ. Press, Cambridge, Massachusetts.

267

This book is an architect's view of the design of large systems (for example, towns). Emphasis is placed on finding natural decompositions of the system into subparts.

Alsberg, P. A., and Mills, C. R. [1969]. "The Structure Of The ILLIAC IV Operating System," *Proc. Second ACM Symp. Operating Systems Principles* (Oct.), 92–96.

The operating system for the ILLIAC IV array computer is described. A Burroughs B6500 is linked to the system and performs most of the operating system functions. The unique underlying hardware makes this system description particularly interesting.

Atwood, J. W. (ed.), Clark, B. L., Grushcow, M. S., Holt, R. C., Horning, J. J., Sevcik, K. C., and Tsichritzis, D. [1972]. *Project SUE Status Rep.,* Tech. Rep. CSRG-11. Comput. Systems Res. Group, Univ. of Toronto, Toronto.

This is the first major document describing Project SUE. The system has evolved considerably since this report, outdating some of its contents.

Baer, J. L. [1973]. "A Survey of Some Theoretical Aspects of Multiprocessing," *ACM Comput. Surveys* 5, No. 1 (Mar.), 31–80.

Programming language features, theoretical models, and analyses of performance for multiprocessor systems are surveyed. An extensive bibliography and an appendix on hardware multiprocessing are included.

Baker, F. T. [1972]. "Chief Programmer Team Management of Production Programming," *IBM Systems J.* 11, No. 3, 56–71.

The chief programmer technique for project management is discussed in the context of the *New York Times* information bank project.

Ballard, A. J., and Tsichritzis, D. [1973]. "Structure and Correctness of Systems," *Proc. Canad. Comput. Conf.,* Edmonton (June), 324–340.

Special problems in the verification of large systems are discussed. An approach to operating system correctness is outlined.

Bard, Y. [1971]. "Performance Criteria And Measurement In A Time-Sharing System," *IBM Systems J.* 19, No. 3, 193–216.

Statistical methods are discussed for evaluating the CP-67 operating system before and after certain modifications. The methods measure the effect of changes and distinguish among sources of the effects.

Belady, L. A. [1966]. "A Study of Replacement Algorithms For A Virtual Storage Computer," *IBM Systems J.* 5, No. 2, 78–101.

Page replacement algorithms are classified based on the amount of information they need about the program. An optimal algorithm is described (see also Mattson *et al.* [1970]) and simulation results for some of the algorithms are discussed.

Belady, L. A., and Kuehner, C. J. [1969]. "Dynamic Space-Sharing In Computer Systems," *CACM* 12, No. 5 (May), 282–288.

A method is proposed for analyzing memory space versus processor time trade-offs. Two page replacement algorithms are compared using this approach (see Section 5.4.4.1).

Belady, L. A., and Lehman, M. M. [1971]. *Programming System Dynamics or the Meta-Dynamics of Systems in Maintenance and Growth,* No. RC3546, IBM Res. Center, Yorktown Heights, New York (Sept.).

A model for the growth of large programming systems is proposed. With time, software is modified and consequently becomes more complex, making it more difficult to maintain. The authors argue that exponential growth in maintenance effort is inevitable in some large software systems. This implies a guaranteed finite life-span for these systems.

Belady, L. A., Nelson, R. A., and Shedler, G. S. [1969]. "An Anomaly In Space-Time Characteristics of Certain Programs Running In A Paging Environment," *CACM* **12**, No. 6 (June), 349–353.

It is shown that for FIFO page replacement, increasing the memory allocation can increase the number of page faults under anomalous referencing patterns. It is shown by Mattson *et al.* [1970] that "stack" algorithms are not subject to this FIFO effect (see also 5.4.2.2).

Bell, C. G., and Gold, M. M. [1971]. "An Introduction to the Structure of Time-Shared Computers," *Advances in Information Sci.* **4**, 161–272.

The structure and external characteristics of time-shared computer system hardware and time-shared operating systems are discussed. A case study of the PDP-10 is included as an example.

Bernstein, A. J., and Sharp, J. C. [1971]. "A Policy-Driven Scheduler For A Time-Sharing System," *CACM* **14**, No. 2 (Feb.), 74–78.

The scheduling algorithm described is based on a policy function associated with each user. Each function specifies how much service a user should receive as a function of time. User priority then varies with the difference between the expected service in the policy function and the actual attained service. The algorithm is analyzed and a specific implementation of it is discussed.

Bernstein, A. J., Detlefsen, G. D., and Kerr, R. H. [1969]. "Process Control And Communication," *Proc. Second ACM Symp. Operating Systems Principles* (Oct.), pp. 60–66.

A mechanism is described for interprocess communication using queues of events. Event operations include CAUSE and MODIFY and their inverse operations UNCAUSE and DELETE. This facility is an interesting alternative to those discussed in Chapter 2.

Bernstein, P. A. [1973]. *Description Problems in the Modeling of Asynchronous Computer Systems,* Tech. Rep. No. 48. Dept. of Comput. Sci., Univ. of Toronto, Toronto.

Twelve models for parallel systems are described and compared, based on their descriptive power. The report includes an extensive bibliography on program schemata.

Brawn, B. S., and Gustavson, F. G. [1968]. "Program Behavior In A Paging Environment," *Proc. AFIPS* 33, Pt. II, *FJCC*, pp. 1019–1032.

Automatic memory management is examined from the user's viewpoint. Results of the study suggest that programming style can be considerably more important than replacement algorithm for overall paging efficiency.

Brinch Hansen, P. [1970]. "The Nucleus Of A Multiprogramming System," *CACM* 13, No. 4 (Apr.), 238–241.

This paper describes the RC4000 nucleus. The system is a hierarchy of cooperating processes which communicate via mailboxes. The system provides a software base on which a variety of operating systems can be built (see also Section 1.4).

Brinch Hansen, P. [1971]. "Short-Term Scheduling In Multiprogramming Systems," *Proc. Third ACM Symp. Operating Systems Principles* (Oct.), pp. 101–105.

A set of algorithms are presented which describe a short-term scheduler for a multilevel scheduling scheme (see also Section 3.4). The algorithms are detailed and lead naturally into an actual implementation.

Buxton, J. N., and Randell, B. (eds.) [1970]. *Software Engineering Techniques.* NATO Sci. Affairs Div., Brussels.

This report documents the 1969 NATO Conference on Software Engineering. The report includes material on program correctness, software portability, and case studies of several large systems.

Calingaert, P. [1967]. "System Performance Evaluation: Survey and Appraisal," *CACM* 10, No. 1 (Jan.), 12–18.

Performance goals of computer systems are defined and basic techniques for analysis, simulation, and synthesis are discussed.

Clark, B. L., and Horning, J. J. [1971]. "The System Language for Project SUE," *ACM SIGPLAN Notices* 6, No. 9 (Oct.), 79–88.

The SUE System language, a system implementation language drawing heavily on PASCAL, is described in this paper.

Coffman, Jr., E. G. [1969]. "Analysis of a Drum Input/Output Queue under Scheduled Operation in a Paged Computer System," *JACM* 16, No. 1 (Jan.), 73–90.

Mathematical models are used to measure utilization, average queue length, and average waiting time for drums operating in the role of auxiliary memory.

Coffman, E. G., Jr. and Denning, P. J. [1973]. *Operating System Theory.* Prentice-Hall, Englewood Cliffs, New Jersey.

Different aspects of modeling and analysis of problems in operating systems are presented. It is a good reference book for an analytic treatment of resource allocation problems.

Coffman, Jr., E. G., and Kleinrock, L. [1968]. "'Computer Scheduling Measures And Their Countermeasures," *Proc. AFIPS* 32, *SJCC*, pp. 11–21.

Major methods of job scheduling are summarized along with user tactics for exploiting the weaknesses of each method.

Coffman, Jr., E. G., and Randell, B. [1971]. "Performance Prediction for Extended Paged Memories," *Acta Informat.* 1, Fasc. 1, 1–13.

The authors develop a model for extending the size of a paged memory. Given the page reference trace of a program, their analytic technique can predict the performance of a paging algorithm when the number of core page frames is increased.

Coffman, Jr., E. G., and Ryan, Jr., T. A. [1972]. "A Study of Storage Partitioning Using a Mathematical Model of Locality," *CACM* 15, No. 3 (Mar.), 185–190.

A mathematical model of partition size in a paged environment is presented. It is shown that fixed partitions are acceptable when variations in working set size are "small."

Coffman, Jr., E. G., and Varian, L. C. [1968]. "Further Experimental Data On The Behavior Of Programs In A Paging Environment," *CACM* 11, No. 7 (July), 471–474.

Experimental results are summarized on the page fault behavior under different replacement algorithms for several programs (see also Section 5.4.4.1).

Coffman, Jr., E. G., Elphick, M., and Shoshani, A. [1971]. "System Deadlocks," *ACM Comput. Surveys* 3, No. 2 (June), 67–78.

This survey briefly describes some of the major work done on deadlocks in systems with serially reusable resources. Deadlock detection is treated for cases where a process's exact resource requirements are known in advance, where only its maximum resource requirements are known in advance, and where resource requirements are not known until requested.

Comeau, L. W. [1967]. "A Study of the Effect of User Program Optimization in a Paging System," *Proc. ACM Symp. Operating System Principles,* 7 pp.

An experiment in user program effects on paging behavior showed that user optimization significantly improved overall performance of the paging system.

Conway, M. E. [1963]. "Design of a Separable Transition Diagram Compiler," *CACM* 8, No. 7 (July), 396–408.

Methods of designing COBOL compilers are discussed. This paper is particularly well known for its introduction of the concept of coroutines.

Conway, M. E. [1968]. "How do Committees Invent?," *Datamation* 14, No. 4 (Apr.), 29–32.

The thesis that the structure of a system resembles the structure of the organization which produces it is presented. The author also discusses effects this observation should have on the structure of the design group.

Conway, R. W., Maxwell, W. L., and Morgan, H. L. [1972]. "On the Implementation of Security Measures in Information Systems," *CACM* 15, No. 4 (Apr.), 211–220.

The security matrix model is defined and is shown to be sufficient to mode a number of existing security systems.

Corbato, F. J. [1969]. "PL/I As A Tool For System Programming," *Datamatio* **15,** No. 5 (May), 68–76.

Reasons why PL/I was chosen as the programming language for the MULTIC project are discussed. The paper is good supplementary reading for Section 9.2.

Corbato, F. J., and Saltzer, J. H. [1969]. "Some Considerations Of Supervisor Prc gram Design For Multiplexed Computer Systems," *Proc. IFIP Congr. 1968,* pp 315–321. North-Holland Publ., Amsterdam.

Problems related to multiplexing and those arising from sharing of informatio are discussed. Time-sharing systems are given special treatment.

Courtois, P. J., Heymans, F., and Parnas, D. L. [1971]. "Concurrent Control wit 'Readers' and 'Writers'," *CACM* **14,** No. 10 (Oct.), 667–668.

Two solutions to the reader–writer problem (discussed in the exercises for Chapte 2) are presented.

Czarnik, B. [editor], Tsichritzis, D., Ballard, A. J., Dryer, M., Holt, R. C., Weiss man, L. [1973]. *A Student Project for an Operating System Course,* CSRG-2§ Computer Systems Research Group, Univ. of Toronto.

This technical report includes a description of the 000/Z toy operating syste▮ project and a users' manual for the TOPPS parallel processing language. Example of 000/Z, written in TOPPS, are included.

Dahl, O.-J., Dijkstra, E. W., and Hoare, C. A. R. [1972]. *Structured Programming* Academic Press, New York.

This book contains three essays on structured programming. The first pape Dijkstra's "Notes on Structured Programming," presents a systematic method ▮ top-down program design. Hoare's "Notes on Data Structuring" presents simila concepts applied to data structures. The third essay synthesizes earlier concep▮ in the context of the Simula 67 language.

Denning, P. J. [1968]. "The Working Set Model For Program Behavior," *CAC▮* **11,** No. 5 (May), 323–333.

This is Denning's original paper outlining the major concepts of the working-s▮ model (see also Section 5.4.1).

Denning, P. J. [1970]. "Virtual Memory," *ACM Comput. Surveys* **2,** No. 3 (Sept. 153–190.

This survey presents an extensive discussion of most aspects of virtual memor systems. It includes a very complete bibliography on the area.

Denning, P. J., and Schwartz, S. C. [1972]. "Properties of the Working Set Model, *CACM* **15,** No. 3 (Mar.), 191–198.

Several mathematical observations about working sets are discussed, includin the relation between working-set size and missing-page rate, the distribution ▮ working-set size, and effects of interpage dependencies on working-set size.

Denning, P. J., Dennis, J. B., Lampson, B. W., Habermann, A. N., Muntz, R. R., and Tsichritzis, D. [1971]. *An Undergraduate Course on Operating System Principles.* Cosine Committee on Education of the Nat. Acad. of Engrng., Washington, D.C.

This report, written by Cosine Task Force VIII, describes a complete course on operating systems. The outline forms the basic organization of this book.

Dennis, J. B. [1965]. "Segmentation And The Design of Multiprogrammed Computer Systems," *JACM* **12**, No. 4 (Oct.), 589–602.

A number of different addressing mechanisms are discussed in the context of name space, memory space, and address space. Flexibility of the address scheme in the context of sharing, protection, and dynamic allocation is emphasized.

Dennis, J. B. [1969]. "Programming Generality, Parallelism And Computer Architecture," *Proc. IFIP Congr. 1968*, pp. 484, 492. North-Holland Publ., Amsterdam.

System parallelism is discussed from the point of view of program schemata.

Dennis, J. B. [1971]. "Coroutines and Parallel Computation," *Proc. Fifth Annu. Princeton Conf. Information Sci. and Systems*, pp. 293–294.

The concept of coroutine [Conway, 1963] is discussed in the context of processes which execute concurrently.

Dennis, J. B., and Van Horn, E. C. [1966]. "Programming Semantics For Multiprogrammed Computations," *CACM* **9**, No. 3 (Mar.), 143–155.

This is one of the first papers describing terminology and concepts in multiprogrammed systems. Capability lists and hierarchical directories are emphasized.

Dijkstra, E. W. [1965]. "Solution to a Problem in Concurrent Programming Control," *CACM* **8**, No. 9 (Sept.), 569.

The n-process mutual exclusion solution, an extension of Dekker's two-process solution, is presented in this paper.

Dijkstra, E. W. [1968a]. "Cooperating Sequential Processes," in *Programming Languages* (F. Genuys, ed.), pp. 43–112. Academic Press, New York.

Semaphores, critical section problems, and deadlock prevention are discussed in this now classic paper on process synchronization.

Dijkstra, E. W. [1968b]. "The Structure Of The T.H.E. Multiprogramming System," *CACM* **11**, No. 5 (May), 341–346.

This paper presents a brief description of the THE system, including a description of the bottom-up design approach and a definition of semaphores.

Dijkstra, E. W. [1968c]. "Go To Statement Considered Harmful," *CACM* **11**, No. 3 (Mar.), 147–148.

In this famous "letter to the editor," Dijkstra outlines his fundamental objections to the GO TO statement.

Dijkstra, E. W. [1971]. "Hierarchical Ordering of Sequential Processes," *Acta Informat.* 1, Fasc. 2, 115–138.

Semaphores and secretaries (that is, Hoare's monitor) are discussed relative to the problem of making nondeterministic hardware interactions into a synchronous virtual machine.

Doherty, W. J. [1970]. "Scheduling TSS/360 For Responsiveness," *Proc. AFIPS* 37, *FJCC*, pp. 97–111.

By careful and methodical adjustments of parameters in the table-driven scheduler for TSS/360, performance was improved considerably. The adjustments were made relative to working-set size and current core allocation. Motivation for the work, the adjustments themselves, and performance results are discussed in detail.

Donovan, J. J. [1972]. *Systems Programming.* McGraw-Hill, New York.

This textbook is an IBM-oriented approach to programming problems in assemblers, linkage editors, loaders, compilers, and operating systems.

Earl, D. P., and Bugely, F. L. [1969]. "Basic Time-Sharing: A System of Computing Principles," *Proc. Second ACM Symp. Operating Systems Principles* (Oct.) pp. 75–79.

This paper is an attempt at systematizing some definitions and design principles of operating systems.

Easton, W. B. [1971]. "Process Synchronization Without Long-Term Interlock," *Proc. Third ACM Symp. Operating Systems Principles* (Oct.), pp. 95–100.

A "version number" is associated with each block of critical data in a file system. A check must be made on the version number before and after accessing a block. The approach is shown to avoid the necessity of locking processes out of a file for long time periods.

Elspas, B., Green, M. W., and Levitt, K. N. [1971]. "Software Reliability," *Computer* 4, No. 1 (Jan.–Feb.), 21–27.

Basic issues in language design and program verification are discussed in the context of software reliability.

Elspas, B., Levitt, K. N., Waldinger, R. J., and Wakeman, A. [1972]. "An Assessment of Techniques for Proving Program Correctness," *ACM Comput. Surveys* 4, No. 2 (June), 97–147.

This extensive survey discusses both the theoretical background and practical considerations in proofs of program correctness, both manually and automatically.

Fabry, R. S. [1973]. "The Case for Capability-Based Computers," *Fourth Symposium on Operating System Principles* (Oct.).

This paper proposes the free use of capabilities as addresses in a computer system. After arguing why such a structure is beneficial, the author discusses implementation considerations in a capability based machine.

Floyd, R. W. [1971]. "Toward the Interactive Design of Correct Programs," *Proc. IFIP 1971*, Booklet TA-1, pp. 1–4.

A conversation between a programmer and an interactive program verifier is hypothesized. The author concludes by outlining what he believes a feasible program verifier might be able to do.

Fontao, R. O. [1971]. "A Concurrent Algorithm For Avoiding Deadlocks," *Proc. Third ACM Symp. Operating Systems Principles* (Oct.), pp. 72–79.

A deadlock prevention algorithm is described which runs in parallel with the process it services. The algorithm maintains a table of safe states which is updated as resource requests and releases are granted.

Foster, C. C. [1971]. "An Unclever Time-Sharing System," *ACM Comput. Surveys* 3, No. 1 (Mar.), 23–48.

UMASS-2, a small time-sharing system for the CDC 3600, is described.

Fuchs, E., and Jackson, P. E. [1970]. "Estimates of Distributions of Random Variables For Certain Computer Communications Traffic Models," *CACM* 13, No. 12 (Dec.), 752–757.

A model for user–computer interactions is proposed and shown to behave consistently with measurements from real systems.

Fuller, S. H., and Baskett, F. [1972]. *An Analysis of Drum Storage Units,* Tech. Rep. No. 26. Digital Systems Lab., Stanford Electron. Lab. Stanford Univ., Stanford, California (Aug.).

FIFO and shortest-latency-time-first drum scheduling algorithms are analyzed by using a probabilistic model.

Gaines, R. S. [1971]. "An Operating System Based On The Concept Of A Supervisory Computer," *Proc. Third ACM Symp. Operating Systems Principles* (Oct.), pp. 17–23.

A small supervisor, similar to the SUE kernel, for an operating system implemented on a CDC 6600 is described and evaluated.

Gear, C. W. [1969]. *Computer Organization and Programming.* McGraw-Hill, New York.

This text provides an introduction to hardware, I/O, assembler, sorting and searching, and compiling.

Gotlieb, C. C., and Borodin, A. [1973]. *Social Issues in Computing.* Academic Press, New York.

This book covers a broad range of issues relating to the effects of computers on society. In particular, the chapter on privacy is relevant to Section 7.6.

Gotlieb, C. C., and MacEwan, G. H. [1970]. "System Evaluation Tools," in *Software Engineering Techniques* (J. N. Buxton, and B. Randell, ed.), pp. 93–99. NATO Sci. Affairs Div., Brussels.

The application of modeling and monitoring to various phases of system design is discussed.

Graham, G. S., and Denning, P. J. [1971]. *Protection: Principles and Practice*, Tech. Rep. No. 101. Dept. of Elec. Enging., Princeton Univ., Princeton, New Jersey (Nov.).

An access matrix model for protection is discussed. Implications of the model for the design of operating systems are also treated.

Graham, R. M. [1968]. "Protection In An Information Processing Utility," *CACM* 11, No. 5 (May), 365–369.

An abstract model for the MULTICS protection mechanism which uses levels called "rings" is described.

Graham, R. M., Clancy, G. J., and DeVancey, D. B. [1971]. "A Software Design and Evaluation System," *Proc. ACM/SIGOPS Workshop on System Performance Evaluation*, pp. 200–213.

This paper describes the DES language for system design, evaluation, and implementation. The main feature of the system is the ability to obtain performance estimates by simulation during the design process.

Gries, D. [1971]. *Compiler Construction for Digital Computers.* Wiley, New York.

This book constitutes an introduction to compiler writing, covering parsing and code generation techniques as well as global organizational considerations.

Habermann, A. N. [1969]. "Prevention of System Deadlocks," *CACM* 12, No. 7 (July), 373–377, 385.

Several algorithms for deadlock prevention are described in relation to a state model of resource allocation. In particular, the notions of safe states and safe transitions are formalized.

Habermann, A. N. [1972]. "Synchronization Of Communicating Processes," *CACM* 15, No. 3 (Mar.), 171–176.

An invariance relation is used to formalize a process synchronization mechanism. The formalism is used to prove some properties about communicating processes.

Havender, J. W. [1968]. "Avoiding Deadlock In Multitasking Systems," *IBM Systems J.* 7, No. 2, 74–84.

The methods used to avoid deadlock in IBM OS/360 MVT are presented.

Hebalkar, P. G. [1970]. "Coordinated Sharing of Resources in Asynchronous Systems," *Record Project MAC Conf. Concurrent Systems and Parallel Comput., Woods Hole, Massachusetts,* pp. 151–168.

A model similar to Petri nets is used to examine deadlock properties in systems where partial descriptions of process behavior are known in advance.

Hoare, C. A. R. [1969]. "An Axiomatic Approach to Computer Programming," *CACM* 12, No. 10 (Oct.), 576–580.

Sets of axioms and rules of inference for programs are defined. These concepts are applied in the hand verification of a simple program.

Hoare, C. A. R. [1971]. "Proof of a Program: FIND," *CACM* **14**, No. 1 (Jan.), 39–45.

In verifying the correctness of a search algorithm, the author develops a general method for hand proofs of program correctness.

Hoare, C. A. R., and Perrot, R. H. (eds.), [1972]. *Operating Systems Techniques*. Academic Press, New York.

The book contains the proceedings of the International Seminar on Operating Systems Techniques held in Belfast, 1971. Excerpts from discussion groups are also included.

Hoffman, L. J. [1969]. "Computers and Privacy: A Survey," *ACM Comput. Surveys* **1**, No. 2 (June), 85–104.

Legal and technical problems relating to privacy are discussed. The article includes a large, annotated bibliography.

Holt, A. W., and Commoner, F. [1970]. "Events and Conditions," *Record Project MAC Conf. Concurrent Systems and Parallel Comput., Woods Hole, Massachusetts*, pp. 3–52.

Petri nets are described, analyzed, and applied to a number of simple problems involving parallel operations.

Holt, R. C. [1972]. "Some Deadlock Properties of Computer Systems," *ACM Comput. Surveys* **4**, No. 3 (Sept.), 179–195.

Several graph theoretic models are used to develop algorithms for deadlock detection and prevention (see also Sections 2.7 and II.3).

Holt, R. C., and Kinread, R. [1972]. "Teaching and Using High Level Concurrent Programming," *Proc. Canad. Comput. Conf., Montreal*, pp. 214202–214212.

A high-level language, called TOPPS, which allows parallel processing is introduced. Using TOPPS, the authors discuss how basic concepts in concurrent programming can be taught.

Horning, J. J., and Randell, B. [1973]. "Process Structuring," *ACM Comput. Surveys* **5**, No. 1 (Mar.). 5–30.

This paper gives precise definitions of many terms relating to parallel processes. Many concepts in system structure, such as virtual machines and levels of abstraction, are also considered.

Huberman, B. J. [1970]. *Principles of Operation of the Venus Microprogram*, MITRE Tech. Rep. MTR-1843. The MITRE Corp., Bedford, Massachusetts.

The microprogrammed and hardware virtual machine of the Venus system is described in detail in this report.

IBM System/360 Operating System: Concepts and Facilities [1965]. Form C28-6535-0. Data Processing Div., IBM Corp. White Plains, New York.

This is an introductory document on the operating system for the IBM/360 family of machines.

Ichbiah, J. D. and Rissen, J. P. [1971]. *Directions de Travail pour un Atelier de Software: Rapport Préliminaire,* Compagnie Internationale Pour l'Informatique, Paris (Oct.), pp. 3–9.

The authors propose a software laboratory environment where tools for reliable software can be constructed.

Karp, R. M., and Miller, R. E. [1969]. "Parallel Program Schemata," *J. Comput. System Sci.* 3, No. 2 (May), 147–195.

This rather difficult paper presents a model for parallel computation similar to that described in Section II.2. It is one of the major papers on the subject of program schemata.

Keefe, D. D. [1968]. "Hierarchical Control Programs For Systems Evaluation," *IBM Systems J.* 7, No. 2, 123–133.

A method of testing system programs is discussed where the system runs in unprivileged mode and a special monitor, running in privileged mode, services the program's I/O and collects data.

Kernighan, B. W. [1969]. "Optimal Segmentation Points For Programs," *Proc. Second ACM Symp. Operating Systems Principles* (Oct.), pp. 47–53.

Programs are modeled as graphs where nodes represent instructions or data items and directed edges represent transitions among them. A linear time algorithm is described which finds the optimal break points in the program for paging behavior under certain assumptions.

Kernighan, B. W., and Plaugher, P. J. [1973]. "Programming Style for Programmers and Language Designers," *Record IEEE Symp. Comput. Software Reliability,* New York, pp. 148–154.

Programs written in a good style are more likely to be good programs than those written in a bad style. A number of principles and examples of programming style are discussed with respect to their effects on program reliability.

Kilburn, T., Edwards, D. B. G., Lanigan, M. J., and Sumner, F. H. [1962]. "One-level Storage System," *IRE Trans. Electron. Comput.* EC-11, No. 2 (Apr.), 223–234.

This paper presents a brief description of the Atlas machine and follows with a general method of constructing a virtual memory using core and drum.

King, J. C. [1969]. *A Program Verifier.* Ph.D. Thesis, Dept. of Comput. Sci., Carnegie-Mellon Univ., Pittsburgh, Pennsylvania.

The author describes the construction of a verifying compiler which, in addition to compiling code, checks that the programmer's assertions are consistent with what the program actually does.

Kleinrock, L. [1970]. "A Continuum Of Time Sharing Scheduling Algorithms," *Proc. AFIPS 36, SJCC,* pp. 453–458.

A class of scheduling algorithms is obtained by varying two parameters of a linear priority function. One of the algorithms, selfish round robin, is given a complete analysis.

Knuth, D. [1966]. "Additional Comments on a Problem in Concurrent Programming Control," *CACM* 9, No. 5 (May), 321–322.

Knuth describes a problem with Dijkstra's solution to the n-process mutual exclusion problem [Dijkstra, 1965] and proposes a solution to it.

Knuth, D. [1968]. "Fundamental Algorithms," *The Art Of Computer Programming*, Vol. I. Addison Wesley, Reading, Massachusetts.

The second half of this excellent book is a complete treatment of data structures and their manipulation. (See also Appendix I.)

Kuck, D. J., and Lawrie, D. H. [1970]. "The Use And Performance Of Memory Hierarchies: A Survey," in *Software Engineering*, Vol. 1, pp. 45–78. Academic Press, New York.

Memory hierarchies are discussed in terms of structure, cost savings, program behavior, and effects on overall system performance. A number of experimental results are cited.

Lampson, B. W. [1968]. "A Scheduling Philosophy For Multiprocessing Systems," *CACM* 11, No. 5 (May), 347–360.

Basic concepts on the protection and scheduling of processes are reviewed, including capabilities, two-level scheduling, and hardware implementation of scheduling algorithms.

Lampson, B. W. [1969]. "Dynamic Protection Structures," *Proc. AFIPS* 35, *FJCC*, pp. 27–38.

A general model for viewing domains, capabilities, and access keys is outlined, with consideration of both theoretical and practical aspects.

Lampson, B. W. [1971]. "Protection," *Proc. Fifth Annu. Princeton Conf. Information Sci. and Systems*, pp. 437–443.

This paper develops most of the major abstract concepts on protection. Protection models for domains, access matrices, capabilities, and memory protection are discussed.

Lewis, P. A. W., and Shedler, G. S. [1971]. "A Cyclic-queue Model Of System Overhead In Multiprogrammed Computer Systems," *JACM* 18, No. 2 (Apr.), 199–220.

A complex probabilistic model of a demand-paged multiprogrammed system is described.

Liptay, J. S. [1968]. "Structural Aspects Of The System/360 Model 85: II The Cache," *IBM Systems J.* 7, No. 1, 15–21.

The cache memory, a high-speed buffer memory between core and the CPU for the IBM 360/85, is described.

Liskov, B. H. [1972]. "The Design Of The Venus Operating System," *CACM* 15, No. 3 (Mar.), 144–149.

This paper presents a description of the essential characteristics of the Venus system's software (see also Chapter 10).

London, R. L. [1970]. "Proving Programs are Correct: Some Techniques and Examples," *BIT* **10**, 168–182.

Five techniques for manual program correctness proofs are outlined and examples of each method are presented.

Lucas, H. C. [1971]. "Performance Evaluation and Monitoring," *ACM Comput. Surveys* **3**, No. 3 (Sept.), 79–91.

This paper presents a nontechnical survey of most well-known performance evaluation techniques.

Luconi, F. L. [1968]. *Asynchronous Computational Structures*, MAC-TR-49. Ph.D. Thesis Dept. of Elec. Engrng., M.I.T., Cambridge, Massachusetts.

The "computational schemata" model for concurrent systems is presented. Certain properties relating to determinism and intercommunication of processes are given a theoretical treatment.

MacDougall, M. H. [1970]. "Computer System Simulation: An Introduction," *ACM Comput. Surveys* **2**, No. 3 (Sept.), 191–209.

General simulation techniques and a model for simulating a disk-based multiprogrammed system are discussed. The paper includes an annotated bibliography on the simulation of computer systems.

McIlroy, M. D. [1969]. "Mass Produced Software Components," in *Software Engineering* (P. Naur and B. Randell, eds.), pp. 138–155. NATO Sci. Affairs Div., Brussels.

This informal paper discusses the feasibility of off-the-shelf modules for software systems and examines questions relating to the production of such modules.

McKeeman, W. M., Horning, J. J., and Wortman, D. B. [1970]. *A Compiler Generator*. Prentice-Hall, New Jersey.

An introductory text on compiler writing based on the XPL compiler writing system.

McKellar, A. C., and Coffman, Jr., E. G. [1969]. "Organizing Matrices and Matrix Operations for Paged Memory Systems," *CACM* **12**, No. 3 (Mar.), 153–165.

By rearranging the pagination of matrices, the authors obtained dramatic improvements in paging behavior.

McKinney, J. M. [1969]. "A Survey of Analytical Time-Sharing Models," *ACM Comput. Surveys* **1**, No. 2 (June), 105–116.

This paper surveys queuing models for scheduling algorithms, including round robin, foreground-background, and feedback queues. The paper concludes with an annotated bibliography.

Madnik, S. E., and Alsop, J. W. [1969]. "A Modular Approach To File System Design," *Proc. AFIPS* **34**, *SJCC*, pp. 1–14.

A multiple-level approach to file system construction is outlined. This is the basis of the structure presented in Chapter 6.

Marshland, T. A., and Tartar, J. [1973]. "A Course in Minicomputer Systems," *ACM SIGCSE Bull.* **5**, No. 1 (Feb.), 153–156.

An outline of a course on minicomputers is described. Goals of the course, project areas, and the selection of an appropriate minicomputer are discussed.

Mattson, R., Gecsei, J., Slutz, D., and Traiger, I. [1970]. "Evaluation Techniques for Storage Hierarchies," *IBM Systems J.* **9**, No. 2, 78–117.

Memory hierarchies in a paged environment are analyzed. Properties of a class of replacement algorithms, called "stack algorithms," are discussed and one stack algorithm is proven to be optimal.

Mealy, G. H. [1967]. "Operating Systems (Excerpts)," in *Programming Systems and Languages* (S. Rosen, ed.), pp. 516–534. McGraw-Hill, New York.

This is a very general, IBM-oriented discussion of operating systems concentrating on I/O and the supervisor.

Mealy, G. H. [1969]. "The System Design Cycle," *Proc. Second ACM Symp. Operating Systems Principles* (Oct.), pp. 1–7.

This paper reviews system development problems which relate to organizational difficulties. Conway's law is cited. The material is related to Section 8.4.

Mealy, G. H., Witt, B. I., and Clark, W. A. [1966]. "The Functional Structure of OS/360," *IBM Systems J.* **5**, No. 1, 2–51.

A unified overview of the OS operating system for the IBM System/360 is presented.

Mills, H. [1971]. "Top Down Programming in Large Systems," in *Debugging Techniques in Large Systems* (R. Rustin, ed.), pp. 41–55. Prentice-Hall, Englewood Cliffs, New Jersey.

The two basic concepts of structured programming, namely, successive refinement and simple control structures, are discussed as part of an overall approach to program design.

Mills, H. [1972]. *Mathematical Foundations of Structured Programming*, N. FSC72-6012. IBM Federal Systems Div.

The paper is centered around a result showing that any program can be written using only IF–THEN–ELSE, BLOCK, and DO–UNTIL control structures (that is, no GO TOs). Fundamental predicates for proving the correctness of a program written top down using these control structures are also presented.

Mills, H. [1973]. "On the Development of Large Reliable Programs," *Record 1973 IEEE Symp. Comput. Software Reliability, New York,* pp. 155–159.

An overview of structured programming techniques and their effects on the construction of large, reliable software systems is presented.

Morenoff, E., and McLean, J. B. [1967]. "An Approach To Standardizing Computer Systems," *Proc. ACM Nat. Conf., 22nd,* pp. 527–536.

In view of frequent hardware changes in many installations, the problem of program compatibility among machines is significant. The authors examine this problem and provide some direction toward eventual standardization.

Morse, P. M. [1958]. *Queues, Inventories, and Maintenance.* Wiley, New York.

This textbook is one of the early documents surveying the theory of queues.

Murphy, J. E. [1968]. "Resource Allocation With Interlock Detection In A Multi-Task System," *Proc. AFIPS* 33, Pt. II, *FJCC,* pp. 1169–1176.

A queue management technique and matrix-based bookkeeping method for resource allocation is discussed. A deadlock detection algorithm using this scheme is presented.

Naur, P., and B. Randell (eds.) [1969]. *Software Engineering.* NATO Sci. Affairs Div., Brussels.

A synopsis of working papers, discussions, and workshops from the 1968 NATO Conference on Software Engineering is reported in this volume.

Neumann, P. G. [1969]. "The Role Of Motherhood In The Pop Art Of System Programming," *Proc. Second ACM Symp. Operating Systems Principles* (Oct.), pp. 13–18.

Common-sense principles of system design and implementation are discussed. About a dozen such principles are presented, and reasons are given why these principles are frequently ignored. The presentation is succinct, amusing, and informative.

Oppenheimer, G., and Weizer, N. [1968]. "Resource Management for a Medium Scale Time-Sharing Operating System," *CACM* 11, No. 5 (May), 313–322.

Problems in scheduling, resource allocation, and memory management are discussed in relation to the design of the RCA Spectra 70/46 Time-Sharing Operating System.

Organick, E. I. [1972]. *The Multics System: An Examination of its Structure.* MIT Press, Cambridge, Massachusetts.

Scattered information about the MULTICS system has been consolidated into this highly readable description. It is among the better published descriptions of a well-known operating system.

Organick, E. I. [1973]. *Computer System Organization—The B5700/B6700 Series.* Academic Press, New York.

This book describes the close interrelation between software structure and the hardware architecture of Burroughs' machines. Segmentation, process structuring, interrupts, and stack instructions are discussed as part of a unified approach to computer system organization.

Pankhurst, R. J. [1968]. "Program Overlay Techniques," *CACM* 11, No. 2, (Feb.), 119–125.

A description of automatic, semiautomatic, and manual overlay techniques is presented. Some implementation questions are also considered.

Parnas, D. L. [1971]. "Information Distribution Aspects of Design ·Methodology," *Proc. IFIP Congr. 1971,* Booklet TA-3, pp. 26–30.

The connectivity between modules is measured by the number of assumptions modules must make about each other. Given this premise, the author discusses its effect on the design and documentation of software systems.

Parnas, D. L., and Darringer, J. A. [1967]. "SODAS And A Methodology For System Design," *Proc. AFIPS* **31,** *FJCC,* pp. 449–474.

This paper discusses the top-down approach to system design in the context of the system design and simulation language SODAS. The paper contains extensive examples of the top-down approach.

Poole, P. C., and Waite, W. M. [1969]. "Machine Independent Software," *ACM Symp. Operating Systems Principles* (Oct.), 19–24.

Modeling of abstract machines and macro processing techniques are used to develop a system for writing machine-independent software. The implemented system has been shown to be effective in several applications for software portability.

Randell, B. [1968]. "Towards A Methodology of Computing System Design," in *Software Engineering* (P. Naur and B. Randell, eds.), pp. 204–208. NATO Sci. Affairs Div., Brussels.

Dijkstra's THE design approach and Parnas and Darringer's SODAS language are compared using the structure developed by Zurcher and Randell [1969] for top-down and bottom-up design.

Randell, B., and Kuehner, C. J. [1968]. "Dynamic Storage Allocation Systems," *CACM* **11,** No. 5 (May), 297–306.

This paper surveys mechanisms for dynamic allocation of storage. Addressing techniques used in seven well-known systems are described.

Rice, D. E., and van Dam, A. [1971]. "An Introduction to Information Structures and Paging Considerations for Online Text Editing Systems," *Advances in Information System Sci.* **4,** 93–159.

The authors apply their experience with text-editing systems to questions of memory organization, such as page size and paging versus segmentation.

Rodriguez, J. E. [1967]. *A Graph Model For Parallel Computation,* MAC-TR-64. Ph.D. Thesis, Dept. of Elec. Engrng., M.I.T., Cambridge, Massachusetts (Sept.).

The "program graph" model for parallel computation is discussed and analyzed. The main feature of the model compared with other program schemata is that control counters are implicitly incorporated into the definition of operation nodes (see also Section II.2).

Rose, C. S. [1972]. "LOGOS and the Software Engineer," *Proc. AFIPS* **41,** Pt. I, *FJCC,* pp. 311–323.

An overview is presented of Project LOGOS, a software environment for hardware and software design. The graph theoretic system representation environment is described in detail.

Rosin, R. F. [1969]. "Supervisory And Monitor Systems," *ACM Comput. Surveys* **1,** No. 1 (Mar.), 37–54.

This paper is a historically motivated survey of operating systems. Emphasis is placed on facilities provided by systems, rather than on their internal structure.

Saltzer, J. H. [1966]. *Traffic Control In A Multiplexed Computer System*, MAC-TR-30. Sc.D. Thesis, Dept. of Elec. Engrng. Cambridge, Massachusetts.

This thesis describes a scheme for multiplexing the processor in a multiprogramming, multiprocessing environment. The proposed traffic controller was implemented in the MULTICS System.

Saltzer, J. H., and Gintell, J. W. [1970]. "The Instrumentation of Multics," *CACM* 13, No. 8 (Aug.), 495–500.

Special hardware devices and software tools are described for use in the evaluation of the MULTICS System.

Sammet, J. E. [1971]. "A Brief Survey of Languages Used in Systems Implementation," *ACM SIGPLAN Notices* 6, No. 9 (Oct.), 1–19.

The basic issues in choosing a high-level language for operating system implementation are discussed. Several specific languages are described, and examples are given of systems written in these languages.

Sayers, A. P. (ed.) [1971]. *The Comtre Corp. Operating Systems Survey*. Auerbach, Princeton, New Jersey.

Basic concepts and facilities of operating systems are surveyed and fourteen "real world" operating systems are described.

Sayre, D. [1969]. "Is Automatic 'Folding' Of Programs Efficient Enough To Replace Manual?" *CACM* 12, No. 12 (Dec.), 656–660.

Performance of demand paging is compared to that of conventional overlay. Paging is shown to have advantages in cost and flexibility.

Seaman, P. H., Lind, R. A., and Wilson, T. L. [1966]. "An Analysis of Auxiliary Storage Activity," *IBM Systems J.* 5, No. 3, 158–170.

A queuing model for direct access peripheral storage systems is used to find estimates of device utilization, response time, and queue lengths.

Schroeder, M. D., and Saltzer, J. R. [1971]. "A Hardware Architecture For Implementing Protection Rings," *Proc. Third ACM Symp. Operating Systems Principles* (Oct.), pp. 42–54.

The concept of protection rings in a segmented address space is discussed, with some emphasis on hardware considerations.

Sevcik, K. C. [1971]. *The Use Of Service Time Distributions In Scheduling*. Ph.D. Thesis, Inst. For Comput. Res., Univ. of Chicago, Chicago, Illinois.

Optimal and nearly optimal scheduling rules for a single processor are analyzed theoretically. Rules are analyzed for various different assumptions. In particular, an optimal rule, called "smallest rank," is introduced which minimizes loss and maximizes service.

Sevcik, K. C., Atwood, J. W., Grushcow, M. S., Holt, R. C., Horning, J. J. and Tsichritzis, D. [1972]. "Project SUE as a Learning Experience," *Proc. AFIPS 41*, Pt. I, *FJCC* pp. 331–339.

Different design alternatives are discussed in the context of the SUE System. Particular mechanisms introduced in the SUE System are outlined.

Sharpe, W. F. [1969]. *The Economics of Computers.* Columbia Univ. Press, New York.

The book begins with background material in economics which is relevant to the economics of computing. Economic issues in the acquisition and use of computers are then discussed in detail.

Shaw, A. C., and Weiderman, N. H. [1971]. "A Multiprogramming System for Education and Research," *Proc. IFIP Congr. 1971,* Booklet TA-7, pp. 110–114.

The authors describe a simple machine simulated in a high-level language which can be used as the base for a small operating system. The system is used for both pedagogical and research purposes.

Slutz, D. R. [1968]. *The Flow Graph Model Of Parallel Computation,* MAC-TR-53. Ph.D. Thesis, Dept. of Elec. Engrng., M.I.T., Cambridge, Massachusetts.

A modified version of Karp and Miller's parallel program schemata [Karp and Miller, 1969] is analyzed with respect to determinacy, equivalence, and equivalence-preserving transformations.

Snowdon, R. A. [1972]. "PEARL: An Interactive System for the Preparation and Validation of Structured Programs," *ACM SIGPLAN Notices* 7, No. 3 (Mar.), 9–12.

This paper describes a system which would aid the programmer in verifying the consistency of each level of refinement during the top-down programming process.

Teichrow, D., and Sayani, H. [1971]. "Automation of System Building," *Datamation* 17, No. 16 (Aug. 15), 25–30.

This informal article is an introduction to the Information System Design and Optimization System (ISDOS) project. The goal of the project is to automate as much of the system design and implementation process as possible.

Teorey, T. J., and Pinkerton, T. B. [1972]. "A Comparative Analysis Of Disk Scheduling Policies," *CACM* 15, No. 3 (Mar.), 177–184.

Five scheduling policies for movable-head disks are evaluated, using analytic and simulation models. The policies are compared with respect to average seek time and average waiting time. A best overall strategy is chosen.

Thompson, K., and Ritchie, D. M. [1973]. "The Unix Time-Sharing System," *Fourth Symposium on Operating System Principles* (Oct.).

This paper describes the essential features of the Unix Time-Sharing System for the DEC PDP-11/40 and 11/45 machines. The description of the Unix hierarchical file system is particularly relevant to Chapter 6.

Turnbull, C. J. M. [1972]. *A Comparative Analysis of Several Disk Scheduling Algorithms,* Tech. Rep. CSRG-16. Comput. Systems Res. Group, Univ. of Toronto, Toronto.

Several disk scheduling policies are analyzed. Results are shown to be consistent with simulation data by Teorey and Pinkerton [1972].

Van Horn, E. C. [1968]. "Three Criteria For Designing Computing Systems To Facilitate Debugging," *CACM* **11**, No. 5 (May), 360–365.

Three criteria for evaluating system features are described in the context of controlling the system's output. The notion of virtual machine is used to explain the criteria.

Varney, R. C. [1971]. "Process Selection In A Hierarchical Operating System," *Proc. Third ACM Symp. Operating Systems Principles* (Oct.), pp. 106–108.

A model for process scheduling is described and applied to the RC4000 process structure.

Weinberg, G. M. [1971]. *The Psychology of Computer Programming.* Van Nostrand-Reinhold, Princeton, New Jersey.

A provocative argument is made that computer programming should be studied as a human activity using psychological methods.

Weingarten, A. [1966]. "The Eschenbach Drum Scheme," *CACM* **9**, No. 7 (July), 509–512.

A paging drum organization is described and analyzed.

Weissman, L., and Stacey, G. M. [1973]. "An Interface System for Improving Reliability of Software Systems," *Record 1973 IEEE Symp. Comput. Software Reliability, New York,* pp. 136–142.

An automatic system for interfacing modules is described. Modules communicate with logical names which the system maps into physical locations. The latter are not directly addressable by the modules.

Wilkes, M. V. [1965]. "Slave Memories And Dynamic Storage Allocation," *IEEE Trans. Computers* **14**, No. 4 (Apr.), 270–271.

This paper is an early description of a small cache memory to speed up average memory access time (see also Kuck and Lawrie [1970]).

Wilkes, M. V. [1968]. *Time Sharing Computer Systems.* Amer. Elsevier, New York.

This book presents a brief user's view of time-sharing systems, with some emphasis on internal memory and file structures.

Wilkes, M. V. [1969]. "A Model For Core Space Allocation In a Time-Sharing System," *Proc. AFIPS* **34**, *SJCC*, pp. 265–271.

A memory structure using a pipeline is described which avoids swapping jobs with small processing requirements, and hopefully eliminates some swapping overhead.

Winograd, J., Morganstein, S. J. and Herman, R. [1971]. "Simulation Studies of a Virtual Memory Time-Shared Demand Paging Operating System," *Proc. Third ACM Symp. Operating Systems Principles* (Oct.), pp. 149–155.

A detailed simulation model of a time-shared operating system is described. Two example simulations are discussed relating to the effects of memory size and paging rate, and batch versus interactive scheduling biases.

Wirth, N. [1968]. "PL360—A Programming Language For the 360 Computers," *JACM* **15**, No. 1 (Jan.), 37–74.

This paper contains a complete description of the PL360 system programming language for the IBM System/360 machines.

Wirth, N. [1969]. "On Multiprogramming, Machine Coding And Computer Organization," *CACM* **12**, No. 9 (Sept.), 489–498.

Programming language structures for parallel processing which avoid explicit use of the interrupt are discussed. Dijkstra's semaphores are applied to a PL360 programming example.

Wirth, N. [1971]. "The Programming Language Pascal," *Acta Informat.* **1**, Fasc. 1, 35–63.

PASCAL, a structured programming language, is described in its entirety in this lucid paper.

Wulf, W. A. [1969]. "Performance Monitors For Multiprogramming Systems," *Proc. Second ACM Symp. Operating Systems Principles* (Oct.), pp. 175–181.

This paper discusses the use of performance monitors for gathering information to be used for influencing scheduling decisions. Specifically, adjusting the allocation policy and modifying the job mix are considered.

Wulf, W., Mitchell, J., Hopkins, M., Horning, J., Wells, M., Berglass, G., Halstead, M., and Karasz, P. [1972]. "Project Rosetta Stone—An Exhibition of Language for System Implementation—Participants Guide." Dept. of Comput. Sci. Carnegie-Mellon Univ., Pittsburgh, Pennsylvania (Sept.).

The Rosetta Stone Project (alias "code-off") for comparison of system implementation languages is described in detail.

Zurcher, F. W., and Randell, B. [1969]. "Iterative Multi-Level Modeling—A Methodology For Computer System Design," *Proc. IFIP Congr. 1968*, pp. 867–871. North-Holland Publ. Amsterdam.

This classic paper presents the top-down approach to system design.

INDEX

Computer Science and Applied Mathematics

A SERIES OF MONOGRAPHS AND TEXTBOOKS

Editor
Werner Rheinboldt
University of Maryland

HANS P. KÜNZI, H. G. TZSCHACH, and C. A. ZEHNDER. Numerical Methods of Mathematical Optimization: With ALGOL and FORTRAN Programs, Corrected and Augmented Edition

AZRIEL ROSENFELD. Picture Processing by Computer

JAMES ORTEGA AND WERNER RHEINBOLDT. Iterative Solution of Nonlinear Equations in Several Variables

A. T. BERZTISS. Data Structures: Theory and Practice

AZARIA PAZ. Introduction to Probabilistic Automata

DAVID YOUNG. Iterative Solution of Large Linear Systems

ANN YASUHARA. Recursive Function Theory and Logic

JAMES M. ORTEGA. Numerical Analysis: A Second Course

G. W. STEWART. Introduction to Matrix Computations

CHIN-LIANG CHANG AND RICHARD CHAR-TUNG LEE. Symbolic Logic and Mechanical Theorem Proving

C. C. GOTLIEB AND A. BORODIN. Social Issues in Computing

ERWIN ENGELER. Introduction to the Theory of Computation

F. W. J. OLVER. Asymptotics and Special Functions

DIONYSIOS C. TSICHRITZIS AND PHILIP A. BERNSTEIN. Operating Systems

ROBERT R. KORFHAGE. Discrete Computational Structures

In preparation

PHILIP J. DAVIS AND PHILIP RABINOWITZ. Methods of Numerical Integration

DATE DUE

MAY 0 5 2003		
OCT 2 5 2003 OCT 0 2 2008		
30 505 JOSTEN'S		